NORTH CAROLINA COAST

JASON FRYE

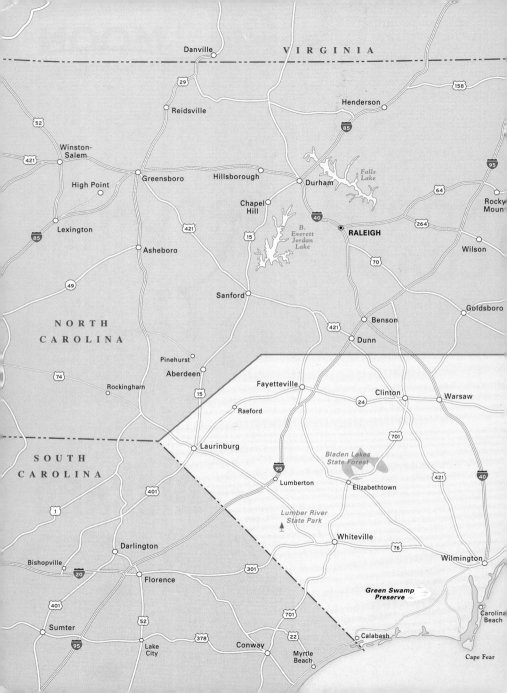

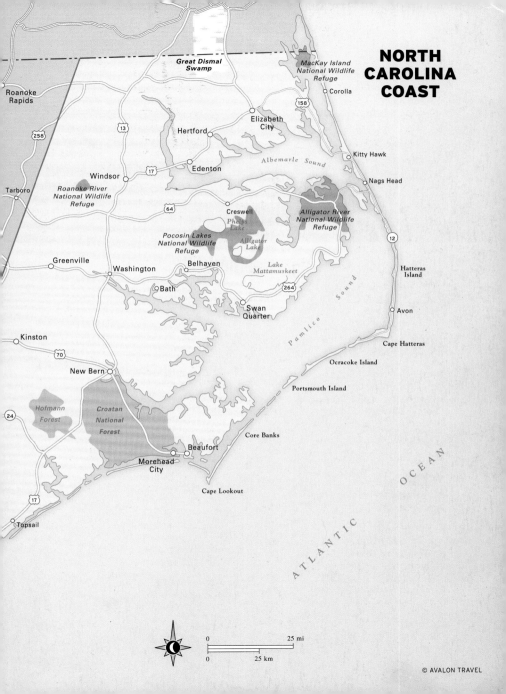

NORTH CAROLINA COAST

Roanoke Rapids

Great Dismal Swamp

MacKay Island National Wildlife Refuge

Corolla

258

13

Hertford

Elizabeth City

158

Kitty Hawk

Tarboro

17

Windsor

Edenton

Albemarle Sound

Nags Head

Roanoke River National Wildlife Refuge

64

Creswell

Phelps Lake

Alligator River National Wildlife Refuge

12

Greenville

Washington

Belhaven

Pocosin Lakes National Wildlife Refuge

Alligator Lake

Lake Mattamuskeet

Hatteras Island

Bath

264

Avon

Kinston

Swan Quarter

Pamlico Sound

Cape Hatteras

70

Ocracoke Island

New Bern

Portsmouth Island

24

Hofmann Forest

Croatan National Forest

Core Banks

Beaufort

Morehead City

17

Cape Lookout

ATLANTIC OCEAN

Topsail

N

0   25 mi

0   25 km

© AVALON TRAVEL

Contents

DISCOVER THE

North Carolina Coast

The first trip I remember taking to North Carolina started in the dark. We left the mountains of West Virginia for the shores of the Outer Banks in the early morning; I slept most of the way. Somewhere around 60 miles from the coast, the heady scent of the Albemarle Sound woke me and announced that we were almost there.

North Carolina has a way of awakening your senses. Sometimes it's a smell: salty water, verdant, unctuous marsh, or a pine-laced breeze. Sometimes it's a sight: a line of pelicans skimming the waves, sunlight filtered through the golden heads of sea oats, or a beach with no end in sight. Maybe it's the sound of gulls, cicadas, a ferry horn, or crashing waves; the feeling of sand, water, sun, and wind on your skin; or the taste of sweet shrimp and delicate scallops – the freshest seafood you've ever eaten.

Once the hook is set, North Carolina always reels you in. While you're here, you can't get enough, and when you're away, you can't wait to get back. You start listening for the surf every time you open a window, watching for sandpipers scurrying from your feet, hoping for the bite of salty air when you leave the house.

From the Outer Banks in the north to the Brunswick beaches in the south, there's a variance to the topography of North Carolina's coast. The Outer Banks hold wild horses, high dunes, and stretches of seashore where not a single home dots the landscape. Along the central Crystal Coast, you'll find winding creeks, vast swaths of swampy forest and marsh, and beaches once roamed by pirates. Near the mouth of the Cape Fear River, revel in lazy beaches, turquoise waters, and a river whose water runs the color of coffee. On the Brunswick beaches, experience maritime forest, sand dollars marking every step, and towns that take you back in time.

I didn't grow up here, but I call North Carolina home all the same. The number of folks like me keeps growing. Some came for the surf, some for school, some for work, some for love, and we stayed. Why? Because that first memory — that first briny breath that pulled us from our slumber — fills us with the irresistible need to be here. Come discover the North Carolina coast for yourself.

Planning Your Trip

Where to Go

The Outer Banks

This beautiful stretch of shoreline is rich with ecological wonders, centuries-old cultural traditions, and unsolved historical mysteries. Around Nags Head and the Cape Hatteras National Seashore, surfers and hang gliders ride the wind and waves. One of the first English settlements appeared and then disappeared on Roanoke Island. Pirates roamed these waters, and Blackbeard lost his head near Ocracoke. Along the vast Pamlico and Albemarle Sounds, colonial towns and fishing villages stand sentinel on deep, still rivers. The Great Dismal Swamp is an eerie, unforgettable place for kayaking and canoeing. Small towns where families have plied the waters for generations line the rivers and sounds of the Inner Banks. Along the Roanoke River are mill towns, fishing villages, and the colonial river town of Halifax, birthplace of the documents that inspired the Declaration of Independence.

Beaufort and the Crystal Coast

Beaufort and New Bern, two of North Carolina's most important early cities, hold some of the most stunning early architecture in the South. Morehead City is a hot spot for scuba diving the countless wrecks offshore

in The Graveyard of Atlantic. Cape Lookout National Seashore has 56 miles of undeveloped shoreline inhabited only by wild horses and birds. Quiet, comfortable beach towns line the Bogue Banks. As in the days of the dread pirates Blackbeard and Stede Bonnet, both regulars in these parts, the Crystal Coast is home to hundreds of species of fish, and great opportunities for inshore and offshore fishing abound.

Wilmington and the Cape Fear Region

Wilmington, an old port city known for antebellum homes and gardens as well as lively shops and restaurants, and the beach towns surrounding the mouth of the Cape Fear River are year-round knockouts. Topsail Island, Wrightsville Beach, and Kure and Carolina Beaches offer some of the most beautiful stretches of sand in the nation. Between Wilmington and the South Carolina line, you'll find Calabash seafood and fantastic golf. Inland, the Waccamaw and Lumber Rivers creep through beautiful blackwater swamps while the Cape Fear River leads upstream to Fayetteville, a military hub and a fun destination for history, gardens, and adrenaline-pumping activities.

When to Go

Spring debuts in the southeast as early as late February. As it creeps up along the coast, temperatures are a pretty consistent 60-70 degrees by mid-April.

Summer means great weather and the high season. The beaches are packed (especially on weekends), and you'll find festivals and events throughout the region. The heat can be brutal, especially when combined with humidity, but the coast stays cooler than inland

destinations, and ocean breezes offer relief. Temperatures range from the upper 60s to the low 90s, with water temperatures in the low 70s to low 80s, making for comfortable beach days.

Autumn reaches the coast by early November, after hurricane season has passed. Autumn weather stays in the high-60s-low-70s, with many days that push into the 80s, making it ideal for outdoor activities. Along

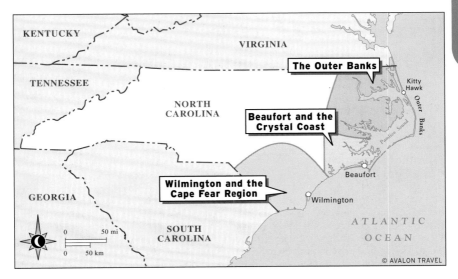

the coast, the water stays swimmably warm past Halloween most years.

Winter is milder here than in many parts of the country. Daytime temperatures are usually in the 40s and 50s between late December and February, with frequent dips below freezing as the season wears on. The coast only gets one or two snow showers every couple of years. Fall and early winter attract anglers, but many coastal businesses reduce their hours or even close entirely during winter.

During the shoulder seasons—late spring and early fall—rental rates are down, beaches are a little less crowded, and visitors can find bargain getaways (although the eastern Sandhills and areas around Pinehurst and Southern Pines can be quite crowded in the spring and fall, when the weather is most beautiful for golfing).

Before You Go

There are some seasonal events that are so large that entire cities or corners of the state can be heavily booked. April is the cruelest month for making short-notice travel arrangements, especially in Wilmington, where the Azalea Festival draws a 100,000 visitors annually. Around the 4th of July, Oak Island, Bald Head Island, and Southport, the epicenter of a massive Independence Day celebration, are jam-packed with visitors enjoying fireworks and celebrations. During festival times like these, it can be difficult to find a motel room, campground, or spot for your RV anywhere near the event. If you'll be visiting the coast in winter, plan ahead for accommodations and dining, as businesses may be closed.

Coastal weather can change dramatically on a whim. Even on hot days, it can be breezy and cool on the water. Bring sun protection no matter when you visit. A water bottle is also handy.

Cell phone signals are pretty consistent throughout North Carolina, but there are pockets on the coast where cell service and 3G, 4G, and LTE connectivity is spotty.

The Best of the North Carolina Coast

North Carolina's coast spans some 300 miles from Virginia to South Carolina. There's tons of beach, marsh, history, food, and fun to be had, but you can make it to all the highlights in a week.

Wilmington and the Cape Fear Region

DAY 1

Easily accessible by road or air, Wilmington, the hub of the southeastern coast, is an ideal starting point. Visit Wrightsville Beach for a morning swim and beach time. Around lunch, pack up and drive 10 minutes to downtown Wilmington for a gyro at The Greeks, a stroll along the Riverwalk, and shopping at The Cotton Exchange. Stay downtown for dinner. Try Phun Seafood Bar for an Asian twist or Caprice Bistro for fine French cuisine, or dine on the river and savor the views. Not ready for bed? Try a cocktail at Manna or a beer at Cape Fear Wine and Beer before retreating to your downtown bed and breakfast or the Hilton Wilmington Riverside.

DAY 2

Make an early tee time at Cape Fear National or one of the Big Cats courses and give Brunswick County your day, or head to the charming fishing village of Southport for a morning of shopping. At lunch, head south to Calabash for a taste of the world-famous style of seafood at Beck's, Ella's, or Coleman's.

Backtrack to Southport (or head there for the first time) and take the ferry to Fort Fisher and walk off lunch at this historic Civil War fort. Next, visit the nearby North Carolina Aquarium for a look at what lies beneath the waves.

Dinner takes you back to Wrightsville Beach. Dine dockside at Dockside, oceanside at Oceanic, or have a fabulous meal of oysters and French-inspired dishes at Brasserie du Soleil.

Beaufort and the Crystal Coast

DAY 3

Drive north on U.S. 17 and U.S. 70 to Beaufort and Morehead City. Learn about

historic downtown Wilmington

Beaufort's pirate history on a walking tour of downtown, then pay your respects to Blackbeard at the North Carolina Maritime Museum, which contains artifacts recovered from his sunken pirate ship. Grab lunch at Front Street Grill or Blue Moon Bistro before heading north on U.S. 70 to New Bern, the second oldest town in the state.

Spend the afternoon exploring art galleries and antique shops in downtown New Bern, and visit the beautiful gardens and home of Tryon Palace. On the way back to your bed and breakfast, drop in the Birthplace of Pepsi to learn about this iconic Southern drink. Dinner will be waterside at Persimmons Restaurant, where fresh seafood and sophisticated preparations are the norm.

DAY 4

Spend your morning at one of the many coffee shops and bakeries in New Bern, then walk off your pastry on a tour of the elegant homes in the neighborhoods on the north side of town. Head inland toward Kinston, about an hour away. From here, it's a 15-minute drive to the famous Skylight Inn, the Eastern end of the North Carolina Barbecue Trail and a great spot for some renowned eastern North Carolina barbecue.

For the afternoon, head to Kinston proper for a look at the remains of a Civil War Ironclad at the CSS *Neuse* Interpretive Center and the full-scale replica of this fearsome ship just a couple of blocks away. Enjoy a beer at Mother Earth Brewing's tap room before dinner at Chef and the Farmer. Spend the night in Kinston.

The Outer Banks

DAY 5

Queen Street Deli has breakfast and eye-opening coffee to fuel you for the three hour push to Roanoke Island on the Outer Banks. Drive northeast to Jamesville and join U.S. 64, which will take you through the rural Inner Banks into Manteo. Along the way, soak up the scenery and stop to stretch your legs at Pettigrew State Park.

You'll arrive on Roanoke Island around lunchtime. Grab a bite to eat at Fisherman's Wharf Restaurant in the fishing village of Wanchese. Sit overlooking the docks and watch fishermen unload the fresh catch they'll be cooking for dinner tonight.

Drive north 15 minutes to Manteo and visit the Elizabethan Gardens and Fort Raleigh National Historic Site. Spend the night at the Tranquil House Inn and enjoy dinner in-house at 1587.

the Bodie Island Lighthouse

the Wright Brothers Memorial

Eat Like A Local

To dine like a local, pick restaurants like the favorites listed below, which use local seafood, meat, and produce while paying homage to the culinary traditions that make each coastal culture distinct. Check out **Outer Banks Catch** (www.outerbankscatch.com), **Carteret Catch** (http://carteretcatch.org), and **Brunswick Catch** (http://brunswickcatch.com) for more restaurants serving local seafood in each region.

THE OUTER BANKS

· **Fisherman's Wharf Restaurant (page 47)** serves traditional Banker seafood and addictive scallop cakes from an original recipe. What else would you expect from one of the Outer Banks' oldest fishing families?

· Enjoy an oyster stout with your dinner at **The Outer Banks Brewing Station (page 37),** where fresh seafood plays a prominent role in the menu.

· **Sam & Omie's (page 37)** opened in 1937 to feed hungry fishermen, and the concept stuck. Try a platter of broiled or fried seafood the way the first patrons ate it—hot and fresh.

· In Duck, **Aqua Restaurant (page 37)**

DAY 6

Pack up and head across the sound toward the beach. Grab breakfast at Sam & Omie's in Nags Head, then walk across the street for some beach time. Drive south on Hwy. 12 to the Bodie Island Lighthouse and climb to the top for a breathtaking view of the Outer Banks.

Take Hwy. 12 north toward Duck. Stop at the Wright Brothers National Memorial and see a replica of the brothers' famed flying machine and the site where those historic first flights took place. Continue north to the village of Duck for lunch at Aqua Restaurant and Spa before checking in to luxe accommodations at the oceanfront Sanderling Resort. Spend the afternoon on the beach or relaxing at the spa, or take serves a small menu of exquisitely prepared dishes that take advantage of the abundant seafood harvested right on the Outer Banks.

BEAUFORT AND THE CRYSTAL COAST

- **Clawson's 1905 Restaurant and Pub (page 93)** serves a number of dishes featuring fresh-caught shrimp, a local delicacy.
- Chef Tim Coyne makes use of the local bounty at his Morehead City eatery, **Bistro by the Sea (page 97)**. It's hard to choose between the crab bisque, grouper, and tuna.
- At **247 Craven (page 81)**, you can't go wrong with seared scallops Fra Diavolo.
- You expect fresh seafood when dining dockside, and New Bern's **Persimmons (page 80)** delivers, with incredibly fresh, immaculately prepared fish.
- In Kinston, **The Boiler Room (page 87)** serves a variety of local and regional oysters.
- Chef Vivian Howard Knight uses local ingredients year-round at Kinston's **Chef and the Farmer (page 87),** where the nouveau-Southern seafood dishes shine.

WILMINGTON AND THE CAPE FEAR REGION

- Chef Keith Rhodes blends Southern cuisine, French technique, and Asian flavors at **Catch (page 131).** The menu features locally caught shrimp, scallops, and fish.
- **Phun Seafood Bar (page 131),** another Rhodes venture, serves Vietnamese-inspired dishes packed with local fish, crabs, and scallops.

- **Manna (page 131)** uses local ingredients exclusively. When they say "catch of the day," they really mean it.
- The haute Southern cooking at **Rx (page 131)** will show you what shrimp and grits is all about.
- At **Brasserie Du Soleil (page 130)** order Chef Tripp Engle's local flounder and try oysters harvested just a few miles away.

an excursion to Corolla, the next town up from Duck, to climb the Currituck Beach Lighthouse or take a wild horse tour on the beach to spot some of the famous Banker Ponies.

Dinner and drinks tonight are across the street from the Sanderling at Kimball's Kitchen, a posh restaurant that makes the most of local seafood, fowl, and produce.

DAY 7

It's about three hours from Duck to Ocracoke, your last stop before heading home, so strike out early and get breakfast at Grits Grill, before following Hwy. 12 south through Cape Hatteras National Seashore. This stretch of beach is wild, and you'll find just a handful of small towns. Close to the southern tip is the Cape Hatteras Lighthouse with its iconic black and white spiral paint job. Snap a photo or to climb to the top. A few miles to the southeast in Hatteras, board the ferry to Ocracoke Island.

On Ocracoke, arrange for a fishing charter or spend the day relaxing on the shell-strewn beach. In the evening, head to the harbor for oysters on the half shell at Topless Oyster Restaurant. Spend the night here (taking time for stargazing, which is especially good outside of town) and begin to make your way home in the morning. A three-hour ferry ride puts you back on the Inner Banks near Beaufort, where you're not far from the airports in Wilmington or Raleigh, as well as I-40 and I-95.

Outdoor Adventure

There's no shortage of outdoor activities along North Carolina's coast. Surfers come in droves, kayakers rave about the marshes, sounds, rivers, and swamps, and hikers and campers find a surprisingly diverse set of environs to explore. Most surprising are the hang gliders who come to Jockey's Ridge on the Outer Banks. This massive sand dune is the perfect launch and landing point for hang gliders of all skill levels.

Kayaking

I've paddled all along the North Carolina coast, and although some prefer to take their kayaks oceanside, I'm happy on the sounds, marshes, creeks, rivers and swamps inland and on the back side of the barrier islands. Everywhere along the coast, outfitters rent kayaks and stand-up paddleboards and often lead visitors on tours.

kayaking in the marsh

Along the Virginia border, the Great Dismal Swamp offers miles of paddling through what is a beautiful swamp, despite its name. Put ins are plentiful, but outfitters are a little ways away. It's best to bring your own gear or make arrangements for day-long or longer rentals.

The same holds true for the Alligator River National Wildlife Refuge, where you stand a good chance of seeing an alligator (be careful if you do and do not approach) or even a black bear. If you take a moonlight paddling tour, listen for the howls of red wolves.

Perhaps the greatest paddle on the coast is exploring the 56 miles of shoreline along the sound at Cape Lookout National Seashore, a long island inhabited only by wildlife, including birds, crabs, and wild horses. The ocean side of Cape Lookout is just ocean, but the sound side is rife with marshes and creeks. Paddle over from Harkers Island and spend a night or two to have enough time for discovering this place.

Near Wilmington, Town Creek winds for many miles from Brunswick County's Green Swamp to the Cape Fear River, ranging from a tight, heavily wooded swamp creek to a wide coastal marsh. The brackish water, stained a rich coffee color by tannins from rotting vegetation, looks like something from *Creature From the Black Lagoon*. Twists and turns and plenty of wildlife, including circling osprey and the occasional snake, keep trips interesting.

Surfing

From powerful storm swells to gentle, easy-to-learn-on beach break, the North Carolina

Historic Lighthouses

the Ocracoke Light at dawn

The lighthouses that guard North Carolina's coast are each distinct and beautiful in the way their function shaped their form.

- The red-brick **Currituck Beach Lighthouse (page 29)** stands at the far north of the Outer Banks. Visitors willing to climb the 214 spiral steps to the top are treated to a dazzling view of Currituck Sound.

- Climb to the top of **Bodie Island Lighthouse (page 48),** which overlooks Lighthouse Bay and the Atlantic Ocean. This black-and-white striped structure has been sending its signal out to sea since 1872, but was closed to the public until 2013.

- With its recognizable black-and-white spiral exterior, **Cape Hatteras Lighthouse (page 49)** is a North Carolina icon. It's also one of the tallest brick lighthouses in the world, and you can climb to the top. (Beware—it's windy up there.)

- Whale oil originally powered the beam of **Ocracoke Light (page 52),** the second-oldest working lighthouse in the United States. Because it's still on duty, visitors can't go inside, but there are lovely places to walk on the grounds and admire this simple, squat white tower.

- As recognizable as Hatteras, **Cape Lookout Lighthouse (page 102)** is festooned with a black-and-white diamond pattern that gives the shoals it warns of their name—Diamond Shoals. The lighthouse stands at the tip of Cape Lookout National Seashore. Visit any time, but climbing is only an option from late spring through early fall.

- **Old Baldy Lighthouse (page 140),** the second of three lighthouses to have graced Bald Head Island, still stands. As the oldest lighthouse in the state, it's something of a monument to North Carolina's seafaring history. How old is it? Commissioned by Thomas Jefferson and completed in 1817; that's how old.

Croatan National Forest

coastline welcomes surfers of all skill levels from all over the world.

The Outer Banks is perpetually popular. The deserted Cape Hatteras National Seashore and the villages of Waves, Buxton, and Salvo are popular basecamps for surf safaris. Bring your boards and drop in along the National Seashore, or head north into the more populated Nags Head and Kill Devil Hills area for good waves closer to numerous surf shops, restaurants, and bars.

For south-facing beaches known for catching swells, head to Emerald Isle on the Crystal Coast and Oak Island, one of the Brunswick beaches. This pair is especially popular when there are storms offshore.

Wrightsville Beach and Topsail Island, near Wilmington, are hot spots along the Cape Fear Coast. At Wrightsville, wide beaches and consistent breaks satisfy experienced and learning surfers. Topsail, a smaller, slightly steeper beach, makes for great sessions for experienced surfers, especially those looking to show off a little.

Hiking

There aren't mountains along the North Carolina coast, so any hiking you do will be relatively flat. And sandy. You can get a little elevation at Jockey's Ridge, the largest sand dune on the east coast, which stands more than 100 feet high and offers amazing views of the sunrise, sunset, shores, and sounds. Wander through this dune system and watch hang gliders, kite flyers, and sand boarders (think snowboarding on a sand dune, sans parka). Notice the changes in vegetation and wildlife as you near the sound, then go for a swim, or just watch the boats and wind surfers go by. Be prepared for lots of sand in your boots.

From dunes and patches of forest to beach, there's plenty to explore at Cape Lookout National Seashore. Get up close and personal to the diamond-patterned Cape Lookout Lighthouse, but keep your distance from the wild Banker Ponies.

Croatan National Forest on the Inner Banks has more than 40 miles of trails, ranging from half a mile to the 20-plus mile Neusiok Trail. Passing through swamp, hummock, and an inland forest, you'll feel like you've been transported into the past. Remember the story of The Lost Colony while you're here.

More than 10 miles of trails circle through Ev-Henwood Nature Preserve, a former farm and turpentine supply point that's now a nature preserve and study center for the University of North Carolina Wilmington.

It's easy to link these trails and explore piney forests, a few stands of hardwoods, and the black headwaters of Town Creek.

The truly adventurous can hike the 11-mile spit of land that connects Bald Head Island to the mainland. The long, hot hike from Fort Fisher along the shore and dunes to the island is best made in the shoulder seasons. Bring water, food, sun protection, and a plan for when you reach the end, because Bald Head Island is closed to cars and accessible only by ferry (or hiking). It's a five-mile trek across the island to the ferry once you arrive, but friendly residents and vacationers offer rides. You may also want to explore the shorter trails that dive into Bald Head Island's maritime forest.

Camping

You can rent a tent or RV site at plenty of campgrounds, but many of North Carolina's best spots put you in reach of true wilderness.

Kayak or take a ferry from Harkers Island to Cape Lookout National Seashore and camp there or to the west at Shackleford Banks. Both islands are inhabited by wild horses and are beautiful places for nights under the stars.

In the Croatan National Forest you'll find several great camping spots, especially along the Neusiok Trail. Select a high and dry spot to camp, or you just may wake up wet.

Hammocks Beach State Park on Bear Island offers paddling campers and ferry-takers alike a place to spend a few nights in the wild. Just north of Topsail Island and just south of Emerald Isle, the beaches here are gorgeous, shell-littered things that few visitors see.

Near Wilmington, Carolina Beach State Park is a popular spot to set up your tent. Hiking trails through pine forests and along the Cape Fear River give you plenty to do, but the campground's close enough to town—just five minutes from a restaurant—to get something to eat or drink in the evenings.

Inland, camp beside one of the strange Carolina Bays at Lake Waccamaw State Park, where you'll find odd plants like the Venus flytrap and a shallow, circular lake of unknown origin.

Best Beaches

The Outer Banks

COROLLA
Best for Wildlife
Visit Corolla to view the Banker Ponies, wild horses that have lived along the Outer Banks for hundreds of years.

DUCK
Best for Sunbathing, Sunsets
The beach at Duck is at a slight incline that provides maximum sun exposure and great ocean views. The wide wash of sound and marsh behind the thin strip of beach makes Duck a favorite for sunsets.

NAGS HEAD AND KILL DEVIL HILLS
Best for Family Fun
Family vacations to the Outer Banks include seafood buffets, golf carts, mini golf, sunburns, and the occasional carnival ride.

Recreate my childhood at Nags Head and Kill Devil Hills, beaches I haunted as a kid.

PEA ISLAND NATIONAL WILDLIFE REFUGE
Best for Wildlife
This refuge on Hatteras Island is an incredible spot for watching migratory waterfowl.

HATTERAS
Best for Beachcombing, Water Sports
The village of Hatteras on Hatteras Island is a popular surfing destination and also good for shelling.

OTHER HATTERAS ISLAND BEACHES
Best for Solitude
The villages of Salvo, Buxton, Rodanthe, Waves, and Avon provide privacy along with modern conveniences.

OCRACOKE
Best for Beachcombing, Solitude, Sunrises
Ocracoke Island has the benefits of a vacation town, but you'll find shell-strewn beaches you have almost all to yourself. Watch the sunrise over what seems like endless miles of ocean.

Beaufort and the Crystal Coast
CAPE LOOKOUT NATIONAL SEASHORE
Best for Long Walks, Solitude
With 56 miles of coastline, you can quickly find yourself alone in nature at Cape Lookout National Seashore. It's hard to beat these unbroken stretches of beach for long walks.

SHACKLEFORD BANKS
Best for Wildlife
Shackleford Banks in Cape Lookout National Seashore is a fantastic place to spot wild Banker Ponies.

ATLANTIC BEACH
Best for Water Sports
For great diving, including the chance to explore offshore wrecks in the Graveyard of the Atlantic, go to Atlantic Beach on the Bogue Banks and arrange for a dive charter to pick you up in nearby Morehead City.

EMERALD ISLE
Best for Family Fun, Water Sports
This Bogue Banks town, popular with surfers for its south-facing beach, is a laid-back, family-friendly getaway.

Wilmington and the Cape Fear Region
TOPSAIL ISLAND
Best for Water Sports
Experienced surfers should head to this island, where the surf is consistent year-round and the wind shapes waves into steep peaks, allowing for aerial maneuvers and sharp cutbacks.

WRIGHTSVILLE BEACH
Best for Sunbathing, Water Sports
This wide, flat beach has sand that's not too packed, not too powdery—perfect for

frolicking in turquoise waters at Wrightsville Beach

catching some sun. It's also popular with new and experienced surfers.

CAROLINA BEACH
Best for Family Fun
Carolina Beach State Park offers an abundance of hotels, a pier for fishing, a boardwalk crowded with shops and arcades, and a small carnival ground—all great for when kids need a break from sea and sand.

BALD HEAD ISLAND
Best for Long Walks, Sunrises, Wildlife
My favorite spot for long walks is the 14 miles of beach on Bald Head Island. On south-facing South Beach and east-facing East Beach, there's ocean on one side and a high dune ridge or maritime forest on the other. More than 225 species of birds have been spotted here. The sunrise over the tumultuous Frying Pan Shoals, which extend toward the ocean from the island's easternmost tip, is a sight to behold.

HOLDEN BEACH, OCEAN ISLE, AND SUNSET BEACH
Best for Beachcombing, Sunsets
These Brunswick beaches are rich with delicate sand dollars. The aptly named Sunset Beach comes to life when the day's last rays stretch over the marsh.

THE OUTER BANKS

The Outer Banks stand off the northeastern corner of North Carolina like a magnificent net. They catch all sorts of things: storms, shipwrecks, horses, history, and the hearts of visitors. This thin strip of islands stretches some 125 miles and an hour-long ferry ride from the Virginia border to the end of Ocracoke Island. Susceptible to profound change brought about by the grind of wind and waves and the force of single storms, the Outer Banks stand guard, protecting the inland and fragile marshland of the Inner Banks. A powerful hurricane can fill a centuries-old inlet in a night and open a new channel a few hundred yards away. As recently as 2012, Hatteras Island was again cut off from the rest of the Outer Banks as Hurricane Sandy washed out roads, damaged bridges, and filled roadways with several feet of sand. The landscape poses challenges to the life it supports, but those same challenges have created an adaptable and hardy group of plants, animals, and people.

Between the Outer Banks and the mainland in the Inner Banks is a collection of sounds known as the Albemarle-Pamlico Estuary. Many travelers ignore the sounds, giving them little more than a glance as they cross on a bridge or a ferry, but they play an enormously important role in the region. The Albemarle-Pamlico Estuary is the second-largest estuarine system in the country after Chesapeake Bay to the north, and it includes Albemarle, Pamlico, Core, Croatan, Roanoke, and Currituck Sounds. Covering more than 3,000 square miles, they drain more than 30,000 square miles and provide diverse marine and terrestrial

THE OUTER BANKS

HIGHLIGHTS

LOOK FOR **(** TO FIND RECOMMENDED SIGHTS, ACTIVITIES, DINING, AND LODGING.

(**Wright Brothers National Memorial:** See where North Carolina earned the slogan "First in Flight" and view a replica of the famed *Wright Flyer* (page 26).

(**Fort Raleigh National Historic Site:** See where the Lost Colony, the first English settlement in the New World, mysteriously disappeared in the 1580s (page 39).

(**Cape Hatteras Lighthouse:** Climb to the top of this iconic lighthouse at the tip of Cape Hatteras in the nation's first National Seashore (page 49).

(**Ocracoke Island:** On this remote island, you'll find a historic village that is the home to one of the country's most unique communities, along with the waters where Blackbeard met his fate and one of the oldest lighthouses in the nation (page 51).

(**The Great Dismal Swamp:** This natural wonder, straddling the Virginia-North Carolina border, is an amazing place for canoeing, kayaking, bird-watching, and sightseeing (page 55).

(**Somerset Place Historic Site:** The graceful architecture and exotic setting of this early plantation contrast with the tragic history of its involvement in slavery (page 64).

(**Pettigrew State Park:** Lake Phelps, the centerpiece of Pettigrew State Park, is an attractive enigma, a body of shallow water with a deep history (page 64).

(**Mattamuskeet National Wildlife Refuge:** The landmark lodge on Lake Mattamuskeet towers over a dramatic waterscape that attracts tens of thousands of migratory birds (page 68).

environments that shelter essential plant and animal life. The vast and beautiful marshlands and wide shallow sounds protect the mainland from storm surges and the Atlantic Ocean from toxins and sediment, all the while providing nursery grounds to countless fish and bird species.

Sheltered from the Atlantic, the Inner Banks are a much more accommodating (ecologically speaking) and familiar landscape than the Outer Banks. Along the marshes and wetlands, hundreds of thousands of migratory birds shelter and rest on their annual journeys, while pocosins (a kind of bog) and maritime forests have nurtured innumerable generations of animals and people. This is where you'll find North Carolina's oldest towns—Bath, New Bern, and Edenton. Settlers established their roots here and the towns have survived for more than 300 years. In Washington County, a rural expanse of farms and wetlands, 4,000-year-old canoes pulled out of Lake Phelps stand witness to the region's unplumbed depths of history. Rivers flow from farther inland, with towns like Roanoke Rapids and Halifax that played a vital role in North Carolina's history and development from colony to state.

PLANNING YOUR TIME

Most visitors plan to come to the coast during late spring and summer, and the reasons are obvious: the beaches, restaurants and attractions that are only open in season, and numerous warm-weather festivals and goings-on. Summer is a great time to visit, but many prefer the shoulder seasons: early to mid-spring and early in the fall. During the fall, the water is still warm, most of the restaurants and attractions are still open, and the crowds are smaller. To many of us who live here, the solitude offered by a winter beach is hard to beat, and a growing number of visitors are coming to love the coast in the off-season as well.

As schools and colleges call students back and the summer season ends, eastern North Carolina's second busy season begins: the tobacco harvest. In rural areas, trucks laden with huge yellow-green tobacco leaves head for the curing barns. The smell of curing tobacco, and later the tight bales of golden leaves, is like none other, and once you smell it, you'll have a taste for fall in this part of the state. Early autumn also brings intermittent clouds of smoke as farmers and backyard-garden hobbyists clear their summer gardens and prepare the ground for cool-weather crops. Beds of lettuce and onions and patches of mustard greens and collards begin to appear alongside houses. Collards, which are at their most flavorful after a touch of fall frost, are a local favorite, although they're popular with North Carolina transplants and visitors searching for an authentic Southern dish. There's no end to the way folks here will prepare collards, but they either accent or mask their mustiness; either way, after a forkful, you'll go back for more. Cotton comes in late in the year and as the bolls ripen, the fields appear snow-covered and quite beautiful.

Spring and fall, and even the occasional winter warm spell, offer many ideal days for exploring eastern North Carolina's rivers, creeks, and swamps in a kayak, canoe, or stand-up paddleboard. Mild temperatures are comfortable enough for a day of paddling, and though the foliage is still green, the absence of summer's leafiness means you can see deeper into the landscape and spy on wildlife from a safe distance. Keep in mind, though, that you can see alligators or even snakes in late fall and throughout the winter. They're never far off, and an especially warm day will have them seeking out sunny patches for basking. If you go for a hike, wear boots, and don't wade or swim in fresh water. Keep an eye out for alligators if you're in, on, or around the water. Gators are hard to spot, especially if you've never looked for them, so watch for their nostrils and the bony ridges of their brow and dorsal spines just above the water's surface.

While the coast can be ideal to visit in the fall, remember that autumn is peak hurricane season in North Carolina. Surfers may love the waves before and after storms, but even people with lots of experience avoid hurricanes. These storms can be beautiful in their ferocity and violence, but anyone who's been through even a weak hurricane will tell you they're no joke. About a week before a fall visit, check the long-term forecasts and call to confirm the weather where you're staying. If authorities issue evacuation orders during your visit, don't hesitate, just pack up and head to safety on the mainland.

INFORMATION AND SERVICES

The **Aycock Brown Welcome Center** (Milepost 1, Kitty Hawk, 877/629-4386, www.outerbanks.org, 9am-5pm daily, closed Thanksgiving and Dec. 25) at Kitty Hawk and the **Outer Banks Welcome Center on Roanoke Island** (1 Visitors Center Circle, Manteo, 252/473-2138 or 877/629-4386, www.outerbanks.org, 9am-5pm daily, closed Thanksgiving and Dec. 25) are the main welcome centers in the Outer Banks, with smaller

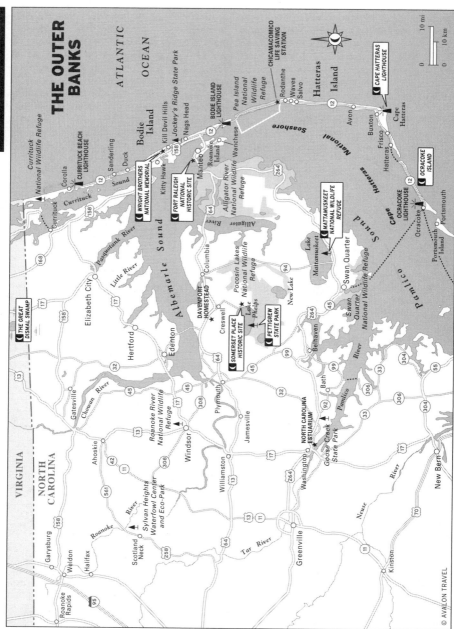

THE OUTER BANKS

© AVALON TRAVEL

PRONUNCIATION PRIMER

North Carolina is full of oddly pronounced place-names, and the farthest northeast corner is a good place to pause for a lesson in talking like a native. The Outer Banks are a garland of peculiar names as well as names that look straightforward but are in fact pronounced in unexpectedly quirky ways. If you make reference publicly to the town of Corolla and pronounce it like the Toyota, you'll be recognized right away as someone "from off." It's pronounced "ker-AH-luh." Similarly, Bodie Island, site of the striped lighthouse, is pronounced "body." That same pattern of pronouncing o as ah is repeated farther down the coast at Chicamacomico, which comes out "chick-uh-muh-CAH-muh-co." But just to keep you on your toes, the rule doesn't apply to Ocracoke, which is pronounced like the Southern vegetable and Southern drink: "O-kra-coke."

Farther south along the banks is the town of Rodanthe, pronounced "ro-DAN-thee." On Roanoke Island, Manteo might resemble a Spanish word but is in fact front-loaded, like so many Carolina words and names. It's pronounced "MAN-tee-oh" or "MAN-nee-oh." Next door is the town of Wanchese, pronounced like a pallid dairy product, "WAN-cheese." Inland, the Cashie River is pronounced "cuh-SHY," Bertie County is "ber-TEE," and Chowan County is "chuh-WAHN." If you think the names around here are unusual, just wait until you get into the mountains.

welcome centers at Hatteras and Whalebone Junction.

Major hospitals include **The Outer Banks Hospital** (4800 S. Croatan Hwy., Milepost 14, Nags Head, 252/449-4500, www.theouterbankshospital.com) in Nags Head, **Albemarle Health** (1144 North Road St., Elizabeth City, 252/335-0531, www.albemarlehealth.org) in Elizabeth City, **Vidant Roanoke-Chowan Hospital** (500 S. Academy St., Ahoskie, 252/209-3000, www.vidanthealth.com) in Ahoskie, **Vidant Chowan Hospital** (211 Virginia Rd., Edenton, 252/482-8451, www.vidanthealth.com) in Edenton, **Vidant Beaufort Hospital** (628 E. 12th St., Washington, 252/975-4100, www.beaufortregionalhealthsystem.org) in Washington, **Vidant Bertie Hospital** (1403 S. King St., Windsor, 252/794-6600, www.vidanthealth.com) in Windsor, and **Halifax Regional Hospital** (250 Smith Church Rd., Roanoke Rapids, 252/535-8011, www.halifaxregional.us) in Roanoke Rapids. On Ocracoke, which is only accessible by air or water, nonemergency medical situations can be addressed by **Ocracoke Health Center** (305 Back Rd., 252/928-1511, after-hours 252/928-7425, www.ocracokeisland.com). Note that 911 emergency service is available on Ocracoke, as it is throughout the state.

Nags Head and Vicinity

Coral reefs anchor most barrier islands, lending them a bit of strength and permanence; not so on North Carolina's Outer Banks. Here, no reef helps shape the islands, and they're more like enormous sandbars, susceptible to the whims of the wind, the sea, and storms. But that's part of the beauty. These natural forces shape the land as well as its history and culture.

Jockey's Ridge, a 100-foot-high dune visible to sailors far out to sea, has been used as a navigational aide for hundreds of years. Legend has it that Nags Head earned its name because of these dunes and the passing ships. Islanders known as proggers (a shipwreck scavenger or land pirate) would lead a nag or mule along the beach and dune ridge, a lantern hung around

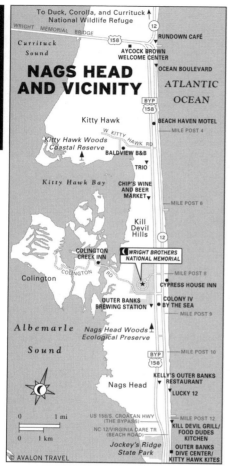

NAGS HEAD AND VICINITY

To Duck, Corolla, and Currituck
National Wildlife Refuge
WRIGHT MEMORIAL BRIDGE
RUNDOWN CAFÉ
AYCOCK BROWN WELCOME CENTER
OCEAN BOULEVARD
Currituck Sound
ATLANTIC OCEAN
Kitty Hawk
BEACH HAVEN MOTEL
MILE POST 4
W. KITTY HAWK RD
Kitty Hawk Woods Coastal Reserve
BALDVIEW B&B
TRIO
Kitty Hawk Bay
CHIP'S WINE AND BEER MARKET
MILE POST 6
Kill Devil Hills
COLINGTON CREEK INN
WRIGHT BROTHERS NATIONAL MEMORIAL
Colington
COLINGTON RD
MILE POST 8
CYPRESS HOUSE INN
OUTER BANKS BREWING STATION
COLONY IV BY THE SEA
MILE POST 9
Albemarle Sound
Nags Head Woods Ecological Preserve
MILE POST 10
KELLY'S OUTER BANKS RESTAURANT
Nags Head
LUCKY 12
0   1 mi
0   1 km
US 158/S. CROATAN HWY (THE BYPASS)
NC 12/VIRGINIA DARE TR (BEACH ROAD)
MILE POST 12
KILL DEVIL GRILL/ FOOD DUDES KITCHEN
Jockey's Ridge State Park
OUTER BANKS DIVE CENTER/ KITTY HAWK KITES
© AVALON TRAVEL

a NASA engineer and inventor of hang gliding. Today, thousands flock to the Wright Brothers Memorial to see where history was made, and even more visit Jockey's Ridge to watch hang gliders or even to take to the sky themselves. With kite-flying, kite-boarding, skydiving, parasailing, and even paragliding, flight enthusiasts love the Outer Banks. Add to this sailing, diving, surfing, paddling, hiking, bird-watching, and, of course, visits to beaches like Duck, which is lovely at sunset, and Corolla, where you can spot wild ponies, and it's obvious that the northern Outer Banks are among the most promising areas in North Carolina for outdoor adventure.

SIGHTS
◖ Wright Brothers National Memorial

In 1903, Orville and Wilbur Wright changed the world in just 12 seconds. Their first flight was short, but it was the culmination of more than three years of failed designs, tests, and travels between their Dayton, Ohio, home and Kitty Hawk, North Carolina, where they tested their gliders on Kill Devil Hill, then the tallest dune on the Outer Banks. A number of Banker families fed and housed them, built them hangars, and assisted with countless trial runs that helped make their experiment a success. On the morning of December 17, 1903, several local people were on hand to help that famous first powered flight get into the air. John Daniels, a lifesaver from a nearby station, took the iconic photo of the airplane lifting off. It was the only photograph he ever took. He was later quoted in a newspaper saying of the flight, "I didn't think it amounted to much." Even though he was unimpressed, the feat is honored at the **Wright Brothers National Memorial** (Milepost 7.5, U.S. 158, Kill Devil Hills, 252/441-7430, www.nps.gov, park daily year-round, visitors center 9am-5pm daily). Replica gliders, artifacts from the original flight, and tools the Wright brothers used to make their flight possible are on display. In the adjacent field a wooden runner and stone markers show their runway, takeoff point, and the spots where

its neck, luring ships into the shallows and shoals where they'd wreck, making their cargo easy pickings. Likewise, the shoals, shallows, and currents gave birth to the heroic members of the United States Lifesaving Service, predecessor to the Coast Guard, who braved many storms to save those shipwrecked.

The relentless wind on the Outer Banks lured Orville and Wilbur Wright to Kill Devil Hills, where they became the first people in history to take flight. It also drew Francis Rogallo,

the Wright Brothers National Memorial

© JASON FRYE

their first four flights landed. Climb to the top of nearby Kill Devil Hill to the 60-foot monument honoring their achievement and marking the spot where they launched hundreds of gliders that preceded that first powered flight. At the foot of the hill, a life-size bronze sculpture of the *Wright Flyer* seconds after liftoff lets you get a sense of the excitement of the moment.

Jockey's Ridge State Park

Jockey's Ridge State Park (Milepost 12, U.S. 158, 252/441-7132, http://ncparks.gov, park 8am-6pm daily Nov.-Feb., 8am-8pm daily Mar.-May, 8am-9pm daily June-Aug., 8am-8pm daily Sept.-Oct., visitors center 9am-5pm daily Nov.-Feb., 9am-6pm daily Mar.-Oct.), contains 420 acres of recreational opportunities in an array of environments. With the big dune, which shifts between 80 and 100 feet high, the smaller dunes surrounding it, the maritime forest, and the sound, you can sand-board (think snowboarding at the beach), fly kites, hike, go for a swim, or even learn to hang glide.

Nags Head Woods Ecological Preserve

Adjacent to Jockey's Ridge, the Nature Conservancy maintains the 1,400-acre **Nags Head Woods Ecological Preserve** (701 W. Ocean Acres Dr., 1 mile from Milepost 9.5 on U.S. 158, 252/441-2525, www.nature.org, dawn-dusk daily year-round). The landscape includes deciduous maritime forest, dunes, wetlands, and interdune ponds, providing a compact look at the diverse environments found on the Outer Banks. It's a bird-watcher's paradise as more than 50 species nest here in season. Ruby-throated hummingbirds, green herons, and red-shouldered hawks are among the easiest to spot, but don't just look for winged wildlife; a number of land animals and reptiles, and even some unusual plants, call this place home. Five miles of public trails wind through the property, starting at the visitors center.

Kitty Hawk Woods Coastal Reserve

Kitty Hawk Woods Coastal Reserve (south of U.S. 158, Kitty Hawk, trail access from Woods Rd. and Birch Lane, off Treasure St., 252/261-8891, http://nccoastalreserve.net, dawn-dusk daily year-round), an 1,822-acre nature preserve maintained by the North Carolina Coastal Reserve, contains one of the largest remaining maritime forests in the Outer Banks. Maritime forests help barrier islands absorb the brunt of powerful storms, and Kitty Hawk Woods contains unusual examples of maritime swale ecosystems, swampy forest sheltered between coastal ridges. Hiking and birding opportunities are abundant, and exploring it from the water via canoe, kayak, or stand-up paddleboard is easy thanks to a put-in. Hunting is permitted in Kitty Hawk Woods, so exercise caution while hiking or paddling during the spring and fall hunting seasons.

Jennette's Pier

My family vacationed on the Outer Banks, and **Jennette's Pier** (7223 S. Virginia Dare Tr., Nags Head, 252/255-1501, www.jennettespier.net, 8am-5pm daily Dec.-Mar.,

sandy trail at Jockey's Ridge State Park

6am-midnight daily Apr., 5am-midnight daily May-Aug., 6am-midnight daily Sept.-Nov., fishing $12, under age 13 $6, walk-on $2 donation) was a fixture on each trip. The then-wooden pier, originally built in 1939, was picturesque but fragile; the owners repaired it after each storm until 2003, when the North Carolina Aquariums bought the pier and Hurricane Isabel demolished 540 feet of the pier structure. Many thought it was the end of this beachside institution, but a new 1,000-foot concrete pier was built. Now an educational and recreational platform managed by the North Carolina Aquarium, the new Jennette's Pier is a LEED Platinum-certified facility and a beautiful lasting structure. Staff here are friendly and accommodating, and during peak season, activities that include summer day camps and nighttime seashore explorations teach kids and adults alike about the ecology of the area.

Currituck Heritage Park

We've come to expect grand ostentatious beachside homes, but on the shore of Currituck Sound, you'll find what may be the original one on the Outer Banks: the **Whalehead Club** (1100 Club Rd., Corolla, 252/453-9040, www.whaleheadclub.org, 9am-5pm Mon.-Sat. summer, 11am-4pm Mon.-Sat. off-season). This art deco home was built in the 1920s as a summer cottage for Edward Collings Knight Jr., an industrialist whose wealth was made in railroads and sugar. The beautiful simple yellow house is the centerpiece of **Currituck Heritage Park,** where visitors can picnic, wade, launch from the boat ramp, or learn about the ghosts (yes, it's rumored to be haunted, and it's no wonder, with so many shipwrecks just off shore).

Next to the Whalehead Club is the **Outer Banks Center for Wildlife Education** (1160 Village Lane, Corolla, 252/453-0221, www.ncwildlife.org, 9am-4:30pm Mon.-Sat., donation). Exhibits focus on native birds, fish, and other creatures in Currituck Sound as well as a huge collection of antique decoys. These decoys represent an important folk-art tradition

THE OUTER BANKS

© JASON FRYE

Jennette's Pier

and way of life for many along the Carolina coast. They're beautiful not just for their design but also for their utility. Naturalists put on a number of nature and art programs throughout the year; check the calendar on the website before you go to see what they have planned.

A favorite spot here is the **Currituck Beach Lighthouse** (1101 Corolla Village Rd., 252/453-4939, www.currituckbeachlight. com, 9am-5pm daily Mar.-Nov., $7, under age 8 free with an adult) and its grounds. Built in 1875, this 158-foot-tall redbrick lighthouse is open to ascend much of the year. As you climb the 214 steps to the top, think about the lighthouse keepers, who for years carried pails of lard, then later pails of kerosene, to the top to fuel the light. Once at the observation deck, take a moment to catch your breath and take in the scenery (and hold onto your hat; it can be windy). The Currituck light is a twin to the Bodie Island Lighthouse, 32 miles south. Upon its completion it lit the last "dark spot" on the North Carolina coast, making for safer navigation.

Corolla Wild Horse Museum

In the town of Corolla you'll find a museum dedicated to some of the more unexpected residents of the Outer Banks. The **Corolla Wild Horse Museum** (1129 Corolla Village Rd., Corolla, 252/453-8002, www.corollawild-horses.com) tells the history of the herd of horses that have lived on the Outer Banks from Corolla to Cape Lookout since the 1600s. The Corolla herd now lives in a preserve north of the town, and several guides offer tours to see the horses in their native habitat.

ENTERTAINMENT AND EVENTS

My favorite spot for wine and beer on the Outer Banks is **Trio** (308 N. Croatan Hwy., Milepost 4.5, 252/261-0277, http://obxtrio. com, 11am-11pm Mon.-Sat., noon-10pm Sun.). The trio the name refers to is wine, beer, and cheese, the passions of the four owners. The selection at Trio is focused and representative of different styles, nations, and grape varietals. Upstairs, North Carolina wine

© JASON FRYE

The distinctive redbrick Currituck Beach Lighthouse is the northernmost lighthouse in the state.

Wine University, offering everything from beginner classes to private tastings.

Food Festivals

As food-centered travel has gained momentum, four festivals taking advantage of this trend have emerged on the Outer Banks. Each draws visitors during the shoulder seasons and showcases something different about the area and its food.

In March, **Taste of the Beach** (www.obxtasteofthebeach.com) features wine tastings, cooking classes by local chefs, cook-offs, dine-arounds, and more, hosted by more than 50 restaurants, breweries, wine shops, and food purveyors on the Banks. The four-day festival (there are plans to make it longer) culminates with the OBX Grand Tasting, where restaurants compete for the best overall dish, best local seafood dish, the Chefs Award, and the People's Choice Award. *Coastal Living* magazine named Taste of the Beach one of the top seafood and wine festivals in the country in 2008, and it has been on the list ever since.

The **Duck and Wine Festival** (www.duckandwine.com), a one-day cook-off held in mid-late April, brings foodies together in the town of Duck to sample dishes that local chefs have created using, you guessed it, duck. The town of Duck shines again in mid-October for the **Duck Jazz Festival** (www.townofduck.com), a one-day festival that features talented national jazz artists and alfresco dining from some of Duck's best restaurants.

Mid-October is also the time for the **Outer Banks Seafood Festival** (www.outerbanksseafoodfestival.org). Although oyster roasts, clam bakes, shrimparoos, and other informal seafood celebrations have been the norm on the Outer Banks for more than a century, 2012 was the first year for this formal seafood festival. More than a dozen restaurants participate in the one-day event, and organizers plan to grow the festival into a marquee event.

Nightlife

One part beach dive bar, one part sports bar, **Lucky 12** (Milepost 12, S. Virginia Dare Tr./

and beer tastings are complimentary and serve as a good introduction to drinks produced across the state. Other tastings include the Trio Passport (focusing on wine from different nations) as well as varietal- and style-specific tastings. Nearly two dozen beers are on tap, and self-serve wine vending stations give you the chance to try tasting-size samples or even full glasses of expensive, hard to find, or interesting wines. Trio serves a selection of small plates, including paninis, salads, cheese plates, and other nibbles that go well with a glass of whatever you're drinking.

Chip's Wine and Beer Market (Milepost 6, Croatan Hwy./U.S. 158, Kill Devil Hills, 252/449-8229, www.chipswinemarket.com) is exactly what its name says. More than 450 craft beers from regional, national, and international breweries along with 2,000-plus wines line the shelves—but don't worry, the knowledgeable staff can find a brew or a bottle that suits your taste. Chip's is also home of the Outer Banks

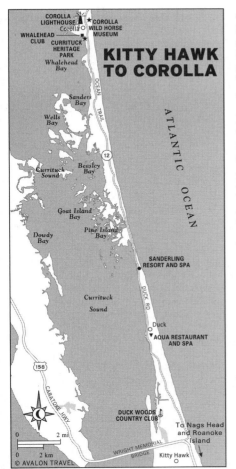

COROLLA LIGHTHOUSE
COROLLA WILD HORSE MUSEUM
Corolla
WHALEHEAD CLUB
CURRITUCK HERITAGE PARK
Whalehead Bay

KITTY HAWK TO COROLLA

Sanders Bay

Wells Bay

OCEAN TRAIL

Currituck Sound

Beasley Bay

ATLANTIC OCEAN

12

Goat Island Bay

Pine Island Bay

Dowdy Bay

SANDERLING RESORT AND SPA

Currituck Sound

DUCK RD.

Duck

AQUA RESTAURANT AND SPA

CAROTAKE HWY

158

DUCK WOODS COUNTRY CLUB

To Nags Head and Roanoke Island

WRIGHT MEMORIAL BRIDGE

Kitty Hawk

0   2 mi.
0   2 km
© AVALON TRAVEL

4:30pm-1am Sun.-Thurs., 4:30pm-2am Fri.-Sat., entrées around $22, tavern fare around $10) is a good bet for live music. Throughout the week karaoke and open-mike nights are the norm, but the weekend feature DJs and bands. With a tavern and a dining-room menu, it's easy to find the right thing to eat.

Ocean Boulevard (Milepost 2.5, N. Virginia Dare Tr./Hwy. 12, Kitty Hawk, 252/261-2546, www.obbistro.com, 5pm-9pm Mon.-Thurs., 5pm-1:30am Fri., 5pm-10pm Sat., 5pm-9pm Sun., entrées $21-31), an upscale but casual martini bar and bistro, features live music on Friday and Saturday during the season, and with the impressive drink menu, it's easy to see why the place is popular with locals and visitors.

Port O' Call Restaurant (Milepost 8.5, S. Virginia Dare Tr./Hwy. 12, Kill Devil Hills, 252/441-7484, http://obxportocall.com, call for hours, entrées $16-28) has been an Outer Banks fixture for more than 50 years. The menu features local seafood and a nice wine list, and live entertainment is available in the bar almost nightly throughout high season.

The Comedy Club (252/207-9950, www.comedyclubobx.com) is, well, a comedy club with two locations on the Outer Banks. Local, up-and-coming, and established comedians perform nightly in summer at the Comedy Club in the Ramada Plaza Hotel (Milepost 9.5, S. Virginia Dare Tr./Hwy. 12, Kill Devil Hills, showtimes vary), and Wednesday in summer at the Currituck Club (620 Currituck Clubhouse Dr., Corolla, showtimes vary). Both clubs serve cocktails and appetizers during the show.

SHOPPING

Much of the shopping on the Outer Banks is focused on beachy souvenir T-shirts and tchotchkes, or beach supplies like towels, boogie boards, and rash guards. There are too many of these mass-market beachwear clearing houses to list, but they're so prolific that they're easy to find. There are also some boutiques, carrying things like bathing suits, art, and jewelry.

Birthday Suits (2000 S. Croatan Hwy./U.S.

Hwy. 12, Nags Head, 252/255-5825, www.lucky12tavern.com, 11:30am-2am daily) is a hit with locals and visitors alike. With 20 beers on tap, another 90 in bottles or cans, a staggering 40-martini drink menu, and more than a dozen TVs, it's the kind of place to watch a game, hang out with friends, and order a pizza (served until 2am).

Kelly's Outer Banks Restaurant and Tavern (Milepost 10.5, U.S. 158, Nags Head, 252/441-4116, www.kellysrestaurant.com,

158, Milepost 10, Kill Devil Hills, 252/441-5338, http://birthday-suits.com, 10am-9pm daily summer, 10am-6pm daily spring, 10am-5pm daily fall) has been in the business of outfitting Bankers and visitors in the best bathing suits for more than 25 years. **Kitty Hawk Kites** (Milepost 12.5, S. Croatan Hwy./U.S. 158, Nags Head, 252/449-2210, www.kittyhawk.com, call for hours) carries swimwear and beach supplies as well as kites, toys, and an assortment of beach games and sports equipment.

In Duck, **Scarborough Faire** (1177 Duck Rd., Duck, 540/272-0974, www.scarborough-faireinducknc.com, hours vary, generally from 10am daily), has served the boutique shopping needs of visitors and residents for over 30 years. More than a dozen shops call Scarborough Faire home, including **Island Bookstore** (252/261-8981, www.islandbooksobx.com, 9am-7pm Mon.-Fri., 9am-6pm Sat.-Sun.), which carries a decent selection of best-sellers and books for kids and teens, and **The Mystic Jewel** (252/255-5515, http://themysticjewel.com, 10am-5pm Mon.-Sat., 11am-4pm Sun.), a jewelry store specializing in unusual stones and limited-edition jewelry pieces by artists from around the world; prices range $20 to around $400.

Fans of local art will want to take a look at **KDH Cooperative Gallery and Studios** (502 S. Croatan Hwy./U.S. 158, Milepost 8.5, Kill Devil Hills, 252/441-9888, www.kdhcooperative.com, 10am-6pm Mon.-Sat.), where more than 40 artists, selected by a jury of their peers to be the best to hang and sell in the gallery, show oil, acrylic, and watercolor paintings, photography, ceramics, sculptures, and more; a few even keep working studios here, providing the opportunity to see them in action. Prices vary as wildly as the media and styles, but if you're an art lover, KDH Cooperative is a must-see.

SPORTS AND RECREATION
Kayaking and Stand-Up Paddleboarding

The Outer Banks combines two very different paddle-sport opportunities, kayaking and stand-up paddleboarding (SUP), in two very different environments—the challenge of ocean paddling and even surfing, and the leisurely drifting tours of salt marshes and creeks. **Kitty Hawk Kites** (Milepost 12.5, S. Croatan Hwy./U.S. 158, Nags Head, 252/449-2210, www.kittyhawk.com, kayak tours $35-55, SUP lessons $59) has locations up and down the Outer Banks where they offer kayak tours, SUP lessons and rentals, and a range of other recreational activities and equipment. *National Geographic Adventure* magazine called them one of the "best adventure travel companies on earth," and they have been in business since the early 1990s.

Kitty Hawk Kayak & Surf School (Milepost 1, N. Croatan Hwy./U.S. 158, Kitty Hawk, 252/261-0145, www.khkss.com, tours $40-60, kayak rentals $99 per week, SUP rentals $150 per week) teaches kayaking and SUP, rents equipment for paddling and surfing, and leads group and private tours, including overnighters. Many of the tours take you to seldom-seen marsh habitats and gorgeous creeks, and even back to the mainland to explore the waterways of the Alligator River National Wildlife Refuge.

Coastal Kayak Touring Company (reservations at North Beach Outfitters, 1240 Duck Rd., Duck, 252/441-3393, www.outerbankskayaktours.com, kayak tours $40-60, SUP tours $50-65) leads groups through some of the beautiful nature reserves on the Outer Banks, namely Kitty Hawk Woods Coastal Reserve and the Pine Island Audubon Sanctuary. Tours range 1.5 to 3 hours.

Outer Banks Stand-Up Paddle (1446 Duck Rd., Duck, 252/305-3639, www.outerbankssup.com, lessons $45-150, rentals from $145 per week) teaches SUP techniques from the basics to the challenge of SUP surfing. Introductory lessons on the sound give first-timers a feel for the board in shallow, wave-free water, where they can build confidence to try ocean-side SUPing on their own with a rented board or with an advanced lesson. The most advanced paddlers will definitely want to take advantage of the SUP surfing lessons.

© JASON FRYE

Kayak the vast sounds along the Outer Banks to experience the barrier islands in a unique way.

Diving

The **Outer Banks Dive Center** (3917 S. Croatan Hwy., 252/449-8349, www.obxdive.com) offers instruction and guided tours of wrecks off the coast of the Outer Banks. Guided wreck dives are only available April-November. All levels of divers are welcome.

Hiking and Tours

At **Jockey's Ridge State Park** (Milepost 12, U.S. 158, 252/441-7132, http://ncparks.gov, park 8am-6pm daily Nov.-Feb., 8am-8pm daily Mar.-May, 8am-9pm daily June-Aug., 8am-8pm daily Sept.-Oct., visitors center 9am-5pm daily Nov.-Feb., 9am-6pm daily Mar.-Oct.), explore the dunes at your own pace or follow one of the trails. The Soundside Nature Trail is about one mile long and takes you through maritime thickets and grassy dunes on a walk through a seldom-seen part of the park. Follow the Tracks in the Sand trail on its 1.5-mile course early in the morning to see undisturbed animal tracks left during the night. Remember,

the dunes can be considerably warmer and the sand can be downright hot, especially during the summer. Bring sunscreen, shoes, and plenty of water if you're trekking around this park.

The **Currituck Banks National Estuarine Preserve** (Hwy. 12, 252/261-8891, www.nccoastalreserve.net) protects some 1,000 acres of woods and water, extending far out into Currituck Sound. A short boardwalk runs from the parking lot to the sound, and a primitive trail runs 1.5 miles through the maritime forest.

You can hike in any park and most of the preserves on the Outer Banks, but nothing compares to seeing the Wild Horses in Corolla. The **Corolla Wild Horse Fund** (1129 Corolla Village Rd., Corolla, 252/453-8002, www.corollawildhorses.com, $45, $20 children) is a nonprofit group dedicated to preserving the herd and its environment, and they lead tours (3 times daily Mon.-Sat.). On the tour you'll ride along with herd managers and conservationists and get a glimpse into how they help keep the horses and their environment safe and healthy.

Back Country Outfitters and Guides (107-C Corolla Light Town Center, Corolla, 252/453-0877, http://outerbankstours.com, wild horse tours $49, $29 ages 3-12, Segway safari $124 over age 12) leads wild horse tours as well as backcountry Segway tours, kayak trips, and other off-road tours.

Surfing

North Carolina has a reputation among surfers for having some of the best waves on the East Coast, making this a top destination for experienced surfers and those new to the sport.

Kitty Hawk Kites (Milepost 12.5, S. Croatan Hwy./U.S. 158, Nags Head, 252/449-2210, www.kittyhawk.com)provides lessons and board rentals. At **Island Revolution Surf Co. and Skate** (252/453-9484, www.island-revolution.com, group lessons $65 pp, private lessons $110), you can take private or group surf lessons, and more experienced surfers can opt to join the Surf Safari, where local surfers teach the finer points of reading local waves and breaks and show you some of the best surf spots on the island. **Farmdog Surf School** (2500 S. Virginia Dare Tr., Nags Head, 252/255-2233, http://farmdogsurfschool.com, $65) and **Corolla Surf Shop** (807 Ocean Tr., Corolla, 252/453-9283, www.corollasurfshop.com, $68) also offer lessons, rentals, and advice.

If you're a veteran surfer and you're bringing your own board, several online resources will help you find the best conditions and the perfect breaks. The websites of the Outer Banks District of the Eastern Surfing Association (www.outerbanksesa.com), OBXSurfInfo (www.obxsurfinfo.com), Surfline (www.surfline.com), and SwellInfo (www.swellinfo.com) will help you find the best places to suit up and drop in.

Hang Gliding

With all the wind on the Outer Banks, everyone thinks about flying a kite, but how about flying a hang glider? **Kitty Hawk Kites** (Milepost 12.5, S. Croatan Hwy./U.S. 158,

hang gliding off Jockey's Ridge

© JASON FRYE

THE OUTER BANKS

Nags Head, 252/449-2210, www.kittyhawk. com, $99) offers dune hang gliding lessons that will give you a taste of the thrill of flight as you lift off over the face of dunes on Jockey's Ridge. More than 300,000 people have learned to hang glide here since the company's Hang Gliding Training Center opened in 1974. Learning to fly on the dunes is quite a thrill, but you can up the thrill factor and try a tandem flight that will have you and an instructor towed up to a mile high before being released to fly back to earth. If you want to pursue advanced certification through the United States Hang Gliding Association, you can do that on the dunes or on a tandem flight; you can even buy a glider and all the accessories you need to get started at the Kitty Hawk Kites retail store across the road from the school.

Golf

There are plenty of mini golf courses on the Outer Banks, but for the full-scale experience, only a handful of courses are open to the public. **Duck Woods Country Club** (50 S. Dogwood Tr., Southern Shores, 252/261-2609, www.duckwoodscc.com, greens fees vary by season, $115 summer) is a 6,000-plus-yard, par-72 course that's challenging but fun any time of year. **Sea Scape Golf Links** (300 Eckner St., Kitty Hawk, 252/261-2158, www.seascapegolf. com, greens fees $50-99) offers 18-hole, par-70 links-style play only a block from the ocean. Be warned, the wind can be a major factor when you play here; keep your ball low.

At another links-style course, the 18-hole, par-71 **Nags Head Golf Links** (5615 S. Seachase Dr., Nags Head, 252/389-9079, www.club-corp.com, greens fees $55-125), the wind is definitely in play; in fact, *Golf Digest* called this course "the longest 6,126 yards you'll ever play."

ACCOMMODATIONS

The **C First Colony Inn** (6720 Virginia Dare Tr., Nags Head, 800/368-9390, www.first-colonyinn.com, $99-299, varies by season) is a wonderful 1932 beachfront hotel. This regional landmark has won historic preservation and landscaping awards for its 1988 renovation, which involved moving the entire building, in three pieces, three miles south of its original location. The pretty and luxurious guest rooms are surprisingly affordable.

In Duck, the **Sanderling Resort and Spa** (1461 Duck Rd., Duck, 855/412-7866, www.sanderling-resort.com, $299-539) reopened in May 2013 after a $6 million renovation. More than a face-lift, the renovation added guest rooms and an adults-only pool, revitalized the dining experience at the resort, created new event spaces, and upgraded the public spaces resort-wide. Kimball's Kitchen, the resort's main restaurant, serves a menu focused on local seafood and grass-fed steaks. The view of Currituck Sound is amazing from every seat in the house, and the restaurant's elegance, view, and level of service make it an experience like no other on the Outer Banks.

There are many bed-and-breakfasts, including the **Cypress Moon Inn** (1206 Harbor Court, Kitty Hawk, 877/905-5060, www.cypressmooninn.com, no children, $135-210, varies by season), a small but beautiful sound-side home featuring three guest rooms. The owners also have three cottages nearby that are perfect for secluded getaways.

The **Cypress House Inn** (Milepost 8, Beach Rd., Kill Devil Hills, 800/554-2764, www.cypresshouseinn.com, $99-219, varies by season) is only 125 yards from the ocean, and that, combined with its central location to Outer Banks attractions and undeniable charm, makes it a desirable B&B. Guests staying in each of the six guest rooms at the 1940s-style inn are treated to complimentary beach chairs and towels. **The Atlantic Street Inn** (Milepost 9.5, Kill Devil Hills, 252/305-0246, www.atlanticstreetinn.com, $69-159) offers similar treatment, with bicycles available for guest use; its six guest rooms can be reserved individually or, if you book far enough ahead, reserve the entire inn or the nearby beach house.

The **Colington Creek Inn** (1293 Colington Rd., Kill Devil Hills, 252/449-4124, www.colingtoncreekinn.com, no children or pets, $178-298, varies by season) has four guest

© JASON FRYE

Sanderling Resort and Spa

rooms with water views of the sound and its namesake creek, along with porches perfect for morning coffee or an evening drink.

At the **Nags Head Beach Inn** (303 E. Admiral St., Nags Head, 252/441-8466, www.nagsheadbeachinn.com, $131-219), a converted beach club dating to the 1930s that's only steps from the beach, all the accoutrements that guest need—chairs, bicycles, body boards, and the like—are available for use. Quaint and comfortable, the Nags Head Beach Inn is one of several cottages known as the "Unpainted Aristocracy." Some of these cottages date back to the 1830s, but they all have common features—weatherworn shake siding and a yesteryear charm.

Throughout Kitty Hawk and Nags Head, you'll find a number of motels, ranging from chains to classic 1950s mom-and-pops. The **Surf Side Hotel** (6701 Virginia Dare Tr., Nags Head, 800/552-7873, www.surfsideobx.com, $79-299, varies by season) has simple, comfortable standard guest rooms and efficiencies in a location only steps from the

beach. At the **Blue Heron** (6811 Virginia Dare Tr., Nags Head, 252/441-7447, www.blueheronnc.com, $58-158, varies by season), every guest room faces the ocean, and for rainy days or off-season visits there is an indoor heated pool.

If you're looking for a motel with that classic beach-motel feel, three spots come to mind. The bargain **Sea Foam Motel** (7111 S. Virginia Dare Tr., Nags Head, 252/441-7320, www.seafoam.com, $68-149, varies by season) is a no-frills motel with a lot of wood paneling and a lot of retro charm. **Beach Haven Motel** (4104 N. Virginia Dare Tr., Kitty Hawk, 252/261-4785, www.beachhavenmotel.com, $77-189, varies by season) offers a little kitsch in the accommodations and even a grill and outdoor picnic area where you can cook your own fresh catch. The wood-paneled walls at **Outer Banks Motor Lodge** (1509 S. Virginia Dare Tr., Milepost 9.5, Kill Devil Hills, 877/625-6343, www.obxmotorlodge.com, $39-225, varies by season) are so tacky that they only add to the place's appeal.

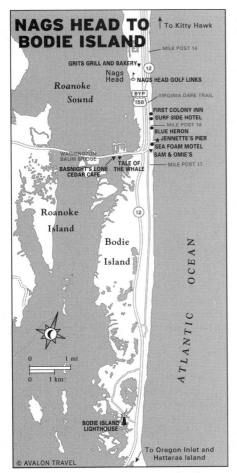

NAGS HEAD TO BODIE ISLAND

To Kitty Hawk

MILE POST 14

GRITS GRILL AND BAKERY

Nags
Head

Roanoke
Sound

NAGS HEAD GOLF LINKS

BYP
158

VIRGINIA DARE TRAIL

FIRST COLONY INN
SURF SIDE HOTEL
MILE POST 16
BLUE HERON
JENNETTE'S PIER
SEA FOAM MOTEL
SAM & OMIE'S
MILE POST 17

WASHINGTON
BAUM BRIDGE

TALE OF
THE WHALE

BASNIGHT'S LONE
CEDAR CAFE

Roanoke
Island

Bodie

Island

Bodie ISLAND
LIGHTHOUSE

To Oregon Inlet and
Hatteras Island

© AVALON TRAVEL

ATLANTIC OCEAN

0   1 mi

0   1 km

FOOD

When I first started visiting the Outer Banks, it seemed that every other restaurant was a seafood buffet. Today, buffets still abound but a number of notable independent restaurants have taken root, and the selection varies from pizza to burgers, gourmet and down home, along with barbecue, fine dining, and a decent representation of international cuisines.

The **Outer Banks Brewing Station** (Milepost 8.5, Croatan Hwy./U.S. 158, Kill Devil Hills, 252/449-2739, www.obbrewing. com, 11:30am-2am daily, entrées $15-31) is an innovative and interesting spot to eat, not just because the food is creative and the beers are adventurous, but because they're wind-powered. Founded by a group of friends who met in the Peace Corps, they combined their love of food, beer, and sustainability to create a hot spot on the Outer Banks' dining and nightlife scenes.

Sam & Omie's (7728 S. Virginia Dare Tr., Nags Head, 252/441-7366, www.samandomies.net, 7am-10pm daily Mar.-mid-Dec., breakfast $1.50-8, dinner $6-26) opened in the summer of 1937 as a place for charter fishing customers and guides to catch breakfast before heading out to sea. They still serve a hearty breakfast heavy on the classics—two eggs your way, pancakes, grits, and the like—but take a look at the specialties, such as crab benedict or the chef's special. Sam & Omie's also serves lunch and dinner, and, as you might expect, both menus emphasize seafood. Sure, you can get a burger, steak, or chicken breast, but why would you when you can get a clam dog, fried oysters, or the massive Whale of a Seafood Platter (which really is more food than one person should eat)?

Owens' Restaurant (Milepost 16.5, Beach Rd., Nags Head, 252/441-7309, www.owensrestaurant.com, 5pm-9pm daily, open later during summer, $20-38) opened in 1946 and has been in continuous operation by the same family ever since. A perennial Outer Banks favorite, Owens serves giant mixed seafood platters, their own version of cioppino and jambalaya, steaks, and more. At Owens' you'll find a treasure trove of photos and artifacts on display, telling the history of the family and the Outer Banks.

A favorite restaurant on the Outer Banks is **Aqua Restaurant and Spa** (1174 Duck Rd., Duck, 252/261-9700, http://restaurantouterbanks.com, lunch 11:30am-3pm daily, dinner 5pm-9pm Sun.-Thurs., 5pm-10pm Fri.-Sat., lunch from $8.50, dinner entrées from $21). It has an interesting concept, with a day spa upstairs and an excellent restaurant downstairs, creating flavorful food using community-sourced organic ingredients and natural meats that will, as the owner puts it, "nourish your body and spirit." Grab a table by the windows or on the deck (weather permitting) and enjoy views of the sound while you dine. The food is straightforward and familiar but flawlessly executed. Try the fresh-catch fish tacos or a salad topped with the catch of the day or crab cakes at lunch, and at dinner it's hard to go wrong with either the duck or the line-caught catch of the day. Vegetarian options are available at both lunch and dinner. Two must-orders are the cone of Aqua fries with truffles, shaved parmesan, and a secret dipping sauce; and the funnel cake, unlike any you've had elsewhere. Light, crispy, chewy, and flavorful even without the homemade ice cream or chocolate drizzle, it's a dessert to share, and one you'll come back for. Aqua also has an exceptionally well-curated wine menu and knowledgeable staff able to steer you toward a glass or bottle that will complement your meal perfectly.

Dining sound-side, especially near sunset, affords two memorable experiences in the food and the view. Another great place to dine on the water is on the causeway at **Tale of the Whale** (7575 S. Virginia Dare Tr., Nags Head, 252/441-7332, http://taleofthewhalenagshead.com, dinner only, hours vary seasonally, around $27). Order a pre-dinner cocktail and enjoy it on the pier that juts out into the Roanoke Sound, or sit and listen to local musicians at the pier-side gazebo. From the dining room, the water view is almost as good as the food. They've got a big menu with everything from off-the-boat fresh fish to grass-fed steaks, pastas, and even vegetarian options. A decent wine list and a creative cocktail menu round out the offerings.

I love a good breakfast place like **Grits Grill** (2000 S. Croatan Hwy., Milepost 14, Nags Head, 252/449-2888, www.gritsgrill.com, 6am-2pm daily, $5-13). The omelets are fluffy, the pancakes are stacked high, and the grits are some of the best I've eaten. Sit at the counter to watch the short-order cooks grill dunes of shredded potatoes into submission as they make countless orders of hash browns. Grits Grill serves lunch—salads, baskets, and sandwiches, including the elusive Monte Cristo—and have breakfast available all day, so it's never hard to find something to eat.

Blue Moon Beach Grill (4104 S. Virginia Dare Tr., Nags Head, 252/261-2583, www.bluemoonbeachgrill.com, 11:30am-9pm daily, $12-25) is rapidly becoming a local favorite. Known for its seafood dishes, Blue Moon is also a popular place to grab a draft beer after work.

Tortuga's Lie (3016 S. Virginia Dare Tr., Nags Head, 252/441-7299, www.tortugaslie.com, 11:30am-10pm Sun.-Thurs., 11:30am-10:30pm Fri.-Sat., about $18) has a good and varied menu specializing in seafood, some of it local, cooked in Caribbean-inspired dishes, along with some good vegetarian options.

For casual and on-the-go chow options at Nags Head, try **Maxximuss Pizza** (5205 S. Croatan Hwy., Nags Head, 252/441-2377, www.nagsheadpizza.com, $6.50-27), which specializes in calzones, subs, and paninis in addition to pizza; **Yellow Submarine** (Milepost 14, U.S. 158 Bypass, Nags Head, 252/441-3511, http://yellowsubmarineobx.com, $7-20), a very casual subs-and-pizza shop.

The **Kill Devil Grill** (2008 S. Virginia Dare Tr., Kill Devil Hills, 252/449-8181, $13-20) serves hearty meals for brunch, lunch, and dinner. Entrées include excellent seafood and steaks. Vegetarians will find limited options, but meat eaters will be well satisfied. **Food Dudes Kitchen** (1216 S. Virginia Dare Tr., Kill Devil Hills, 252/441-7994, 11:30am-9pm Mon.-Sat., 11am-9pm Sun., $10-17) has great seafood, wraps, and sandwiches. **Rundown Café** (5218 N. Virginia Dare Tr., Kitty Hawk, 252/255-0026, 11:30am-late Mon.-Sat., noon-late Sun., $10-15) is a popular local eatery with affordable Caribbean-influenced fare.

One other interesting dining option is joining **Outer Banks Restaurant Tours** (252/722-2229, www.outerbanksrestauranttours.com, tours from $45) on a dine-around excursion in Kitty Hawk, Duck, or Corolla. Each tour consists of four to six stops at restaurants, wine shops, bakeries, and specialty food markets. Other tours include the Brews-Day Tuesday Beer Tour, winery tours, cooking classes, and dessert-only tours.

GETTING THERE AND AROUND

The closest major airport to this region is **Norfolk International Airport** (ORF, 2200 Norview Ave., Norfolk, VA, 757/857-3351, www.norfolkairport.com), approximately an hour from the northern Outer Banks.

Raleigh-Durham International Airport (RDU, 2600 W. Terminal Blvd., Morrisville, 919/840-2123, www.rdu.com) is three to five hours' drive from most Outer Banks destinations.

Only two bridges exist between the mainland and the northern Outer Banks. U.S. 64/264 crosses over Roanoke Island to Whalebone, just south of Nags Head. Not too far north of there, U.S. 158 crosses from Point Harbor to Southern Shores. Highway 12 is the main road all along the northern Outer Banks.

Roanoke Island

The first nonnative residents of the Outer Banks, and perhaps the most famous, called Roanoke Island home for a brief time in the 1580s. These intrepid English colonists found the island protected from the brunt of storms by Albemarle, Roanoke, and Croatan Sounds and the mass of Bodie Island. They established Fort Raleigh, where Virginia Dare, the first European born on the new continent, came into the world. The community then vanished completely, known to history as the Lost Colony. No one knows what happened to them.

Visitors to Roanoke Island today will find what the colonists found: a beautiful, welcoming island ripe for exploration. The relative abundance of bed-and-breakfasts, restaurants, and shops make staying on Roanoke Island much easier than it was four centuries ago.

At the northern end of Roanoke Island the Fort Raleigh National Historic Site marks the last known location of the Lost Colony, and the nearby town of Manteo offers a day or two of dining and distractions. Most of the island's offerings for visitors are concentrated here, although a visit to the tiny town of Wanchese at the southern end of the island is worthwhile. Here, some of Dare County's oldest immigrant families continue to ply their ancestral trades of boatbuilding and fishing.

◖ FORT RALEIGH NATIONAL HISTORIC SITE

Fort Raleigh National Historic Site (1401 National Park Dr., Manteo, 252/473-2111, www.nps.gov, 9am-5pm daily, closed Dec. 25, free) includes much of the original site of the first English settlement in the New World. Archaeologists still conduct digs here, regularly unearthing new artifacts and assembling clues about the Lost Colony's fate, but sections of the earthworks associated with the original 1580s fort remain and have been preserved, making it easy to imagine the site as a working fort on the frontier of an unknown land. In the visitors center, which underwent an extensive renovation in early 2013, artifacts and interactive displays tell the story of the fort and the missing colonists, and of the freedman's colony—a colony of freed and displaced slaves established on the island during the Civil War. Two nature trails in the park allow you to explore the natural landscape and the site of a Civil War battle.

Within the National Historic Site, two of Manteo's most famous attractions operate autonomously. Nearly 60 years ago, **Elizabethan Gardens** (1411 National Park Dr., Manteo, 252/473-3234, http://elizabethangardens. org, 10am-4pm daily Dec.-Feb., 9am-5pm daily Mar.-May, 9am-6pm daily Apr.-May, 9am-7pm daily June-Aug., 9am-6pm daily Sept., 9am-5pm daily Oct.-Nov., $9, $6 ages 6-17,

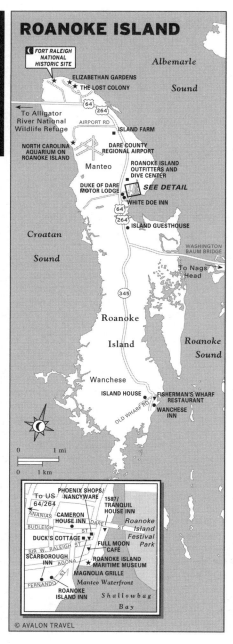

ROANOKE ISLAND

under age 6 free, $3 pets) was conceived by the Garden Club of North Carolina as a permanent memorial to the settlers of Roanoke Island. As a tribute, they planted the types of gardens and plants that would have been common in the colonists' native England in the 16th century. There are many corners to explore in this 10.5 acre garden, and many treasures both natural and artificial to discover: an ancient live oak so huge that many believe it has been standing since the colonists' days; a sunken garden containing Renaissance-era statuary; a Shakespearian herb garden; an impressive display of camellias and azaleas; and a 19th-century statue of Virginia Dare. The statue was underwater off the coast of Spain for two years, was salvaged, and made it to Massachusetts, where it was nearly lost in a fire. It finally arrived in North Carolina in the 1920s, where modest residents, shocked by the statue's nudity, passed it around the state for years until it found a permanent home in Elizabethan Gardens.

Also within the park is the Waterside Theatre. North Carolina has a long history of outdoor performances celebrating regional heritage and history, and the best known of these is Roanoke Island's *The Lost Colony* (1409 National Park Dr., Manteo, 252/473-2127, http://thelostcolony.org, from $24). Playwright Paul Green was commissioned to write a drama about the colony in 1937 to celebrate the 350th anniversary of the birth of Virginia Dare. What he thought would be a single-season production has turned into a fixture, with performances every year since, except when extraordinary circumstances, like German U-boats prowling off the coast during World War II, interrupted the production schedule.

OTHER SIGHTS

The **Roanoke Island Maritime Museum** (104 Fernando St., Manteo, 252/475-1750, http://roanokeisland.com, hours vary, free) is a unique working boat shop and repository for artifacts that offer a look at local and regional maritime heritage. Traditional boat

THE LOST COLONY

On July 4, 1584, an English expedition commissioned by Walter Raleigh dropped anchor in the sound near Hatteras Island. Within a couple of days, local Native Americans were coming and going from the English ships, making trades and some of the first offers of Southern hospitality. They got on famously, and when the English returned home to tell the court of the land they'd found, two indigenous Roanoke men, Manteo and Wanchese, came along as guests. It seems that Wanchese was a bit taciturn and found London not to his liking, but Manteo was amazed at what he saw and found the English to be all right.

A year later, a new expedition set out for Roanoke, this time with the intentions of establishing a permanent settlement. When they reached the Pamlico Sound, their bad luck began. Most of their food stores were soaked and ruined when seawater breeched the ship, so from the moment they set foot on land, they were dependent on the mercy of the indigenous inhabitants. Manteo and Wanchese went to Roanoke chief Wingina to discuss the colonists' plight. Wanchese was a man of superior insight, told Wingina of what he had seen, and begged Wingina to withhold help for the colonists. Manteo, however, pled their case well, and the colonists were made welcome.

The colonists grew dependent on the Roanoke people's generosity and had done very little to become self-sufficient by the time winter arrived. That's when a silver cup disappeared from the English compound. They believed the thief to be from a nearby Native American village, which they promptly burned to the ground. Wingina, worried for the fate of his people, shut down his assistance in hopes that the English would either starve or leave. They did neither, and instead killed the generous chief. Three weeks later an English supply ship arrived with reinforcements of soldiers, materiel, and food stores, only to find the colony totally deserted.

Another attempt at colonizing Roanoke was made, this time with families rather than rowdy gangs of single men. A young couple, Eleanor and Ananais Dare, were expecting a child, and soon after they landed on Roanoke, Virginia Dare, the first English child born in the New World, arrived. The situation with the Native Americans grew worse, though, and the Roanoke people, now under the leadership of Wanchese, were unwilling to aid the second wave of colonists. Manteo, ever the optimist and still friendly with the English, tried to enlist the help of his people, but they were facing lean times as well. John White, leader of the colonial expedition and grandfather to Virginia Dare, returned to England on what he planned to be a fast there-and-back voyage for supplies. It was three years before he returned, and when he did, he found no signs of the settlers—no bodies, no bones, no sign except the letters "CRO" carved on a tree and "CROATOAN" on a palisade stake.

And so began 400 years of mystery and speculation that will probably never be resolved. Some believe the English were killed, others that they were captured and sold into slavery to indigenous people farther inland, still others believe they left under the protection of nearby Native Americans known to be friendly, and then died off or assimilated into Indian society. Several communities in the South of uncertain or mixed racial heritage believe themselves to be descendants of the lost colonists, and some evidence suggests that this may be true. Although answers may never be found, the mystery hangs heavily over Roanoke Island and its two towns, Manteo and Wanchese.

builders offer classes in boat building and handling at the George Washington Creef Boathouse, but visitors not enrolled in the classes are still welcome to come and observe. Also on the grounds is the **Roanoke Marshes**

Lighthouse. The large lighthouses protecting the outer Atlantic coast are well known, but a number of smaller river and marsh lighthouses also once dotted the coast. This structure is a reconstruction of the square

© JASON FRYE

Elizabethan Gardens at Fort Raleigh National Historic Site

cottage-style lighthouse that was decommissioned in 1955.

Island Farm (1140 U.S. 64, Manteo, 252/473-6500, www.theislandfarm.com, 10am-4pm Wed.-Sat. Apr.-Nov., closed Thanksgiving Day, $6 adults, free under age 5) is a living-history site that transports you back to a Roanoke Island farm circa 1850. Reproduction outbuildings include the smokehouse, cookhouse, and slave house alongside the original farmhouse, built between 1845 and 1850. Period interpreters lead tours and talks that focus on the gardening, cooking, and day-to-day doings on a farm in the pre-Civil War Outer Banks.

The **North Carolina Aquarium on Roanoke Island** (374 Airport Rd., Manteo, 252/473-3494, www.ncaquariums.com, 9am-5pm daily year-round, closed Thanksgiving, Dec. 25, and Jan. 1, $8, $7 over age 61, $6 ages 3-12, free under age 3) is one of three state aquariums on the North Carolina coast. A great place for kids, the aquarium is home to all sorts of marine fauna and tells the aquatic story of North Carolina from the deep sea to freshwater tributaries. See river otters, alligators, freshwater fish, sharks, and more in traditional and touch-tank aquariums. Don't miss the daily dive shows in the huge 285,000-gallon Graveyard of the Atlantic tank. Displays in the aquarium detail the U.S. Lifesaving Service, and outside is the grave of Richard Etheridge, the first African American to captain a Lifesaving Station, on Pea Island, just south of the Bodie Island Lighthouse.

Roanoke Island Festival Park (across the water from downtown Manteo, 252/475-1500, http://roanokeisland.com) is a state-operated living-history site in Manteo. The highlight here is the *Elizabeth II,* a reconstruction of a 16th-century ship like those that brought Walter Raleigh, the members of the Lost Colony, and so many others to the New World. A museum, reconstructed settlement, and costumed interpreters help tell the story of the Roanoke colony, focusing more on their daily life than on their mysterious fate.

© JASON FRYE

Island Farm, a living-history site

SPORTS AND RECREATION

Roanoke Island Outfitters and Dive Center (312 U.S. 64, Manteo, 252/473-1356, www.roanokeislandoutfittersanddivecenter.com) is a one-stop shop for outdoor activities on Roanoke Island. They rent out kayaks, stand-up paddleboards, bicycles, and camping equipment and offer lessons and tours for kayaks and paddleboards, even teaching scuba diving at all levels. Experienced divers looking for a thrill will want to take advantage of their spearfishing charters (they don't rent out spear guns, so bring your own).

Spearfishing is just one way to catch a big one on the Outer Banks. On Roanoke Island it's easy to catch fish with a rod and a reel thanks to a number of inshore and offshore charters that are available year-round. The Outer Banks Visitors Bureau (www.outerbanks.org) has a comprehensive list of charters; look under "Fishing" for operators and rates.

Daring travelers can take in the sights of Roanoke Island and the Outer Banks from 9,000 feet with **Skydive OBX** (410 Airport Rd., Manteo, 252/678-5867, www.skydiveobx.com, $249). Each tandem jump provides 30 seconds of free fall at 120 mph and plenty of time to admire the view. Discounts are offered on same-day second jumps.

TOURS

The **Downeast Rover** (sails from Manteo waterfront, 252/473-4866, www.downeastrover.com, daytime cruises $30 adults, $15 ages 2-12, sunset cruises $40) is a 55-foot reproduction of a 19th-century schooner. Cruises last two hours and depart three times daily at 11am, 2pm, and sunset. To see the Outer Banks from the air, options include a World War II biplane or a closed-cockpit Cessna through **OBX Air Charters** (410 Airport Rd., Manteo, 252/256-2322, www.outerbanksaircharters.com, $210 for up to 5 people).

The gardens and quaint waterfronts on Roanoke Island are charming for adult visitors, but not so much for kids; thankfully, two tours fulfill the fun quotient for the young ones. On **Captain Johnny's Outer Banks Dolphin Tours**

WATERMAN RICHARD ETHERIDGE

The Outer Banks is a land of firsts: one of the first English settlements in the nation, the first flight, and another first that transcended racial boundaries in the tumultuous years after the Civil War. Richard Etheridge, Keeper of the Pea Island Life-Saving Station, was born as a slave on Roanoke Island in 1842 and became the first African American to command a Life-Saving crew, one made up entirely of African Americans.

Slavery on the Outer Banks was different than it was across most of the South. The absence of large plantations kept the numbers of slaves low, and the demands of the Banker lifestyle—scratching a farm out of the sand, subsistence fishing, crabbing, and foraging—kept slave owners and slaves in constant close company. The children of enslaved people often grew up alongside their slave-owning counterparts, and a few, like Etheridge, were rumored to have white fathers and received special treatment, even learning, as Etheridge did, to read and write. Etheridge worked alongside possible half brothers, fishing, farming, hunting, scavenging shipwrecks, and learning the finer points of being a waterman: how to read currents, swim, predict the weather, and navigate boats in breakers and under perilous conditions.

During the Civil War, one of the first Union victories occurred on Roanoke Island. General Ambrose Burnside freed the enslaved people here, established a massive freedman's colony (a sort of homestead for displaced and freed slaves), and recruited soldiers for the 36th U.S. Colored Troop, in which Etheridge enlisted. He saw action across North Carolina and Virginia, and after the war served in Texas in the Cavalry units that came to be known as the Buffalo Soldiers. He returned home a free man, married, and worked as a fisherman. In 1875 he joined the U.S. Life-Saving Service, precursor to the modern-day Coast Guard, serving as a Surfman at the Bodie Island Life-Saving Station.

As a Surfman, Etheridge served on a "checkerboard crew" made up of black and white Surfmen under the command of a white Keeper. He repeatedly garnered attention, not all of it positive, from his fellow Surfmen and superiors. By 1879 he was serving in another checkerboard crew at Pea Island station, and was promoted to Keeper after the white Keeper was fired. Despite the Emancipation Proclamation, the Union's victory in the war, Etheridge's possible parentage, and his expertise as a Surfman, he was not permitted to command white men; his command had to be formed entirely of black Surfmen. Only five months after taking command of the Pea Island station and becoming the first African American Keeper (and the first commander of the first all-African American crew), the smoldering racism of Jim Crow burned his station to the ground.

Etheridge served as Keeper for 21 years, never letting racism stand in the way of his duties as a member of the Life-Saving Service. In October 1896, in the midst of a storm so bad Etheridge had suspended the nightly beach patrols, the *E. S. Newman* grounded south of his station. The Pea Island crew leapt into action, but the waves were too high to launch their rescue surfboat. Two of his crew swam to the ship to secure a rescue line and made the trip back and forth nine times in order to rescue the passengers and crew, including the captain's three-year-old daughter. It was Etheridge's, and his crew's, finest moment.

Etheridge died of a fever in 1900. He's buried with his family in Manteo on Roanoke Island, outside the North Carolina Aquarium. In 1996 the Coast Guard posthumously awarded Keeper Etheridge and his crew the Gold Life-saving Medal, the service's highest peacetime honor. In 2011 the Coast Guard launched a cutter named after Etheridge, extending their respect to this groundbreaking American hero.

(Manteo Waterfront, 252/473-1475, www.outerbankscruises.com, from $28, $18 children), you'll get up close to bottlenose dolphins in their native habitat and watch as they swim, leap, hunt, and sometimes even inspect the boat on each two-hour tour. Kids get the chance to transform themselves into pirates with **Pirate Adventures of the Outer Banks** (408 Queen Elizabeth Ave., Manteo, 252/473-2007, www.piratesobx.com, tours 9:30am, 11am, 12:30pm, 2pm, 3:30pm, and 5pm daily, $20, $12 under age 3). Aboard the *Sea Gypsy*, a 40-foot pirate ship replete with a water cannon and a costumed pirate crew, kids get the chance to dress like pirates with face-painted mustaches, beards, and fearsome scars, read a treasure map, hunt down an enemy pirate, engage in a water-cannon battle, find sunken treasure, and have a pirate party. These 1.25-hour tours sail six times daily, seven days a week, giving parents opportunities to take an hour to explore the Manteo waterfront.

If you don't mind a scare, take a 90-minute stroll through Manteo with **Ghost Tours of the OBX** (399 Queen Elizabeth Ave., Manteo, 252/573-1450, www.ghosttoursoftheobx.com, $13, $8 under age 11). Visit the village cemetery, look for the ghosts of pirates and lost sailors along the shore and waterfront, and learn about supernatural creatures in the surrounding woods on one of three chilling but kid-friendly tours.

ENTERTAINMENT AND EVENTS

Roanoke Island is a pretty tame place, with most of the events and activities of a family-oriented nature. To that end, on the first Friday of the month April-December, the town of Manteo celebrates **First Friday,** a free downtown festival. In addition to live music on the streets, many restaurants and shops feature their own musical acts, sales, and refreshments. The **Dare County Arts Council Gallery** (300 Queen Elizabeth Ave., Manteo, 252/473-5558, www.darearts.org, 10am-6pm Mon.-Fri., 10am-8pm 1st Fri., noon-4pm Sat.) always hosts a reception during First Friday

that showcases a new exhibit by a local or regional artist.

One of the best spots for nightlife is **Poor Richard's Sandwich Shop** (303 Queen Elizabeth Ave., Manteo, 252/473-3333, www.poorrichardsmanteo.com, dining room breakfast and lunch 8am-3pm Mon.-Sat., bar 5pm-2am Mon.-Sat., entrées around $6). During the summer season they have live entertainment in the bar most nights; they also serve one of the best breakfasts in town.

SHOPPING

Roanoke Island is a haven for artists, with many calling Manteo home. Downtown are several studios and galleries featuring local artists' paintings, drawings, pottery, and jewelry. A favorite is the pottery studio of Nancy Huse, **Nancyware** (402 Queen Elizabeth Ave., Manteo, 252/473-9400, www.nancywareobx.com, call for hours), where she shapes, glazes, and fires beautiful and functional pots, trivets, decorative pottery pieces, ornaments, and earrings. The small but impressive **Gallery 101** (101 Budleigh St., Manteo, 252/473-6656, www.gallery101mante.com, call for hours) has a mix of original watercolors, oils, acrylics, photographs, and other objets d'art for sale.

The **Phoenix Shops** (Budleigh St. and Queen Elizabeth Ave.) are home to an eclectic mix of boutiques, galleries, and home-goods stores. **Duck's Cottage Downtown Books** (105 Sir Walter Raleigh St., Manteo, 252/473-1056, www.duckscottage.com, 10am-5pm Mon.-Sat. summer, 10am-5pm Tues.-Sat. off-season) is a small but well-stocked bookstore, with more than just the best-sellers; there is quite a selection of books by local and regional authors. The staff are friendly and knowledgeable and can point out easy summer reads.

ACCOMMODATIONS

The **White Doe Inn** (319 Sir Walter Raleigh St., Manteo, 800/473-6091, www.whitedoeinn.com, from $175 off-season, $350 summer) is one of North Carolina's premier inns. The 1910 Queen Anne is the largest house on the island and is listed on the National Register of Historic Places. Guest rooms are exquisitely furnished in turn-of-the-20th-century finery. Guests enjoy a four-course breakfast, evening sherry, espresso and cappuccino any time, and a 24-hour wine cellar. Spa services are available on-site, and you need only step out to the lawn to play croquet or boccie.

The **Roanoke Island Inn** (305 Fernando St., 877/473-5511, www.roanokeislandinn. com, $150-200) has been in the owner's family since the 1860s. It's a beautiful old place, with a big porch that overlooks the marsh. They also rent out a single cottage on a private island, five minutes away by boat, and a nice cypress-shingled bungalow in town. Another top hotel in Manteo is the **Tranquil House Inn** (405 Queen Elizabeth Ave., 800/458-7069, www.1587. com, $109-239). It's in a beautiful location, and downstairs is one of the best restaurants in town, 1587. The **Scarborough Inn** (524 U.S. 64, 252/473-3979, www.scarborough-inn.com, $75-125, varies by season) is a small hotel with 12 guest rooms and great rates. It's the sort of old-time hotel that's hard to find these days.

The **Cameron House Inn** (300 Budleigh St., Manteo, 800/279-8178, http://cameronhouse-inn.com, $130-210) is a cozy 1919 arts and crafts-style bungalow. All of the indoor guest rooms are furnished in a lovely and understated craftsman style, but the nicest guest room in the house is the porch, which has an outdoor fireplace, fans, and flowery trellises.

The **Island Guesthouse** (706 U.S. 64, 252/473-2434, www.theislandmotel.com, rooms from $60 off-season, from $85 summer, cottages from $125 off-season, from $200 summer, additional fee for pets) offers simple and comfortable lodgings with two double beds, air conditioning, and cable TV in each guest room. They also rent out three cute tiny cottages. Another affordable option is the **Duke of Dare Motor Lodge** (100 S. U.S. 64, 252/473-2175, from $42 summer), a 1960s motel that's not at all fancy but a fine budget choice.

The **Wanchese Inn** (85 Jovers Lane, Wanchese, 252/475-1166, www.wancheseinn. com, from $69 off-season, from $129 summer) is a simple and inexpensive bed-and-breakfast

in a nice Victorian house with modern guest rooms. There's a boat slip and on-site parking for a boat and trailer. The **Island House** (104 Old Wharf Rd., 866/473-5619, www.island-house-bb.com, $85-175) was built in the early 1900s for a local Coast Guardsman with wood cut from the property and nails forged on-site. It's very comfortable and quiet, and a big country breakfast is served every day.

FOOD

Located in the Tranquil House Inn with a great view of Shallowbag Bay, **1587** (405 Queen Elizabeth Ave., 252/473-1587, www.1587.com, dinner entrées $17-42) is widely regarded as one of the best restaurants in this part of the state. The menu has hearty chops and seafood, with local ingredients in season; a full vegetarian menu is available, and the wine list is a mile long.

Basnight's Lone Cedar Café (Nags Head-Manteo Causeway, 252/441-5405, www. lonecedarcafe.com, dinner from 4:30pm daily, brunch 11am-3pm Sun., dinner entrées $14-32, brunch entrées $8-14) is a water-view bistro that specializes in local food—oysters from Hyde and Dare Counties, fresh-caught local fish, and North Carolina chicken, pork, and vegetables. It's one of the most popular restaurants on the Outer Banks, and they don't take reservations, so be sure to arrive early. The full bar is open until midnight.

The **Full Moon Café** (208 Queen Elizabeth St., 252/473-6666, www.thefullmooncafe. com, 11:30am-9pm daily summer, call for off-season hours, $10-30) is simple and affordable, specializing in quesadillas and enchiladas, wraps, sandwiches, a variety of seafood and chicken bakes, and quiches. Despite the seemingly conventional selection, the food is so good that the Full Moon has received glowing reviews from the *Washington Post* and the *New York Post*—quite a feat for a little café in Manteo. On the brewery side of Full Moon, they brew their own British- and Irish-style beers, and they carry a variety of other North Carolina brews. Ask for a taste or order a tasting flight before committing to a full pint; the bartenders will be happy to accommodate you and help you find a beer you'll enjoy.

The **Magnolia Grille** (408 Queen Elizabeth St., 252/475-9787, www.roanokeisland.net, 7am-8pm Tues.-Sat., 7am-4pm Sun.-Mon.) is a very inexpensive place for your three daily meals and snacks in between. They've got a great selection of breakfast omelets, burgers, salads, soups, and deli sandwiches, with nothing priced over $7.

In Wanchese, the Daniels family has been fishing the waters of the Outer Banks since the 1930s and cooking up their catch since 1974. **Fisherman's Wharf Restaurant** (4683 Mill Landing Rd., Wanchese, 252/473-6004, www.fishermanswharfobx.com, 11am-9pm Mon.-Sat., lunch entrées $9-25, dinner entrées $15-25) serves fresh seafood in traditional Banker preparations. The Fisherman's Fried Platter is a feast unto itself, with fresh flounder, shrimp, sea scallops, clam strips, and crab bites. The Scallop Cakes, a Daniels family original, are not to be missed.

Avenue Grille (207 Queen Elizabeth Ave., Manteo, 252/473-4800, www.avenueeventsobx.com, 11am-9pm Mon.-Sat. summer, call for hours off-season, lunch entrées $8-18,

dinner entrées $11-28) serves modern coastal cuisine in a modern dining room overlooking the bay. Their slider trio includes a crab cake, an angus burger, and duck confit to give you a taste of how they treat fish, beef, and fowl, but their Tuna Oscar or crab cakes, both of which use locally-sourced seafood, steal the show.

GETTING THERE AND AROUND

Coming from the mainland, you first reach the town of Mann's Harbor on the inland side of the Croatan Sound; from there you have two choices to cross to Roanoke Island. If you take U.S. 64/264, to the north (left), you'll cross the sound to the north, arriving in Manteo. If you drive straight ahead at Mann's Harbor, you'll be on the U.S. 64/264 Bypass, which crosses to the middle of the island, south of Manteo. Proceed until you get to the main intersection with Highway 345, where you can turn left onto U.S. 64/264 to go to Manteo, or right onto Highway 345 to Wanchese.

To reach Roanoke Island from the Outer Banks, take U.S. 158 or Highway 12 to Whalebone Junction, south of Nags Head, and cross Roanoke Sound on the U.S. 64/264 bridge.

Cape Hatteras National Seashore

Most Americans recognize Cape Hatteras as a name often heard during hurricane season. Hatteras stretches farther south and east than any other part of the United States, jutting out into the Atlantic far enough to be a prime landmark for mariners, meteorologists, and storms.

Because of its position near the Gulf Stream, a treacherous zone of shifting sandbars called Diamond Shoals extends from the cape and it's pristine beaches to the warm Gulf Stream currents. Only two channels—Diamond Slough and Hatteras Slough—offer water deep enough for ships to traverse Diamond Shoals safely; ships that miss either slough end up shoaled on sandbars if they're lucky, and become one more

shipwreck in the Graveyard of the Atlantic if they are not so fortunate. Countless ships have gone down here over the centuries, including the 1837 wreck of the steamboat *Home* in which 90 passengers lost their lives. The wreck, which received considerable media attention, led Congress to pass the Steamboat Act, which established the requirement of one life vest per passenger on all vessels.

In 2003, Hurricane Isabel struck Hatteras Island, opening a 2,000-foot-wide channel where none had been before, separating the towns of Hatteras and Frisco, and causing major inconveniences for weeks. The inlet was filled in and the island remained intact for

© JASON FRYE

Bodie Island Lighthouse

that the Confederates blew it up themselves. The third light still stands, although a flock of geese nearly put it out of commission soon after its first lighting when they collided with and damaged the lens.

In 2013 the Bodie Island Lighthouse opened to the public for the first time after extensive renovations by the National Park Service. Ranger-led tours (daily late Apr.-early Oct.) take you on a strenuous climb up the lighthouse, but it is worth it for the view. Solid shoes are required to climb the lighthouse, so no heels, flip-flops, or bare feet.

The nearby Lighthouse Keeper's Cottage serves as a visitors center, and it is also the trailhead for self-guided nature trails to Roanoke Sound. These trails wind through beautiful marsh on the sound side of Bodie Island.

The **Oregon Inlet Campground** (Hwy. 12, 877/444-6777, www.recreation.gov, $20), operated by the National Park Service, offers camping behind the sand dunes, with coldwater showers, potable water, and restrooms.

several years until Hurricane Sandy in 2012. Sandy washed out roads, deposited sand several feet deep across Highway 12, and wreaked general mayhem up and down the island, all without a direct hit. The destruction from these two hurricanes demonstrates the vulnerability of the Outer Banks.

BODIE ISLAND

You'll spot the horizontal black-and-white stripes of the 170-foot **Bodie Island Lighthouse** (6 miles south of Whalebone Junction, 252/473-2111, www.nps.gov/caha, lighthouse climbs $8 adults, $4 seniors and under age 12) from several miles away. The Bodie Light's huge Fresnel lens first beamed in 1872, but this is the third lighthouse to guard this stretch of coast from this location. The first iteration of the Bodie Light (pronounced "body") was built in the 1830s, but due to engineering errors and shifting sand it leaned like the Tower of Pisa and didn't last too long. The next one stood straight but proved such a tempting target for the Yankee Navy during the Civil War

HATTERAS ISLAND

As Cape Hatteras arches dramatically along the North Carolina coast, it shelters Pamlico Sound from the ocean like a giant cradling arm. The cape itself is the point of the elbow, an exposed and vulnerable spit of land that's nearly irresistible to passing hurricanes. Most of the island is included in Cape Hatteras National Seashore, the first of its kind in the country, although a handful of small towns—Rodanthe, Waves, Salvo, Avon, Buxton, Frisco, and the village of Hatteras—dot the coastline. For the most part Hatteras Island isn't much wider than the dune line and Highway 12, which makes for a great deal of dramatic scenery on all sides.

Chicamacomico Life Saving Station

Lifesaving operations are an important part of North Carolina's maritime heritage. Corps of brave men occupied remote stations along the coast, ready at a moment's notice to risk their lives to save foundering sailors in the relentlessly dangerous waters off the Outer Banks.

In Rodanthe, the **Chicamacomico Life Saving Station** (Milepost 39.5, Hwy. 12, Rodanthe, 252/987-1552, www.chicamacomico.net, 10am-5pm Mon.-Fri. Apr.-Nov., $6, $4 under age 17 and over age 62) preserves the original station building, a handsome gray-shingled 1874 building, the 1911 building that replaced it and which now houses a museum of fascinating artifacts from maritime rescue operations, and a complex of other buildings and exhibits depicting the lives of lifesavers and their families.

◖ Cape Hatteras Lighthouse

At 208 feet tall, **Cape Hatteras Lighthouse** (near Buxton, 252/473-2111, www.nps.gov/caha, 9am-4:30pm daily late Apr.-June and early Sept.-early Oct., 9am-5:30pm June-early Sept., $8, $4 children and seniors, children under 42 inches tall not permitted) is the tallest brick lighthouse in the United States, and its distinctive black-and-white spiral paint job makes it easy to see from miles away on land or sea. It was built in 1870 to protect ships at sea from coming upon the shoals unaware. It still stands and is open for climbing during the warm months. If you have a healthy heart, lungs, and knees and are not claustrophobic, get your ticket and start climbing. Tickets are sold on the premises beginning at 8:15am, and climbing tours run every 10 minutes starting at 9am. Winds at the top can be ferocious, so hold onto your hats, cameras, phones, and anything else you don't want to fly away.

Sports and Recreation

Pea Island National Wildlife Refuge (Hwy. 12, 10 miles south of Nags Head, 252/987-2394, www.fws.gov/peaisland) occupies the northern reach of Hatteras Island. Much of the island is covered by ponds, making this an exceptional place for watching migratory waterfowl. Two nature trails link some of the best bird-watching spots, including the 0.5-mile fully wheelchair-accessible North Pond Wildlife Trail. Viewing and photography blinds are scattered along the trails for extended observation.

The Outer Banks owe their existence to the

© JASON FRYE

Cape Hatteras Lighthouse

volatile action of the tides. The same forces that created this habitable sandbar also make it an incredible place for water sports. **Canadian Hole,** a spot in the sound between Avon and Buxton, is one of the most famous windsurfing and sailboarding places in the world (and, of course, it's perfect for flying kites). The island is extraordinarily narrow at Canadian Hole, so it's easy to tote your board from the sound side over to the ocean for a change of scene.

It's important to know your skill level and choose activities accordingly. Beginners and experts alike can benefit from the guidance of serious water-sports instructors. **REAL** (25706 Hwy. 12, Waves, 866/732-5548, www.realkiteboarding.com) is the largest kite-surfing school in the world. They offer kite-surfing camps and classes in many aspects of the sport for all levels as well as surfing and stand-up paddleboarding lessons and rentals. **Outer Banks Kiting** (Avon, 252/305-6838, www.outerbankskiting. com) also has lessons and two-day camps and carries boarders out on charter excursions to find the best kite-surfing spots.

Among the ways to tour Hatteras, **Equine Adventures** (Frisco, 252/995-4897, www. equineadventures.com, tours from $30) leads two-hour horseback tours through the maritime forests and along the beaches of Cape Hatteras. With **Hatteras Parasail** (Hatteras, 252/986-2627, www.hatterasparasail.com, $65 parasail ride, $55 WaveRunner rental, $35 kayak tour, $275 per day boat rental) you can ride 400 feet in the air over the coast; go even higher with **Burrus Flightseeing Tours** (Frisco, 252/986-2679, www.outerbanksairtours.com, $45-80 pp).

Hatteras Watersports (Milepost 42.5, Hwy. 12, Salvo, 252/987-2306, www.hatteraswatersports.com) offers sailboat, Jet Ski, and kayak rentals as well as guided and self-guided kayak tours. Their location on shallow Pamlico Sound is a perfect spot to head out in any of their watercraft, even for novices.

Shopping
In a place this beautiful and inspiring, it's no surprise that you'll find a number of galleries

showcasing the works of local and regional artists. The **Pea Island Art Gallery** (27766 Hwy. 12, Salvo, 252/987-2879, call for hours) has works from over 100 artists in a range of media in a gallery that's a replica of a 19th-century Lifesaving Station. **SeaWorthy Gallery** (58401 Hwy. 12, Hatteras, 252/986-6511, www.seaworthygallery.com, call for hours) carries pieces ranging from fun, cartoonish folk art representations of area wildlife to painstaking paintings of area landmarks, seascapes, and landscapes. **Blue Pelican Gallery** (57762 Hwy. 12, Hatteras, 252/986-2244, www.bluepelicangallery.com, call for hours) carries jewelry from local glassblowers, lockets filled with objects found on and inspired by the shore, jewelry, and a beautiful selection of yarn and supplies for knitting and other needle arts.

The indie **Buxton Village Books** (47918 Hwy. 12, Buxton, 252/995-4240, www.buxtonvillagebooks.com, 10am-5pm daily) carries a large selection of books about the Outer Banks and by regional authors, along with the latest in contemporary and Southern fiction. The staff are knowledgeable and can point you to beach reads or something deeper.

Accommodations
Among the lodging choices on Hatteras Island is the very fine **Inn on Pamlico Sound** (49684 Hwy. 12, Buxton, 866/726-5426, www.innonpamlicosound.com, $100-350, varies by season). The inn is right on the sound, with a private dock and easy waterfront access. The dozen suites are sumptuous and relaxing, many with their own decks or private porches. Another good choice is the **Cape Hatteras Bed and Breakfast** (49643 Old Lighthouse Rd., Buxton, 252/995-6004, www.capehatterasbandb.com, Apr.-late Nov., $120-210), which is only a few hundred feet from the ocean. Guests rave about the breakfast.

Simpler motel accommodations include the clean, comfortable, and pet-friendly **Cape Pines Motel** (47497 Hwy. 12, Buxton, 866/456-9983, www.capepinesmotel.com, $49-199, varies by season, pets $20); the **Outer Banks Motel** (47000 Hwy. 12, Buxton,

252/995-5601 or 800/995-1233, www.outer-banksmotel.com, $69-365, varies by season), with both motel rooms and cottages; and the **Avon Motel** (Avon, 252/995-4123 or 252/995-5774, www.avonmotel.com, $39-140, varies by season, pets $10 per day), a pet-friendly motel that has been in business for more than 50 years.

CAMPING
Rodanthe Watersports and Campground (24170 Hwy. 12, 252/987-1431, www.watersportsandcampground.com, $19.25 for 2 people, $4.75 per additional adult, $3 children and dogs, add $4.75 for electrical hookup) has a campground on the sound for tents and RVs under 25 feet, with water and electrical hookups and hot showers.

The National Park Service operates two campgrounds in this stretch of the National Seashore: **Frisco Campground** (late Apr.-mid-Oct., $20), where you actually camp in the dunes, and **Cape Point Campground** (46700 Lighthouse Rd., Buxton, and 53415 Billy Mitchell Rd., Frisco, 877/444-6777, late-May-Aug., $20), with level campsites located behind the dunes. Both have cold showers, restrooms, and potable water. **Frisco Woods Campground** (Hwy. 12, Frisco, 800/948-3942, www.outer-banks.com/friscowoods, $30-90, varies by season) has a full spectrum of camping options, including no-utilities tent sites, RV sites with partial or full hookups, and one- and two-bedroom cabins. The campground has wireless Internet access, hot showers, and a coin laundry.

Cape Hatteras KOA (2509 Hwy. 12, Rodanthe, 252/987-2307 or 800/562-5268, www.koa.com, from $56) offers campsites, RV sites, and small cabins along with a pool, a play area for kids, a small commissary, and direct beach access.

Food
Dining options are limited on Hatteras Island, but there are plenty of places to eat. The **Restaurant at the Inn on Pamlico Sound** (Hwy. 12, Buxton, 252/995-7030, www.

innonpamlicosound.com, 5pm-9pm daily, $25-35) is primarily for guests of the inn, but if you call in advance, you might be able to get a reservation for dinner, even if you're staying elsewhere. The chef likes to use fresh-caught seafood, sometimes caught by the guests themselves earlier in the day. Vegetarian fare and other special requests are available.

For breakfast, try the **Gingerbread House** (52715 Hwy. 12, Frisco, 252/995-5204, http://gbhbakery.com, breakfast 7am-11am, dinner 4:30pm-9pm Tues.-Sat., breakfast around $6, dinner around $18), which serves great baked goods made on the premises. In the evenings, try pan and hand-tossed pizza made using fresh dough; in addition to the usual toppings, they offer a whole-wheat crust and a number of specialty pies topped with local shrimp, clams, crab, or barbecued chicken. **StingWrays's Bar and Grill** (24394 Hwy. 12, Rodanthe, 252/987-1500, 4pm-11pm Mon.-Wed., 11am-11pm Thurs.-Sun. entrées $10-30) is a laid-back place with a great outdoor deck and great sunset views, along with a good selection of North Carolina beers on tap.

◖ OCRACOKE ISLAND
Ocracoke Island, one of the most geographically isolated places in the state, is the southernmost part of the Cape Hatteras National Seashore. Accessible only by water and air, this 16-mile-long island seems charmingly anchored in the past. Regular ferry service didn't start until 1960, as most residents were content to stay on their island, separate from the rest of the state, and they didn't have a paved highway until 1963. The natural beauty of the island is mostly intact, and some areas look much like they did in 1585 when the first English colonists ran aground. It may have been during their time on Ocracoke (called Wococon at the time) that the ancestors of today's wild ponies first set hoof on the Outer Banks. Theirs was not the last shipwreck at Ocracoke, nor was it the first; Spanish explorers reportedly ran aground here too, and it's possible the now-feral Banker ponies came from their ships. As on the northern stretches

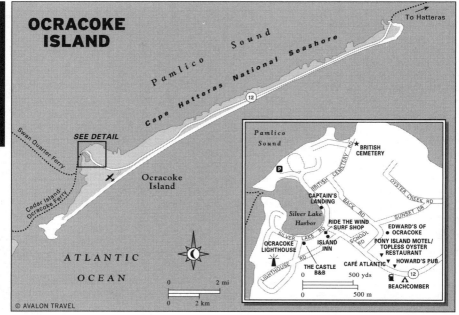

of the Outer Banks, Ocracokers subsisted partially on the flotsam and goods that would wash up after shipwrecks, so wherever the wild horses came from, like other gifts from the sea they have become part of the island's history and lifestyle.

In some ways, Ocracoke is a little creepy. Its isolation has something to do with that, but so do its legends and ghosts. During the early 18th century, Ocracoke was a favorite haunt of the pirate Edward Teach, better known as Blackbeard. He lived here from time to time, married his 14th wife here, and died here. He met his fate in Teach's Hole, a spot just off the island, when a band of privateers (pirate hunters) hired by Virginia's Governor Spottswood finally cornered and killed him. According to legend, he didn't go down without a fight; it took five musket shots, more than 20 stab wounds, and a near beheading before his fight was over. Afterward, Spottswood's privateers took Blackbeard's head as a trophy and dumped his body overboard where, legend has

it, it swam around the ship seven times before going under.

All of **Ocracoke Village,** near the southern end of the island, is on the National Register of Historic Places. While the historical sites of the island are highly distinctive, the most unique thing about the island and its people is the culture that has developed over the centuries. Ocracokers have a "brogue" or dialect of their own, similar to those of other Outer Banks communities but distinctive and unique to the island.

Ocracoke Lighthouse

A lighthouse has stood on Ocracoke since at least 1798, but due to the constantly shifting sands, the inlet that it protected kept sneaking away. Barely 20 years after that first tower was built, it was almost a mile from the water. The current **Ocracoke Lighthouse** (Ocracoke Village, 888/493-3826) was built in 1823 and originally burned whale oil to power the beam. It is still in operation, the oldest continuously operating light in North Carolina and the second-oldest in the nation. Because it's on active duty, it is not publicly accessible, but a boardwalk nearby gives nice views.

British Cemetery

The **British Cemetery** (British Cemetery Rd.) is not, as one might suppose, a colonial graveyard but rather a vestige of World War II, when the Carolina coast was lousy with German U-boats. Many old-timers today remember catching a glimpse of a furtive German sub casing the beach. Defending the Outer Banks became a pressing concern, and on May 11, 1942, the HMS *Bedfordshire,* a British trawler sent to aid the U.S. Navy, was torpedoed by the German *U-558.* The *Bedfordshire* sank, killing all 37 men on board. Over the course of the next week, four bodies washed up on Ocracoke—those of Lieutenant Thomas Cunningham, Ordinary Telegraphist Stanley Craig, and two unidentified sailors. An island family donated a burial plot, where the four men lie today, memorialized with a plaque that bears a lovely verse by Rupert Brooke, a young World War I British sailor and poet who died of disease on his way to the battle of Gallipoli.

Sports and Recreation

Ride the Wind Surf Shop (486 Irvin Garrish Hwy., 252/928-6311, www.surfocracoke.com) gives individual and group surfing lessons for adults and children ($75 per hour for 1 person, $35 per hour each additional person), covering ocean safety and surfing etiquette in addition to board handling. A three-day surf camp for kids ages 9-17 ($85 per day, $200 per week) gives an even more in-depth tutorial. Ride the Wind also leads sunrise, sunset, and full-moon kayak tours ($35) around the marshes of Ocracoke. Kayak, stand-up paddleboard, surfboard, and boogie-board rentals ($12-55 per day, $28-150 per week) are available.

The *Windfall II* (departs from Community Store Dock, Ocracoke, 252/928-7245, www.schoonerwindfall.com), a beautiful 32-foot lazy jack schooner, sails out into the Pamlico Sound to visit Teach's Hole, where Blackbeard

was brought to justice, and conducts daily sunset cruises. The *Wilma Lee,* a 46-foot skipjack that can accommodate up to 42 passengers, also sails for pleasure cruises, sunset cruises, weddings at sea, and other private functions. Passengers are encouraged to try their hand at the wheel or trimming the sails.

Tradewinds Tackle (1094 Irvin Garrish Hwy., 252/928-5491, www.fishtradewinds. com) offers fishing tips and sells all the gear you'll need, including fishing licenses, to land a big one. The Ocracoke Island fishing experts at Tradewinds can tell you where to catch what and how, or they can simply send you to a good fishing guide. A comprehensive list of fishing charters and guides is available on the Ocracoke Village website (www.ocracokevillage.com).

Accommodations

The **Captain's Landing** (324 Hwy. 12, 252/928-1999, www.thecaptainslanding.com, from $280 summer, from $110 off-season), with a perch right on the harbor (called Silver Lake) looking toward the lighthouse, is a modern hotel owned by a descendant of Ocracoke's oldest families. Suites have 1.5 baths, full kitchens, comfortable sleeper sofas for extra guests, and decks with beautiful views. They also have a bright airy penthouse with two bedrooms, an office, a gourmet kitchen, and even a laundry room. The Captain's Cottage is a private two-bedroom house, also right on the water, with great decks and its own courtyard.

The **Pony Island Motel and Cottages** (785 Irvin Garrish Hwy., 252/928-4411 or 866/928-4411, www.ponyislandmotel.com, from $115 summer, from $60 off-season) has been in operation since the late 1950s and run by the same family for more than 40 years. It has regular and efficiency motel rooms and four cottages on the grounds. Clean guest rooms, a good location, and reasonable rates year-round make this a top choice on the island.

Edwards of Ocracoke (226 Old Beach Rd., 252/928-4801 or 800/254-1359, www.edwardsofocracoke.com, from $54 spring and fall, from $90 summer, weekly rentals $445-2,095) has several cozy bungalows typical of coastal

Carolina, referred to here as "vintage accommodations." The mid-20th-century vacation ambiance is pleasant, the cabins are clean and well-kept, and the rates are great. Private cottages are available, as are two homes perfect for larger groups traveling together.

The pet- and child-friendly **Island Inn** (25 Lighthouse Rd., 252/928-4351, www.ocracokeislandinn.com, from $49 off-season, from $89 summer) is on the National Register of Historic Places and bills itself as the oldest operating business on the Outer Banks. It was built in 1901, first used as an Oddfellows Hall, and later used as a barracks during World War II. The building is made of salvaged shipwreck wood, which everyone knows brings strange juju; add that to the 1950s murder of a caretaker and the discovery of colonial bones under the lobby, and it's a given that the place is considered haunted. The resident wraith is believed to be a woman, because she seems to enjoy checking out female guests' cosmetics and clothes, which will sometimes turn up in the morning in places other than where they were left the night before. No one has ever seen her, but her footsteps are sometimes heard in empty guest rooms, and odd happenings are attributed to her—most notably the unraveling of an entire roll of toilet paper in the presence of a terrified guest. Like many hotel ghosts, she is most active during the inn's less crowded seasons.

The Castle B&B (155 Silver Lake Rd., 252/928-3505 or 800/471-8848, www.thecastlebb.com, from $189 summer, from $139 off-season) is a beautiful home with well-appointed guest rooms, spectacular views, a pool, and, of course, breakfast. Get to breakfast early, when the biscuits are hot; they're legendary around these parts.

CAMPING

At **Ocracoke Campground** (4352 Irvin Garrish Hwy., Ocracoke, 252/928-6671, www.recreation.gov, $23), campsites are right by the beach and behind the dunes. Remember to bring extra-long stakes or sand anchors to stake your tent in the sand.

Beachcomber Campground (990 Irvin Garrish Hwy., 252/928-4031, www.ocracokecamping.com, tents from $31, RVs from $42) is open year-round and is conveniently located near both the Cape Hatteras National Seashore and Ocracoke Island's only gas station, perfect for those late-night munchies. Throughout the season they feature live music. There isn't a lot of shade, so it is more pleasant during the shoulder seasons, when the weather is milder.

Food

Ocracoke's **Café Atlantic** (1129 Irvin Garris Hwy., 252/928-4861, www.ocracokeisland. com, dinner daily, lunch Sun., $14-21) has a large and eclectic menu, with tastes venturing into Italian, Nuevo Latino, and local fare. Lunch and dinner choices may include a BLT, a crab cake (with Pamlico Sound crabmeat), or a *caciucco,* an Italian seafood stew. While many restaurants will accommodate vegetarians with a single pasta dish at the end of the list of entrées, Café Atlantic has several options without meat or seafood. There's also an extensive wine list.

Topless Oyster Restaurant (875 Irvin Garrish Hwy., 252/928-2800, 11am-2am daily, $10-30) serves, you guessed it, oysters on the half shell. Oysters purists will probably order them plain, but for those with an adventurous palate, several types of specialty oysters (topped with crab, ceviche, and the like) are available. Topless Oyster also serves burgers, ribs, barbecue, and more.

Howard's Pub & Raw Bar Restaurant (1175 Irvin Garrish Hwy., 252/928-4441, www.howardspub.com, 11am-10pm daily, entrées $15-26) serves steaks, burgers, salads, sandwiches, and a wide assortment of appetizers. Try the homemade hush puppies and the conch fritters; they'll get you ready for a memorable meal.

GETTING THERE AND AROUND

The northern part of Cape Hatteras National Seashore can be reached by car, following Highway 12 south from Nags Head. Along Highway 12 you'll go through the towns of Rodanthe, Waves, Salvo, and Avon, and then around the tip of the cape to Buxton, Frisco, and Hatteras, where the highway ends. From here, you have two choices: backtrack or take a ferry to Ocracoke.

Ocracoke can only be reached by ferry. The Hatteras-Ocracoke Ferry (800/368-8949, www.ncdot.gov/ferry, 1 hour, free) is the shortest route to Ocracoke. On some maps, Highway 12 is shown crossing from Ocracoke to Cedar Island, as if there were an impossibly long bridge over Pamlico Sound. In fact, that stretch is a ferry route too. The **Cedar Island-Ocracoke Ferry** (800/293-3779, www.ncdot. gov/ferry), a 2.25-hour ride, costs $15 one-way for a regular-size vehicle. There's also an **Ocracoke-Swan Quarter Ferry** (800/293-3779, 2.5 hours, $15 regular-size vehicle one-way).

Across the Sounds

Traditionally called the Albemarle, although today sometimes called the Inner Banks, the mainland portion of northeastern North Carolina is the heart and hearth of the state's colonial history, the site of its first colonial towns and earliest plantations, and the seat of power for the largely maritime economy.

Inland, early European Carolinians and Virginians named a region they thought of as a diseased and haunted wasteland "the Great Dismal Swamp." They planned to drain it and create more hospitable places to settle, and to a point they succeeded in doing so, but enough of the swamp remains today that it is recognized it as one of the state's prettiest places, valued by human visitors almost as much as by the bears and wolves that live there.

Early cities like Edenton and Bath were influential centers of commerce and government, and today they preserve some of the finest examples of colonial and early Federal architecture in the Southeast. Inland, along the Roanoke River, the small town of Halifax played a key role in American history; in a tavern in Halifax, representatives from North Carolina wrote and ratified the Halifax Accords, the first documents to denounce British rule over the colonies and to declare American independence. The Halifax Accords were read at the Continental Congress in Philadelphia, which led to the Declaration of Independence and the Revolutionary War.

The vast networks of rivers and creeks feeding the Roanoke River and other major waterways include some of the state's best places for inland canoeing and kayaking. Along the Albemarle Regional Canoe-Kayak Trail, a number of camping platforms allow paddlers to spend an unforgettable night listening to owls hoot and otters splash. The abundant water also irrigates the vast farms in this corner of the state, and if a small town has a restaurant, it'll be either a country kitchen or a fish shack. Either way, you'll get to sample the region's inland seafood traditions.

◖ THE GREAT DISMAL SWAMP

Thought of for centuries as an impediment to progress, the Great Dismal Swamp is now recognized for the national treasure that it is, and tens of thousands of its acres are protected. There are several points to access the interior of the Dismal Swamp. On U.S. 17 a few miles south of the Virginia-North Carolina border is the **Dismal Swamp Welcome Center** (2294 U.S. 17 N.) as well as the **Dismal Swamp Visitors Center** (2356 U.S. 17 N., South Mills, 877/771-8333, www.dismalswamp. com, 9am-5pm daily June-Oct., 9am-5pm Tues.-Sat. Nov.-May). Arriving by water, you'll find the Welcome Center at Mile 28 on the Intracoastal Waterway. You can tie up to the dock and spend the night, or wait for one of the four daily lock openings (8:30am, 11am, 1:30pm, and 3:30pm) to proceed. There are also picnic tables and grills, and restrooms open 24 hours.

Another area of the swamp to explore is

the **Great Dismal Swamp National Wildlife Refuge** (3100 Desert Rd., Suffolk, VA, 757/986-3705, www.fws.gov, dawn-dusk daily), which straddles the state line. Two main entrances are outside of Suffolk, Virginia, off White Marsh Road (Hwy. 642). These entrances, Washington Ditch and Jericho Lane, are open 6:30am-8pm daily April 1-September 30, and 6:30am-5pm daily October 1-March 31. In the middle of the refuge is Lake Drummond, an eerie 3,100-acre natural lake that's a wonderful place for canoeing. Contact refuge headquarters for directions on navigating the feeder ditch into Lake Drummond. You may see all sorts of wildlife in the swamp, including poisonous cottonmouths, canebrake rattlers, copperheads, and possibly even black bears. Controlled hunting is permitted on certain days in October-December, so if you visit in the fall, wear bright-colored clothing and contact refuge staff before your visit to find out about closures.

GATESVILLE

Near the town of Gatesville, west of South Mills on U.S. 158, is another gorgeous natural swamp area, **Merchant's Millpond State Park** (176 Millpond Rd., Gatesville, 252/357-1191, http://ncparks.gov, office 8am-4:30pm Mon.-Fri. except holidays, park 8am-6pm daily Nov.-Feb., 8am-8pm daily Mar.-May and Sept.-Oct., 8am-9pm daily June-Aug.). There is an amazing variety of wildlife, particularly among reptiles, with many species snakes (most are harmless) and turtles (harmless, except for the snappers), and despite the relatively northerly clime, alligators (most emphatically not harmless). Other denizens include salamanders, mink, and nutrias.

This is a great spot for canoeing or kayaking, with miles of beautiful blackwater backwaters. For those unfamiliar with blackwater, it looks like it sounds: black water. Tannins from decaying vegetation leech into the water, turning it a dark tea or coffee color and creating a beautiful, but eerie, effect. The park has canoe rentals ($5 1st hour, $3 per additional hour, $20 per day for campers). There are nine

miles of hiking trails, all classified as easy, but rangers strongly caution hikers to be careful to avoid ticks. Wear bug spray, tuck your pant legs into your socks, wear light-colored clothing to see the ticks better, and when you return, do a tick check by running your fingers over every inch of your body.

Merchant's Millpond has several campsites ($13-20): The family campground, near the park office, is easily accessible, accommodates tents and RVs, and has a washhouse with restrooms, showers, and drinking water. Off the park's Lassiter trail are five backpack campsites, where all supplies, including water, must be packed in; there is a pit toilet nearby. There are also two canoe camping areas accessed by canoe trails, with pit toilets; campers must bring water and other supplies.

ELIZABETH CITY

The **Museum of the Albemarle** (501 S. Water St., 252/335-1453, www.museumofthealbemarle.com, 10am-4pm Tues.-Sat.) covers the four centuries since the first English settlers arrived at Roanoke. Come to learn about the Lost Colonists, the pirates who swarmed the region, and the folkways of the Sound country.

To stay in Elizabeth City, the **Pond House Inn** (915 Rivershore Rd., 252/335-9834, www.thepondhouseinn.com, $99-165) is on the banks of the Pasquotank River. Each of the large guest rooms has its own fireplace in this pleasant 1940s house. The **Culpepper Inn** (609 W. Main St., 252/335-9235, www.culpepperinn.com, $110-135), just a few blocks from Albemarle Sound, has several comfortable guest rooms in the main house as well as cozy accommodations in a carriage house and a cottage.

There are also chain motels in the area, including the **Travelers Inn** (1211 N. Road St., 252/338-5451, www.travelersinn.webs.com, around $70) and **Econo Lodge** (510 S. Hughes Blvd., 252/338-4124, www.econolodge.com, around $70), both of which allow small pets, the **Holiday Inn Express** (306 S. Hughes Blvd., 252/338-8900, www.ihg.com, $75-125), and **Hampton Inn** (402 Halstead Blvd.,

252/333-1800, www.hamptoninn3.hilton.com, around $130).

Toyama Japanese Restaurant (218 N. Poindexter St., 252/338-5021, lunch 11am-2:30pm daily, dinner 4:30pm-10pm Mon.-Thurs., 4:30pm-11pm Fri.-Sun., entrées $8-20) has a fantastic reputation for quality sushi on a staggeringly lengthy menu. Don't worry if you're not a sushi fan; there's plenty on the menu that's not raw fish.

Cypress Creek Grill (113 Water St., 252/334-9915, www.cypresscreekgrill.com, 11am-9pm Mon.-Thurs., 11am-10pm Fri., 5pm-10pm Sat., entrées $11-27) is close to downtown and serves gulf-style seafood, Tex-Mex cuisine, and a few creole dishes. The owners are from Texas, and they've blended their native flavors with the local ingredients of eastern North Carolina to make for some tasty dining.

HERTFORD

If you're traveling between Edenton and Elizabeth City, don't miss Hertford, a pretty little Spanish moss-draped town on the Perquimans (per-KWIH-muns) River. The historic **Newbold-White House** (151 Newbold-White Rd., 252/426-7567, www.newbold-whitehouse.org, guided tours 10am-4pm Tues.-Sat. Apr.-Nov., $5 adults, $3 students) is the oldest brick house in North Carolina, built in 1730 by one of the region's early Quakers. The grounds include a seasonal herb garden and a 17th-century Quaker graveyard.

Stop in at **Woodard's Pharmacy** (101 N. Church St., 252/426-5527, 9am-6pm daily, under $10), an old-fashioned lunch counter and soda fountain in the heart of downtown, where you can grab a pimiento cheese sandwich and an ice cream cone. If you're making it an overnight, stay at **1812 on the Perquimans** (385 Old Neck Rd., 252/426-1812, $80-85), or at the **Beechtree Inn** (948 Pender Rd., 252/426-1593, www.beechtreeinn.net, $80-90), where guests stay in restored pre-Civil War cottages and children and pets are welcome. The **Beautiful Moon Café** (252/426-2500, www.beautiful-moon-cafe.com, 5:30pm-8pm Mon.-Thurs., 5:30pm-9pm Fri.-Sat., $12-19) is at the

Beechtree Inn and serves a small, simple menu of steak, chicken, and some seafood.

EDENTON

Incorporated in 1722 but inhabited by colonists for 50 years before that, Edenton was not only North Carolina's first permanent settlement, it was also one of the most important colonial towns in the state. This beautiful waterside town served as the colonial capital until 1743, and the state's oldest courthouse, built in 1767, is still in use today.

Historic District

All of Edenton is lined with historic buildings, and several especially important sites are clustered within a few blocks of the waterfront. The easiest starting point for a walking tour is the headquarters of the **Edenton State Historic Site** (108 N. Broad St., 252/482-2637, www.nchistoricsites.org, 9am-5pm Tues.-Sat., guided tours $1-10), also referred to as the Edenton Visitors Center. The 1782 **Barker House** (505 S. Broad St., 252/482-7800, http://ehcnc.org, 10am-4pm daily), a stunning Lowcountry palazzo, was the home of Penelope Barker, an early revolutionary and organizer of the Edenton Tea Party. It's now the headquarters of the Edenton Historical Commission and the location of their bookstore. The 1758 **Cupola House** (408 S. Broad St., tickets and information at Edenton Visitors Center, 108 N. Broad St., 252/482-2637, www.cupolahouse.org, 9am-4:30pm daily) is a home of great architectural significance and a National Historic Landmark. Although much of the original interior woodwork was removed in 1918 and sold to the Brooklyn Museum in New York, where it remains, Cupola House has been meticulously restored inside and out and its colonial gardens recreated. Also a designated National Historic Landmark is the **Chowan County Courthouse** (117 E. King St., 252/482-2637, www.edenton.nchistoricsites.org, hours vary), a superb 1767 brick building in the Georgian style. It's the best-preserved colonial courthouse in the United States.

Downtown you'll find yourself surrounded

by beautiful examples of Jacobean, Georgian, Federal, and Victorian homes as well as a number of other important historical sites, including **St. Paul's Episcopal Church** (W. Church St. and N. Broad St., 252/482-3522, http://stpauls-edenton.org), the second-oldest church structure in the state, and **Colonial Waterfront Park** (Edenton waterfront, parking on W. Water St. and S. Broad St.), a stop on the Underground Railroad. African American workers would find sailors sympathetic to the cause of freeing slaves and arrange their passage on ships to a free state. Harriet Jacobs's description of her 1842 escape by sea from Edenton is one of the few existing written accounts. Learn more about her story at http://harrietjacobs.org or on a guided or self-guided walking tour (tours begin at the Edenton State Historic Site) that highlights her years in Edenton.

Sports and Recreation

Right on the water, Edenton is surrounded by miles of paddling trails (www.visitedenton.com), but there is only one kayak and canoe rental outfit, the **Edenton Town Harbor Dock Master** (Edenton Harbor, 252/482-2832, www.visitedenton.com, kayaks from $5 per hour, canoes $10 per hour).

The **Chowan Golf & Country Club** (1101 W. Sound Shore Dr., 252/482-3606, http://chowangolfandcountryclub.com, 18 holes, par 72, greens fees $25 with cart, $15 walking) is the only golf course around, and it's a friendly, very playable course with beautiful water views from a few holes. Rental clubs are available ($10).

Accommodations and Food

◖ **The Pack House Inn** (103 E. Albemarle St., 252/482-3641, www.thepackhouse.com, from $99) occupies three exceptional historic buildings: the 1900 grand Victorian mansion known as The Proprietor's; the 1915 Pack House, which started its life as a tobacco packing house on a nearby plantation; and the 1879 Tillie Bond House cottage. Each is artfully restored with soft and restful furnishings. A three-course breakfast, which features gluten-free and vegetarian selections if arranged

in advance, is served every morning in the Tillie Bond Dining Rooms. Lunch and dinner are also available at the Proprietor's Table Restaurant.

The **Granville Queen Inn** (108 S. Granville St., 866/482-8534, www.granvillequeen.com, $105-155) is a rather splendid early-20th-century mansion decorated in a variety of period styles. Breakfasts are as ornate and elegant as the house itself, featuring poached pears, potato tortillas, and crepes. Children are welcome most of the year, but there are occasions when their presence isn't appropriate; let the innkeepers know about any children in your party when making reservations.

WINDSOR

A small historic town on the Cashie (Cuh-SHY) River, Windsor is the seat of Bertie (Ber-TEE) County. Historic architecture, good food, and wetlands exploration are equally compelling reasons to visit this lesser-known treasure of the Albemarle region.

Sights

Hope Plantation (132 Hope House Rd., 252/794-3140, www.hopeplantation.org, visitors center 9am-4pm Mon.-Fri., 10am-4pm Mon.-Sat., 2pm-5pm Sun. Apr.-mid-Dec., 10am-4pm Sat., 2pm-5pm Sun. mid-Dec.-Mar. 31, $10, $8 seniors, $5 students and children) was built in 1803 for David Stone. Stone did not live to see his 50th birthday, but by the time of his death he had been governor of North Carolina, a U.S. senator and representative, a state senator, a Superior Court judge, and had been elected seven times to the State House. He graduated from Princeton and passed the bar when he was 20, fathered 11 children, and was one of the founders of the University of North Carolina. As busy as he was, he managed to oversee the construction of this impressive house. Characterized by a mixture of Georgian and Federal styles with significant twists of regional and individual aesthetics, Hope House is on the National Register of Historic Places. Also on the register and now on the grounds of the plantation is the brick-end, gambrel roof

King-Bazemore House, built in 1763 and also a significant example of its type.

The **Roanoke-Cashie River Center** (112 W. Water St., Windsor, 252/794-2001, www.partnershipforthesounds.org, 10am-4pm Wed.-Fri., 10am-2pm Sat. Apr.-Oct., 10am-4pm Tues.-Fri. Nov.-Mar., $2, $1 children) has interpretive exhibits about this region's history and ecology. There is a canoe ramp outside where you can access the Cashie River, and canoe rentals ($10 per hour, $25 half-day, $35 full-day) are available.

Southeast of Windsor on the Cashie River, the **San Souci Ferry** (Woodard Rd. and Sans Souci Rd., 252/794-4277, 6:30am-6pm Mar. 16-Sept. 16, 6:45am-5pm Sept. 17-Mar. 15) operates, as it has for generations, by a cable and a honk of the horn. To cross the river, pull up to the bank and look for the ferry. If it's across the river, honk your horn and wait. The ferry operator will cross to you and pull you to the opposite bank. There's only room for two cars at a time, but it's a charming way to cut 20 miles off your journey.

Recreation

The headquarters of the **Roanoke River National Wildlife Refuge** (114 W. Water St., 252/794-3808, www.fws.gov/roanokeriver) is located in Windsor. The refuge stretches over nearly 21,000 acres in Bertie County, through the hardwood bottomlands and cypress-tupelo wetlands of the Roanoke River Valley, an environment that the Nature Conservancy calls "one of the last great places." The refuge is an exceptional place for bird-watching, with the largest inland heron rookery in North Carolina, a large population of bald eagles, and many wintering waterfowl and neotropical migratory species.

Food

Bunn's Bar-B-Q (127 N. King St., 252/794-2274, 9am-5pm Mon.-Tues., 9am-2pm Wed., 9am-5pm Thurs.-Fri., 9am-2pm Sat., from $5) is a barbecue and Brunswick stew joint of renown, an early gas station converted in 1938 to its present use. Service here is blazing fast,

primarily because there are just a few choices on the menu. Super-finely chopped barbecue is the specialty, and you get it with or without Brunswick stew, on a plate or a sandwich, with tart or creamy coleslaw and cornbread. It comes lightly sauced, the way the locals like it, but if you want more, or hotter, sauce, you'll find a bottle close at hand.

SCOTLAND NECK

In the little Halifax County community of Scotland Neck, west of Windsor, is the **Sylvan Heights Waterfowl Center and Eco-Park** (500 Sylvan Heights Park Way, off Lees Meadow Rd., 252/826-3186, www.shwpark.com, 9am-5pm Tues.-Sun. Apr.-Sept., 9am-4pm Tues.-Sun. Oct.-Mar., $9 adults, $5 ages 2-12, $7 over age 62, free under age 2), a center for the conservation of rare species of birds and home to the world's largest collection of waterfowl, comprising more than 1,000 birds of 170 different species. You'll see birds native to every continent except Antarctica; it gets a little hot here for penguins. A visit to Sylvan Heights is an unbeatable opportunity to get up close to birds you won't encounter elsewhere, as well as for wildlife photography—you won't even need your zoom lens.

HISTORIC HALIFAX AND ROANOKE RAPIDS

Sometimes the biggest things come from the smallest places. Less than 300 people call the tiny hamlet of Halifax home, but it is the birthplace of a nation, where the first official documents calling for independence from British rule were written. Once an important town due to its proximity to the river and trade routes, Halifax dwindled as nearby Roanoke Rapids rose in significance. Today, Halifax is not much more than a state historic site, with the vast majority of local shopping, dining, and infrastructure located in Roanoke Rapids.

In its heyday Roanoke Rapids was home to several textile mills, but, like so many other Southern towns, the mill jobs left and the town suffered. More recently a canal, once part of a complex series of locks allowing river traffic to

ROANOKE RIVER

After a long journey down from the Blue Ridge Mountains of Virginia, the waters of the Roanoke River cross into North Carolina just northwest of the town of Roanoke Rapids and travel another 130 miles before emptying into Albemarle Sound. The Roanoke River played a crucial role in the region's history as a major route for transportation and commerce in colonial times. It is also a river of tremendous ecological importance; its floodplain represents the Mid-Atlantic's largest and most pristine bottomland hardwood forest ecosystem. It's a region of beautifully primitive dark swamps and towering ancient trees.

More than 100,000 acres surrounding the river are preserved as wilderness. The **Roanoke River National Wildlife Refuge** (114 Water St., Windsor, 252/794-3808, www. fws.gov) comprises more than 20,000 acres in three separate tracts–Broadneck Swamp, Company Swamp, and Conine Island–between the towns of Hamilton and Windsor. Limited road access is available from U.S. 17 north of Windsor, but the best way to experience the refuge is by water. The Nature Conservancy also owns tens of thousands of acres of forests and wetlands along the river. These areas can be explored on field trips led by the North Carolina chapter of the **Nature Conservancy** (www. nature.org).

For a lover of river journeys by canoe or kayak, this is an irresistible place, and thanks to a network of area environmental and commu-nity organizations, it is increasingly a destination for paddlers. **Roanoke River Partners** (252/792-0070 or 252/724-0352, www. roanokeriverpartners.org) has designated a paddle trail through this wild region. They've also constructed more than a dozen camping platforms at locations along the river from Weldon, near the Virginia line, to Albemarle Sound. Every camping platform is different, but most are sturdy wooden decks over the cypress swamps or in the woods near the river on which campers can pitch their tents. Others are positively cushy screened houses in which campers can sleep protected from hovering bugs.

Reservations are required to use the platforms, and there's a lot to learn before you embark on a Roanoke River trip. For instance, do you know what to do if a bear pays a visit to your campsite? At some of the campsites, that information may come in handy. Read the information on the Roanoke River Partners website or call to find out more. Some stretches of the trail are best suited to experienced paddlers and campers. Novices can enjoy the river too by signing up for guided trips with conservation organizations such as the Nature Conservancy, paddle clubs such as the **Roanoke Paddle Club** (www.roanokeriver.com), or commercial river guides. Williamston-based **Roanoke Outdoor Adventures** (252/809-9488, http://roanokeoutdooradventures.com), for example, leads trips on many stretches of the Roanoke.

bypass the falls on the Roanoke River, has become a museum and a well-used walking and cycling trail.

Sights

The main attraction is **Historic Halifax** (25 St. David St., Halifax, 252/583-7191, www. nchistoricsites.org, 9am-5pm Tues.-Sat., free). Several colonial-era buildings still stand, including a prominent merchant's home and the Tap Room tavern, both from 1760, and the 1790 Eagle Tavern; there are also several early-19th-century buildings, including a home, an attorney's office, the clerk's office, and the jail. Tours (30 minutes) run throughout the day. On April 12 the Halifax Day celebration commemorates the date of the 1776 Halifax Resolves, which may have been signed in the Eagle Tavern. Events, speakers, tours, and usually costumed Colonial-era reenactors fill the day with the sights, sounds, smells, and activities that would have given the community so much energy so long ago.

In Roanoke Rapids, the **Roanoke Canal**

THE HALIFAX RESOLVES

On April 12, 1776, in a bar in the tiny town of Halifax, one of the most important but little-known documents in the history of the United States was ratified. At the Sign of the Thistle tavern, 83 members of the Fourth Provincial Congress of North Carolina met in secret to write and unanimously ratify the Halifax Resolves, the first official provincial action to declare independence from Great Britain. Three delegates from North Carolina delivered the Resolves to the Continental Congress in Philadelphia, and a few months later, word spread that the Declaration of Independence had been signed.

Museum and Trail (15 Jackson St. Ext., 252/537-2769, www.roanokecanal.com, museum 10am-4pm Tues.-Sat., trail dawn-dusk daily, museum $4, trail free) calls itself the world's longest museum as it included the 7.5-mile nature trail. At the trailhead, a museum tells the story of this 200-year-old canal, originally opened to allow river traffic to bypass the falls, and all its subsequent incarnations. In 1882 investors developed it into an early hydroelectric power source, and by 1900 two powerhouses were in full operation. The investors couldn't maintain it, and it was sold to a power company that operated it for several decades. In 1976 what remained of the canal was placed on the National Register of Historic Places. Learn about this in greater detail in the museum, which also provides an overall feel for the history of the Roanoke River Valley.

Sports and Recreation

The **Roanoke Canal Trail** (15 Jackson St. Ext, trailheads at Roanoke Rapids Lake, near Oakwood Ave., Roanoke Rapids; and Rockfish Dr., near U.S. 158/301, Weldon, dawn-dusk daily) runs for 7.5 miles along the tow path beside the 19th-century canal. Expect river views and secluded woodsy sections along the path; bring water and bug spray.

Every spring, anglers from around the country come to nearby Weldon to catch striped bass, known here as rockfish; as they travel up the river to spawn, the fishing is excellent. The Roanoke River's other fish species include shad, largemouth bass, and catfish. Outfitters can provide gear as well as the requisite fishing license. A comprehensive list of outfitters and guides is maintained by the **Halifax County Convention and Visitors Bureau** (www.visithalifax.com).

If kayaking is more your speed, **Roanoke River Partners** (www.roanokeriverpartners.org) maintains an index of outfitters and guides happy to help you with a solo or guided exploration of the river.

Shopping

At the western end of the Roanoke Canal Trail is **Riverside Mill** (200 Mill St., Weldon, 252/536-3100, www.riversidemill.net, 10am-6pm daily), an antiques mall and artisans gallery in a historic cotton mill. It's a fun place to explore because of the eclectic mix of local pottery, paintings, crafts, and antiques.

Along King Street in Halifax, you'll find a number of antiques stores that pop up for a year or two and are then replaced just as quickly by others. One of the permanent residents on this "antiques row" is **Ernie's Place** (18 King St., 252/583-2110, 9am-5pm Tues.-Sat.), a consignment shop that carries works by 30 or 40 local artisans.

Accommodations and Food

Most of the bed-and-breakfasts in the area are on the smaller side; the lone B&B in Roanoke Rapids is the charming **Twin Magnolias Bed & Breakfast** (302 Jackson St., Roanoke Rapids, 252/308-0019, $80), with just two guest rooms, a quaint garden, and a porch lined with chairs and tables that provide plenty of room to spread out.

© JASON FRYE

Historic Halifax contains colonial buildings.

Nearby Enfield, just a few miles south of Roanoke Rapids, is home to two B&Bs. **Bellamy Manor and Gardens Bed and Breakfast** (613 Glenview Rd., Enfield, 252/445-2234, www.manorbnb.com, $145) has four charming guest rooms in a beautiful home. Extensive gardens provide a place to walk and unwind, and if you're the sporting type, request a skeet-shooting outing when you make your reservation. The smaller **Healthsville Haven Bed and Breakfast** (25560 Hwy. 561, 252/445-5448, www.healthsvillehaven.com, from $70) has three guest rooms and serves breakfast in the dining room or on the deck, terrace, or garden (weather permitting), or even in your room if you're in the Executive Suite. The innkeepers are devoted to healthy eating and clean living to the point that if you want artificial sweetener for your coffee, you'll have to bring your own.

King Street Deli (20 S. King St., Halifax, 252/583-2112, 10am-2pm Mon.-Sat., around $8) specializes in rotisserie and fried chicken. The house-made potato chips are always good,

and if you want fried pickles, this is the only place in town to get them. **Abner's Drive In** (93 Roanoke Ave., Roanoke Rapids, 252/519-1296, 6:30am-2:30pm daily, $7) may lack aesthetics but they serve a great breakfast; try the pancakes.

WILLIAMSTON AND VICINITY

Williamston is at the junction of U.S. 17 and U.S. 64. If you're passing through town, Williamston is a great place to stop for barbecue or a fresh seafood meal.

Sights

A little west of Williamston on U.S. 13/64 is the town of Robersonville and the **St. James Place Museum** (U.S. 64 and Outerbridge Rd., by appointment with Robersonville Public Library, 252/795-3591, year-round). A Primitive Baptist church built in 1910 and restored by a local preservationist and folk-art enthusiast, St. James Place is an unusual little museum that fans of Southern craft will not want to miss. A serious collection of traditional quilts is the main feature of the museum. Of the 100 on display, nearly half are African American quilts, which are much less likely to survive and find their way into museum collections than their counterpane counterparts made by white quilters. Getting a glimpse of the two traditions side by side is an education in parallel Southern aesthetics.

Also on U.S. 13/64 west of Williamston is **East Carolina Motor Speedway** (4918 U.S. 64, 252/385-2018, www.ecspeedway.com, pits from 3:30pm, grandstands from 5pm, green flag 7:30pm Sat., pits from 10am, practice noon, green flag 2:30pm Sun., usually Apr.-Oct., $24 pit access, $10 adults, $5 ages 6-12, free under age 6, no one under age 12 in the pits), a 0.4-mile hard-surface track featuring several divisions, including late-model stock, street stock, mini stock, and U-Car divisions. U-Cars are fun to watch; they are front-wheel-drive vehicles like Ford Escorts, Dodge Daytonas, and Toyota Tercels that have been upfitted with safety measures and race on short tracks. Drivers range in age from 14-50 and are divided into classes by age. Fast and fun, this racing division has been gaining more fans every year.

One of the oddest sights in eastern North Carolina may be **Deadwood** (2302 Ed's Grocery Rd., 252/792-8938, www.deadwoodnc.com, from 5pm Thurs.-Sat., noon-9pm Sun. year-round), a tiny amusement park with an Old West flair. The owner calls this 10-acre park as "a weird, out-of-hand backyard project" inspired by Dolly Parton's Dollywood in Tennessee. Amusements here include miniature golf, a miniature train ride, a kid-friendly roller coaster, and a murder-mystery dinner show (first Sat. of the month, $30), complete with pratfalls, a gunfight, and a hearty dinner. It's well worth the stop, even if all you do is play a round of mini golf and eat ice cream.

Food

Come to Williamston on an empty stomach: It has an assortment of old and very traditional eateries. The ◖ **Sunny Side Oyster Bar** (1102 Washington St., 252/792-3416,

www.sunnysideoysterbarnc.com, from 5:30pm Mon.-Sat., from 5pm Sun. Sept.-Apr., $6.50-25) is the best-known, a seasonal oyster joint open in the months whose names contain the letter *R*—that is, oyster season. It has been in business since 1935 and is a historic and gastronomic landmark. Oysters are steamed behind the restaurant and then hauled inside and shucked at the bar. Visit the restaurant's website to meet the shuckers. In eastern North Carolina, a good oyster shucker is as highly regarded as a good artist or athlete, and rightly so. The Sunny Side doesn't take reservations, and it soon fills to capacity, so come early.

Down the road a piece, **Martin Supply** (118 Washington St., 252/792-2123, 8am-5pm Mon.-Fri., 8am-1pm Sat.), an old general store, is a good place to buy local produce and preserves, honey, molasses, and hoop cheese, and a place to stock up on hunting, fishing, and sporting supplies. **Griffin's Quick Lunch** (204 Washington St., 252/792-0002, 6am-8:30pm Mon.-Fri., 6am-2pm Sat., under $10) is a popular old diner with good barbecue and a devoted following. Back on U.S. 64, **Shaw's Barbecue** (202 West Blvd., 252/792-5339, 6am-7pm Mon.-Sun., $3-8) serves eastern North Carolina-style barbecue, fried chicken, and all the fixin's. They're open early, so if you're passing through to or from the Outer Banks, stop in for a good greasy breakfast—two eggs over easy, bacon, grits, and toast.

East of Williamston at the intersection of U.S. 64 and Highway 171, a most unusual restaurant in the small Roanoke River town of Jamesville draws attention from all over the country. The ◖ **Cypress Grill** (1520 Stewart St., off U.S. 64, 2nd Thurs. in Jan.-Apr., 11am-2pm and 5-8pm Mon.-Sat., under $10) is an unprepossessing wooden shack on the river, a survivor of the days when Jamesville made its living in the herring industry, dragging the fish out of the water with horse-drawn seines. Herring—breaded and seriously deep-fried, not pickled or sweet—is the main dish, although they also serve bass, flounder, perch, oysters, and catfish. The Cypress Grill is open for the a few months of the year and provides an intensely authentic small-town dining experience.

The Smokehouse Grill (252/792-8516, www.deadwoodnc.com, dinner from 5pm Thurs.-Sat., noon-9pm Sun., $9-23), in the Deadwood amusement park, serves steaks, ribs, chicken, and shrimp, and Tex-Mex specialties in a kitschy but charming Old West venue.

EAST ON U.S. 64

The eastern stretch of U.S. 64 runs along the Albemarle Sound between Williamston and the Outer Banks, passing through the towns of Plymouth, Creswell, and Columbia before it crosses to Roanoke Island. Here you'll encounter evidence of North Carolina's ancient past in old-growth forests, its recent past in the form of a plantation with a long and complex history of slavery, and its present in art galleries and abundant wildlife-watching and recreational opportunities.

Plymouth

Plymouth is an attractive little town on the Roanoke River with a rich maritime and military history. Most notably it was the site of the 1864 Battle of Plymouth, the second-largest Civil War battle in North Carolina, fought by more than 20,000 soldiers. At the **Roanoke River Lighthouse and Maritime Museum** (W. Water St., 252/217-2204, www.roanokeriverlighthouse.org, 11am-3pm Tues.-Sat. and by appointment, $3 adults, $2 students), visitors can explore a pretty replica of Plymouth's 1866 screw-pile lighthouse and, across the street in an old car dealership, the maritime museum, featuring artifacts and photographs from the region's water-faring heritage. On East Water Street is the **Port O'Plymouth Museum** (302 E. Water St., 252/793-1377, www.livinghistoryweekend.com, 9am-4pm Tues.-Sat., $3 adults, $2 students). This tiny museum is packed with Civil War artifacts, including a collection of beautiful pistols, telling the story of the Battle of Plymouth.

Davenport Homestead

West of Creswell is the **Davenport Homestead** (3 miles south from U.S. 64's exit 554 on Mt. Tabor Rd., 252/793-1377), a small 18th-century cabin built by Daniel Davenport, the first state senator from Washington County. In 1800 this diminutive homestead was home to 14 people—six members of the Davenport family and eight enslaved people. Visitors can take a self-guided tour of the Davenport Homestead, but for a closer look, ask Loretta Phelps, who lives across the road and is a Davenport descendant, to unlock the buildings and show you around.

Somerset Place Historic Site

Somerset Place Historic Site (2572 Lake Shore Rd., Creswell, 252/797-4560, www. ah.dcr.state.nc.us, 9am-5pm Tues.-Sat., free) was one of North Carolina's largest and most profitable plantations for the 80 years leading up to the Civil War. In the late 18th and early 19th centuries, 80 Africa-born men, women, and children were brought to Somerset to labor in the fields. The grief and disorientation they experienced and the subsequent trials of the slaves, whose numbers grew to include more than 300 people, are told by the historian Dorothy Spruill Redford in the book *Somerset Homecoming*. Somerset is a significant historical place for many reasons, but the story of its African Americans makes it one of this state's most important historic sites.

Somerset Place is a lovely but eerie place to visit. The restored grounds and buildings, including the Collins family's house, the slave quarters, and several dependencies, are deafeningly quiet, and the huge cypress trees growing right up to the quarters and the mansion make it feel almost prehistoric. Visitors can walk around the estate at their leisure. A small bookshop on the grounds is a good source for books about North Carolina history in general and African American history in particular.

Pettigrew State Park

Pettigrew State Park (2252 Lakeshore Rd., Creswell, 252/797-4475, http://ncparks.gov), on the banks of **Lake Phelps,** preserves an unusual ancient waterscape that's unlike anything else in the state. Archaeology reveals that there was a human presence here at least 10,000 years ago. The lake, which is five miles across and never more than nine feet deep, is only fed by rainfall and has yielded more than 30 ancient dugout canoes, some as old as 4,400 years and measuring more than 30 feet. The natural surroundings are ancient too, encompassing some of eastern North Carolina's only remaining old-growth forests. **Pungo Lake,** a smaller body of water within the park, is visited by 50,000 migrating snow geese over the course of the year, an unforgettable sight for wildlife watchers.

Visitors can camp at the family campground ($20), which has drive-in sites and access to restrooms and hot showers, or at primitive group campsites (from $13).

Art Galleries

Eastern North Carolina has always had a folk-art tradition. **Pocosin Arts** (Main St. and Water St., Columbia, 252/796-2787, www. pocosinarts.org, 10am-5pm Tues.-Sat.) has helped keep the tradition of arts and crafts alive, teaching community classes in ceramics, fiber arts, sculpture, jewelry making, metal-work, and other media. The sales gallery has beautiful handmade items, and the main gallery displays many examples of folk art from eastern North Carolina.

Sports and Recreation

Palmetto-Peartree Preserve (entrance on Pot Licker Rd./Loop Rd./State Rd. 1220, east of Columbia, 252/796-0723 or 919/967-2223, www.palmettopeartree.org) is a 10,000-acre natural area, wrapped in 14 miles of shoreline along Albemarle Sound and Little Alligator Creek. Originally established as a sanctuary for the red cockaded woodpecker, this is a great location for bird-watching and spotting other wildlife, including alligators, wolves, bears, and bobcats, as well as hiking, cycling, and horse-back riding along the old logging trails through the forest and canoeing and kayaking. The preserve's excellent paddle trail passes by Hidden Lake, a secluded cypress-swamp blackwater lake. There is an overnight camping platform

© JASON FRYE

Lake Phelps

at the lake, which can be used in the daytime without a permit for bird-watching and picnicking. To stay overnight, arrange for a permit through **Roanoke River Partners** (252/792-3790, www.roanokeriverpartners.org, $20 single campers, $10 pp multiple campers).

Once the southern edge of the Great Dismal Swamp, **Pocosin Lakes National Wildlife Refuge** (205 S. Ludington Dr., 6 miles south of Columbia, 252/796-3004, www.fws.gov/pocosinlakes) is an important haven for many species of animals, including migratory waterfowl and reintroduced red wolves. Five important bodies of water lie within the refuge: Pungo Lake, New Lake, the 16,600-acre Lake Phelps, and stretches of the Scuppernong and Alligator Rivers. All of these areas are good spots for observing migratory waterfowl, but Pungo Lake is special in the fall and winter, when snow geese and tundra swans visit in massive numbers—approaching 100,000—on their arctic journeys.

The landscape here was drastically altered by a tremendous wildfire in summer 2008, blanketing towns as far away as Raleigh with thick smoke. You can still observe some of the damage today, from burn marks on some of the larger trees to the growth patterns of the smaller trees, shrubs, and grasses. Wildfire is an important part of the natural cycle, however, and now is a unique opportunity to watch the regeneration of an ecosystem.

Also east of Columbia on U.S. 64 is the **Alligator River National Wildlife Refuge** (between Columbia and Roanoke Island, 252/473-1131, http://alligatorriver.fws.gov). The large refuge covers most of the peninsula bounded by the Alligator River to the west, Albemarle Sound to the north, Croatan Sound to the east, and Pamlico Sound to the southeast. This large swath of woods and pocosin represents one of the most important wildlife habitats in the state, home to over 200 species of birds as well as alligators, red wolves, and more black bears than anywhere in the coastal Mid-Atlantic. In the 1980s, red wolves were introduced into the Alligator River Refuge as they became extinct in the wild elsewhere in their original range.

Rangers lead "howlings" (reservations required, $7), nighttime expeditions into the refuge to hear the wolves' calls. The Columbia-based **Red Wolf Coalition** (252/796-5600, http://redwolves.com) works to educate the public about the wolves in the hope of helping to establish free-ranging, self-sustaining red wolf populations at a number of sites.

There are many other ways to enjoy the Alligator River National Wildlife Refuge, including hiking, kayaking, and bird-watching. The refuge does not have a physical headquarters or traditional visitors center, but detailed directions and visitor information are available on the website.

WASHINGTON, BATH, AND BELHAVEN

North of the Pamlico River, as you head toward the Mattamuskeet National Wildlife Refuge and the Outer Banks, the towns of Washington, Bath, and Belhaven offer brief but beautiful diversions into the nature and history of the region.

North Carolina Estuarium

The **North Carolina Estuarium** (223 E. Water St., Washington, 252/948-0000, www.partnershipforthesounds.org, 10am-4pm Tues.-Sat., $4, $2 children, free under age 5) is a museum dedicated to both the natural and cultural history of the Tar-Pamlico River basin. In addition to the exhibits, which include live native animals, historic artifacts, a 0.75-mile boardwalk along the Pamlico River, and hands-on displays, the Estuarium operates pontoon-boat tours (10:30am Wed.-Sat., 1:30pm Wed.-Fri., reservations required, free).

Moss House

Located in the historic district a block from the river, the **Moss House** (129 Van Norden St., 252/975-3967, www.themosshouse.com, $125-145) dates to 1902 and is now a cozy bed-and-breakfast with airy guest rooms and delicious breakfasts, often including hot cross buns. An easy walk from the Moss House is **Bill's Hot Dogs** (109 Gladden St., 252/946-3343),

ACROSS THE SOUNDS   **67**

a longtime local favorite for a quick snack. It's been around since 1928, so they've got their process down—you can only order when they ask for your order—and they know how to produce the dogs on the double.

Goose Creek State Park

Goose Creek State Park (2190 Camp Leach Rd., 252/923-2191, http://ncparks.gov, 8am-6pm daily Nov.-Feb., 8am-8pm daily Mar.-May and Sept.-Oct., 8am-9pm daily June-Aug., closed Dec. 25) is on the banks of the Pamlico River where Goose Creek joins it. It's an exotic environment of brackish marshes, freshwater swamps, and tall pine forests that are home to a variety of wildlife, including bears, a multitude of bird species, and lots of snakes. Eight miles of hiking trails as well as boardwalks and paddle trails traverse the hardwood swamp environment, and miles of shoreline and creek await exploration from a kayak or canoe (bring your own). Twelve primitive campsites (year-round, $13) are available, with access to toilets and water, including one campsite that is wheelchair-accessible.

Historic Bath

North Carolina's oldest town, Bath was chartered in 1705. The town has changed so little that even today it is mostly contained within the original boundaries laid out by the explorer John Lawson. For its first 70 years Bath enjoyed the spotlight as one of North Carolina's most important centers of trade and politics, home to governors, a refuge from the Indian wars, and frequently host to and victim of the pirate Blackbeard. Bath faded into obscurity as the town of Washington grew in the years after the Revolution, and today almost all of Bath is designated as **Historic Bath** (252/923-3971, www.nchistoricsites.org, visitors center and tours 9am-5pm Mon.-Sat., 1pm-5pm Sun. Apr.-Oct., 10am-4pm Tues.-Sat., 1pm-4pm Sun. Nov.-Mar., admission charged for the Palmer-Marsh and Bonner Houses). Important sites on the tour of the village are the 1734 St. Thomas Church, the 1751 Palmer-Marsh House, the 1790 Van Der

Veer House, and the 1830 Bonner House. Bath, like any self-respecting town of its age, has its fair share of legends, including a set of indelible hoof prints said to have been made by the devil's horse and "Teach's light"—the head of the pirate Blackbeard, often seen near his former home.

While in Bath, drop in at the **Old Town Country Kitchen** (436 Carteret St., 252/923-1840, 7am-8:30pm daily, under $12) for some country cooking and seafood. If you decide to stay the night, try the **Inn on Bath Creek** (116 S. Main St., 252/923-9571, www.innonbathcreek.com, 2-night minimum Fri.-Sat. Apr.-Nov., $130-225). This bed-and-breakfast, built on the site of the former Buzzard Hotel, fits in nicely with the old architecture of the historic town, but because it was built in 1999, it has modern conveniences to make your stay comfortable. Breakfast is big—think scratch-made blueberry pancakes, scrambled-egg wraps, and quiche along with the usual fruit, coffee, and pastries; vegetarian options are available.

Belhaven

Belying its innocuous name, **Belhaven Memorial Museum** (210 E. Main St., 919/943-6817, www.beaufort-county.com, 1pm-5pm Thurs.-Tues., free) is actually a very strange little institution that houses the collection of Miss Eva—Eva Blount Way, who died in 1962 at the age of 92—a most accomplished collector of oddities. In 1951 the local newspaper described her: "housewife, snake killer, curator, trapper, dramatic actress, philosopher, and preserver of all the riches of mankind, inadequately describes the most fascinating person you can imagine." Miss Eva kept among her earthly treasures a collection of pickled tumors (one weighs 10 pounds), a pickled one-eyed pig, a pickled two-headed kitten, cataracts (pickled), and three pickled human infants. There's also a dress that belonged to a 700-pound woman, a flea couple dressed in wedding togs, 30,000 buttons, and assorted snakes that Miss Eva determined needed killing. It must have taken a very long time to carry everything over here, but Miss Eva's collection is now on public display, the core of the Belhaven Memorial Museum's collection.

Belhaven has an especially nice inn, the **Belhaven Water Street Bed and Breakfast** (567 E. Water St., 866/338-2825, www.belhavenwaterstreetbandb.com, $85-125). The guest rooms in this 100-year-old house face Pantego Creek and have their own fireplaces and private baths as well as wireless Internet access.

⟨ MATTAMUSKEET NATIONAL WILDLIFE REFUGE

Near the tiny town of Swan Quarter, **Mattamuskeet National Wildlife Refuge** (856 Mattamuskeet Rd., off Hwy. 94, between Swan Quarter and Englehard, 252/926-4021, www.fws.gov/mattamuskeet) preserves one of North Carolina's most remarkable natural features as well as one of its most famous buildings. Lake Mattamuskeet, 18 miles long by 6 miles wide, is the state's largest natural lake, and at an average of 1.5 feet deep—5 feet at its

deepest point—it is a most unusual environment. The hundreds of thousands of waterfowl who rest here on their seasonal rounds make this a world-famous location for bird-watching and wildlife photography.

Old-timers in the area have fond memories of dancing at the **Lodge at Lake Mattamuskeet,** one of eastern North Carolina's most recognizable buildings. The huge structure was built in 1915 and at the time was the world's largest pumping station, moving over one million gallons of water per minute. In 1934 it was bought by the federal government along with the wildlife sanctuary, and the Civilian Conservation Corps transformed it into the lodge, a favorite gathering place for the next 40 years. Efforts have been made to return the lodge to its former glory, but with the economic downturn that began in 2008, state budget shortfalls have kept the project from getting the resources necessary to complete the restoration.

Hiking and biking trails thread through the

the Lodge at Lake Mattamuskeet

© JASON FRYE

refuge, but camping is not permitted. In hunting season, which runs during spring and autumn months, beware of hunters (wearing a bright color like safety orange isn't a bad idea) and keep an eye out as well for copperheads, cottonmouths, two kinds of rattlesnakes, and alligators. Bears and red wolves abound here as well.

Within the administration of the Mattamuskeet Refuge is the **Swan Quarter National Wildlife Refuge** (252/926-4021, www.fws.gov/swanquarter), located along the north shore of the Pamlico Sound, and accessible only by water. It is a gorgeous waterscape full of wildlife and worth exploring if you have the time and the means to get here.

While you're here, stop in one of the handful of roadside produce stands you'll pass and inquire about getting some Mattamuskeet onions. Much like the famed Vidalia onion, the Mattamuskeet onion has a sweet, distinctive flavor farmers and foodies swear is endemic to the region thanks to the makeup of the soil.

GETTING THERE AND AROUND

This remote corner of North Carolina is crossed by two major north-south routes, U.S. 17 and U.S. 168, both from Chesapeake, Virginia. U.S. 168 passes to the east through Currituck, and U.S. 17 is the westerly route, closest to the Dismal Swamp and Elizabeth City, passing through Edenton, Windsor, and Williamston. At Williamston, U.S. 17 meets U.S. 64, a major east-west route that leads to Plymouth, Creswell, and Columbia to the east.

If you continue south on U.S. 17 from Williamston, the next major town is Washington, where you can turn east on U.S. 264 to reach Bath and Belhaven. Alternately, you can reach U.S. 264 from the other direction, taking Highway 94 at Columbia and crossing Lake Mattamuskeet.

There is one state ferry route in this region, at the far northwest corner between Currituck and Knotts Island (877/287-7488, 45 minutes, six trips daily, free).

BEAUFORT AND THE CRYSTAL COAST

Long before you smell the ocean salt on the air, you can feel the ocean drawing near. The sky seems wider and it takes on a deeper shade of blue. Hardwoods and hills give way to towering pines and flat fields, and then more and more water—creeks, wetlands, and widening rivers. Somewhere between Kinston and New Bern, still an hour's drive from the beaches and sounds of Carteret County, you can sense the Atlantic.

Along the Crystal Coast, as North Carolina's central coast is known in tourism literature, you'll find New Bern and Beaufort, two old North Carolina towns that were centers of colonial commerce and access to the Atlantic. These two towns are beautifully preserved, with great examples of historic commercial and residential architecture dating as far back as three centuries, including one home believed to have belonged to the dreaded pirate Blackbeard.

The Neuse River winds through pine forests, passing Kinston—a town with an unusual Civil War past and a food scene that's more than worth the visit—and widening as it enters the coastal plain, feeding the primeval forest, creeks, hidden lakes, and tiny towns in the Croatan National Forest. To the northeast, the Cedar Island National Wildlife Refuge is a vast swath of marshes, gradually easing into the Pamlico Sound, where Cape Lookout National Seashore shelters the mainland from storms. Along the seashore are miles of beach where the only occupants are wild horses, the Banker ponies, and the beautiful diamond-patterned Cape Lookout Lighthouse. You

© JASON FRYE

HIGHLIGHTS

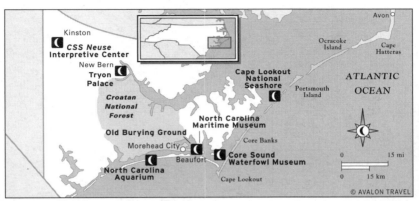

© AVALON TRAVEL

LOOK FOR **(€** TO FIND RECOMMENDED SIGHTS, ACTIVITIES, DINING, AND LODGING.

(€ Tryon Palace: The splendid, and in its day controversial, seat of colonial government is re-constructed in New Bern's historic district, worthy of a day's leisurely exploration (page 75).

(€ CSS *Neuse* Interpretive Center: Far up the Neuse River a Confederate ironclad was built, fought, scuttled, and burned to prevent its capture. It stayed in the river for nearly a century before being salvaged for historic preservation. This museum tells its story, complete with the recovered hull (page 84).

(€ North Carolina Maritime Museum: North Carolina's seafaring heritage, ranging from pirate history to its fishing legacy to current maritime culture, is represented by fascinating exhibits and activities at this great museum (page 89).

(€ Beaufort's Old Burying Ground: One of the prettiest and most storied cemeteries in the South, this churchyard is home to the "Little Girl Buried in a Barrel of Rum" and other fascinating residents (page 90).

(€ Core Sound Waterfowl Museum: Actually a museum about people rather than ducks, the Waterfowl Museum eloquently tells of the everyday lives of past generations of Down Easterners while bringing their descendants together to reforge community bonds (page 98).

(€ Cape Lookout National Seashore: The more than 50 miles of coastline along Core and Shackleford Banks, now home only to wild horses and turtle nests, were once also the home of Bankers who made their livings in the fishing, whaling, and shipping trades (page 100).

(€ North Carolina Aquarium: Sharks, jellies, otters, and their aquatic kin show their true beauty in underwater habitats at the aquarium. Hiking trails and boat tours lead to the watery world outdoors (page 103).

BEAUFORT

BEAUFORT

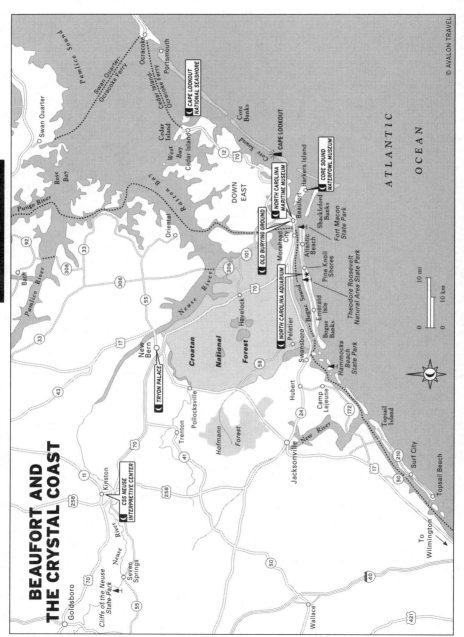

© AVALON TRAVEL

won't find homes here. Portsmouth Village, a once-thriving whaling port washed away by a series of storms, is now nearly empty except for seagulls.

Sometimes people in North Carolina refer to any part of the coast, from Wilmington to Nags Head, as "Down East." In the truest sense of the term, Down East refers to northeast Carteret County, the area north of Beaufort. Here the islands, marshes, and towns bordering Core Sound are undergoing colossal cultural shifts as people from "up North" (meaning "anywhere but here") move into the area and local youth leave generations of family life for greener economic pastures. Changes in global trade and in the environment have made traditional maritime occupations like fishing and shrimping untenable. Nonetheless, Down Easterners work to preserve the treasure of their home, the Core Sound, with conservation and historic preservation as well as folkways education. Witness the Core Sound Waterfowl Museum on Harkers Island, where community members have assembled an interesting collection of family photos, quilts, baseball uniforms, oyster knives, net hooks, and other treasures to tell their story.

PLANNING YOUR TIME

Beach-season rules apply along the coastal areas and river towns, meaning that prices increase dramatically between Memorial Day in May and Labor Day in early September. Conversely, prices drop to rock bottom during the off-season. Visiting during shoulder seasons can mean warm water, empty beaches, and no waiting for restaurant tables, but your accommodations and dining choices can be limited, particularly in smaller towns.

When you visit, try the fresh local seafood. To ensure you're getting the best local catch, **North Carolina Sea Grant** (www.ncseagrant. org) provides downloadable cards and information on the seasonally fresh seafood caught in the area.

Across the Southeast, late summer and early autumn are hurricane season. The paths of hurricanes can be quite unpredictable, so if you're planning a week at the beach at this time of year, be aware that even if reports say a storm will dissipate over Cuba, that doesn't mean it won't turn into a hurricane and head for the Carolina coast. Chance are that you'll have sufficient warning before any major storm, but it's advisable to keep an eye on the weather forecast. A storm that stays offshore, even at some distance, can cause foul beach conditions; surfers love the big waves that precede a storm, but they know the danger of powerful tides, strong undertow, rip currents, and the general unpredictability that storms bring. Not unique to this region, the risk is the same anywhere on the North Carolina coast.

Barring storms, fall is a fabulous time to visit. Days and nights are still warm, the ocean is swimmable, and the crowds are smaller. Mild weather often holds through the end of October into November, but the water becomes chilly for swimming then, although air temperatures are still nice for strolling on the sand.

INFORMATION AND SERVICES

Hospitals in the area include **Carteret General Hospital** (3500 Arendell St., 252/808-6000, www.ccgh.org) in Morehead City, **Carolina East Medical Center** (2000 Neuse Blvd., 252/633-8111, www.carolinaeasthealth.com) in New Bern, **Vidant Duplin Hospital** (401 N. Main St., 910/296-0941, www.vidanthealth. com) in Kenansville, **Lenoir Memorial Hospital** (100 Airport Rd., 252/522-7000, www.lenoirmemorial.org) in Kinston, and **Wayne Memorial Hospital** (2700 Wayne Memorial Dr., 919/736-1110, www.wayne-health.org) in Goldsboro.

Extensive travel information is available from the **Crystal Coast Tourism Authority** (3409 Arendell St., 800/786-6962, www.crystalcoastnc.org) in Morehead City.

New Bern

New Bern's history attracts visitors, but the natural beauty of this artistic community keeps many of them returning year after year. Situated at the confluence of the Trent and Neuse Rivers, it's a prime spot for sightseeing and retirement living. Despite the attention it gets and the consequent traffic, New Bern has retained its charm and is still a small and enormously pleasant town. An important note: It's pronounced "NYEW-bern" or "NOO-bern," sometimes even like "neighbor," but never "New-BERN."

At the junction of two major highways, New Bern is easily reached by car. U.S. 17 passes through New Bern north-south, and U.S. 70 crosses east-west, with Beaufort and Morehead City to the east and Kinston to the west.

HISTORY

New Bern's early days were marked by tragedy. It was settled in 1710 by a community of Swiss

and German colonists under the leadership of English surveyor John Lawson (author of the 1709 *A New Voyage to Carolina,* available today in reprint) and Swiss entrepreneur Christoph von Graffenried (from Bern, Switzerland). More than half of the settlers died en route to the New World, and those who made it alive suffered tremendous hardship in the first years. Lawson and Graffenried were both detained in 1711 by the indigenous Tuscarora people, whom the colonists had evicted from their land without compensation. Graffenried was released, according to some accounts because he wore such fancy clothes that the Tuscarora feared executing such a high-ranking official. Lawson was tried and burned at the stake, and the conflict escalated into the Tuscarora War.

Despite early disasters, New Bern was on its feet again by the mid-18th century, when it was home to the colony's first newspaper and its first chartered academy. It also became

© JASON FRYE

North Carolina's capital, an era symbolized by the splendor of Tryon Palace, one of the most recognizable architectural landmarks in the state.

During the Civil War, New Bern was captured early on by Ambrose Burnside's forces, and despite multiple Confederate attempts to retake the city, it remained a Union stronghold for the balance of the war. It became a center for African American resistance and political organization through the Reconstruction years, a story grippingly told in historian David Cecelski's book *The Waterman's Song.*

SIGHTS
◖ Tryon Palace
Tryon Palace (529 S. Front St., 252/639-3500 or 800/767-1560, www.tryonpalace.org, 9am-5pm Mon.-Sat., noon-5pm Sun., last guided tour 4pm, gardens 9am-7pm Mon.-Sat., noon-7pm Sun. summer, museum shop 9am-5pm Mon.-Sat., noon-5pm Sun., full admission $20 adults, $10 schoolchildren, galleries and gardens only $12 adults, $4 children, gardens only $6 adults, $3 children) is a remarkable feat of historic re-creation, a reconstruction of the 1770 colonial capitol and governor's mansion done from the ground up. It was a magnificent project the first time around too, when Governor William Tryon bucked the preferences of Piedmont Carolinians and had the colonial government's new home built here on the coastal plain. He hired English

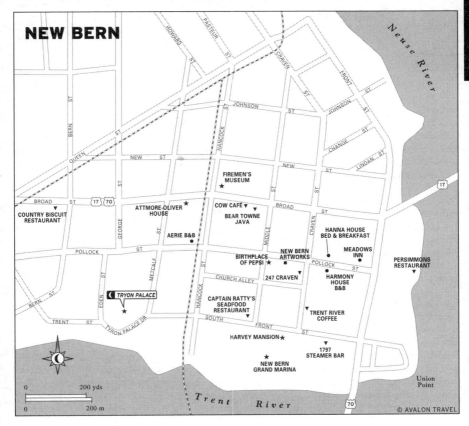

BEAUFORT

© JASON FRYE

Tryon Palace is a re-creation of North Carolina's colonial capitol.

architect John Hawks to design the complex, a Georgian house on an estate laid out in the Palladian style. The palace's first incarnation was short-lived, standing for a scant 25 years before burning down in 1798. As the new state had relocated its governmental operations to Raleigh, there was no need to rebuild the New Bern estate, but it was not forgotten. In the early 20th century a movement arose to rebuild Tryon Palace. By the 1950s both the funds and, incredibly, Hawks's original drawings and plans had been secured, and the palace was rebuilt over a period of seven years using the drawings as well as the stables, the only original building not destroyed in the fire, as a model. Today, it is once again one of the most striking and recognizable buildings in the state.

Tryon Palace is open for tours year-round, and it hosts various lectures and living-history events throughout the year. One of the best times to visit is during the December holiday season, when the estate is decorated beautifully and a recreated **Jonkonnu,** a colonial African American celebration once seen throughout the Caribbean and Southeast, is celebrated. Also known by the name Junkanoo, John Canoe, and several other variations, enslaved Africans and African Americans would put on a Mardi Gras-like festival with deep African roots, parading through plantations with music and wearing outlandish costumes, some representing folk characters associated with the celebration. Like Mardi Gras, it was a sort of upside-down day, when the social order was temporarily inverted and enslaved people could boldly walk right onto the master's porch and demand gifts or money. Some slave owners got into the spirit of the celebration and played along with the remarkable pantomime. It was a tradition fraught with both joy and sorrow. Tryon Palace puts on a lively and enlightening re-creation.

Tryon's living-history interpreters do a wonderful job of enlightening visitors to certain aspects of colonial life, on a guided tour of the palace and on a walk through the nearby kitchen. In the kitchen, costumed interpreters show what was involved in running an

© JASON FRYE

BEAUFORT

period gardens at Tryon Palace

18th-century household, utilizing the nearby kitchen garden for most of what they cook with during the demonstrations. Lately the cooking demonstrations have expanded, pairing the beauty of the palace with the talents of a local chef to put on dinner events, including the on-site Savoring Spring event that makes use of the bounty of the kitchen garden.

At the Tryon Palace ticket office is the **North Carolina History Center,** a collection of galleries and exhibits that illustrate the history of the region and New Bern in particular. The **Pepsi Family Center** is a hit with kids, as interactive displays transport you back to 1835, when the region was busy producing valuable things like turpentine for the nation's young navy. Visitors interested in Jonkonnu will find enlightening exhibits on the festival, and art lovers will appreciate the best of the region in the **Duffy Exhibit Gallery.** Admission to the Pepsi Family Center, Duffy Exhibit Gallery, and Regional History Museum are included in the admission cost for Tryon Palace.

Visiting Tryon Palace and its gardens along

with the North Carolina History Center can fill an afternoon or even a full day. When you're done exploring, the surrounding neighborhood contains some wonderful old homes.

New Bern Firemen's Museum

The **New Bern Firemen's Museum** (408 Hancock St., 252/636-4087, www.newbern-firemuseum.com, 10am-4pm Mon.-Sat., $5 adults, $2.50 children, free under age 6) is a fun little museum for gearheads that has an antiquarian bent. The museum houses a collection of 19th- and early-20th-century fire wagons and trucks and chronicles the lively and contentious history of firefighting in New Bern. The city was the first in North Carolina and one of the first in the country to charter a fire department. After the Civil War, three fire companies operated in New Bern; one was founded before the war, one was founded after, and the third was a boys bucket brigade, a training program for junior firefighters. During Reconstruction, every fire became a competition among the companies, as residents would gather to see which would get to a blaze first—the "good old boys" (white Southerners) or the "carpetbaggers" (Northerners who came to the South during Reconstruction for economic opportunities).

Attmore-Oliver House

The beautiful 1790 **Attmore-Oliver House** (512 Pollock St., 252/638-8558, www.newbernhistorical.org, 10am-4pm Mon.-Fri., guided tours by appointment, free) is a historic house museum with exhibits about New Bern's Civil War history. It's also the headquarters of the New Bern Historical Society.

Birthplace of Pepsi

We often think of Coca-Cola as the quintessential Southern drink, but it was here in New Bern that Caleb Bradham, a drugstore owner, put together what he called Brad's Drink—later Pepsi-Cola. The Pepsi-Cola Bottling Company operates a soda fountain and gift shop at the location of Bradham's pharmacy, called the **Birthplace of Pepsi** (256 Middle St., 252/636-5898, www.pepsistore.com). A few Pepsi antiques sit in display cases, but the pièce de résistance is the mural showing the original recipe for a production batch of Brad's Drink.

ENTERTAINMENT AND EVENTS

New Bern's historic Harvey Mansion has a cozy old-fashioned pub in its cellar, the **1797 Steamer Bar** (221 S. Front St., 252/635-3232, 5pm-2am daily). As you might guess, the pub serves steamed seafood and other light fare. This basement bar is a rarity for houses of such an age; it was originally the house's kitchen, which in the 18th century was typically in a separate building because of the danger of fire. Today, it's a perfect hangout—the low ceiling, exposed beams, and copper-topped bar make it cozy.

Captain Ratty's Seafood Restaurant (202-206 Middle St., 252/633-2088 or 800/633-5292, www.captainrattys.com, 11:30am-9:30pm Mon.-Fri., 8am-9:30pm Sat.) has a rooftop bar that's a popular gathering spot

for locals and travelers alike, and the impressive wine list, combined with a few choice appetizers, make this a great place to watch the sun go down.

SHOPPING

Given its age, the fact that New Bern is a great place for antiques shopping comes as no surprise. Check out **New Bern Antiques** (1000 Greenleaf Cemetery Rd., 252/672-1890, www.new-bern-antiques.com, 9:30am-5:30pm Mon.-Sat., 1pm-5pm Sun.) and the adjacent **New Bern Flea Mall** (4109 U.S. 17 S., 252/636-1855, http://new-bern-flea-mall-complex.com, 10am-5pm Mon.-Sat.), with nearly 40,000 square feet of antiques, collectibles, and vendors. **Tom's Coins and Antiques** (244 Middle St., 252/633-0615, hours vary) carries an impressive array of antique coins and currency as well as a good selection of small mementos and antiques. There are also periodic antiques shows and even a salvaged antique architectural hardware show at the New Bern Convention Center (www.visitnewbern.com).

Tryon Palace is a fun shopping spot for history buffs and home-and-garden fanciers. The historical site's **Museum Shop** (Jones House, Eden St. and Pollock St., 252/514-4932, 9am-5pm Mon.-Sat., noon-5pm Sun.) has a nice variety of books about history and architecture as well as handicrafts and children's toys and games. In season, the **Garden Shop** (610 Pollock St., 252/514-4932, 10am-5pm Mon.-Sat., 1pm-5pm Sun.) sells special bulbs and plants grown in Tryon Palace's own greenhouse. Out of season you can still find a nice variety of gardening tools and accessories. A Shop Pass is available at the Museum Shop; it allows you to visit the shops at Tryon Palace without paying the entrance fee.

Strolling the streets of New Bern, you'll notice a number of art galleries. One of the best is **New Bern Artworks and Company** (323 Pollock St., 252/634-9002, www.newbernartworks.com, 10am-6pm Mon.-Fri., 10am-5pm Sun.), a well-curated gallery and working studio with architecture almost as beautiful as the artwork. The gallery is in a former jewelry store and has the original antique cases and even the safe. This is a great stop for art and architecture buffs.

Carolina Creations Fine Art and Contemporary Craft Gallery (317-A Pollock St., 252/633-4369, www.carolinacreationsnewbern.com, 10am-6pm Mon.-Thurs., 10am-8pm Fri., 10am-6pm Sat., 11am-4pm Sun. spring-summer, 10am-6pm Mon.-Sat., 11am-3pm Sun. winter) has a mix of fine arts and functional craft items. You'll find everything from turned wooden bowls to oil paintings and hand-forged menorahs.

SPORTS AND RECREATION

Right on the river and near miles of tributaries to explore by boat, it's no surprise that watersports dominate New Bern's outdoor offerings. Familiarize yourself with the area on a two-hour tour waterfront tour on the catamaran *Lookout Lady* (New Bern Grand Marina, 100 Middle St., Dock F, 252/728-7827, www.tournewbern.com, $25 adults, $15 children, sunset cruises $26 adults, $16 children). Tours pass Millionaire's Row, where author Nicholas Sparks has a home, and are narrated by knowledgeable local residents.

Head out on the water on your own aboard a kayak or stand-up paddleboard and discover New Bern by water. Kayakers will want to head to the Grand Marina, where **Captain Fins** (New Bern Grand Marina, 100 Middle St., Dock F, 252/876-2288, http://kayaknewbern.com, single kayaks $30 for 2 hours, $40 half-day, $55 full-day, double kayaks $40 for 2 hours, $55 half-day, $70 full-day) rents out kayaks and provides some guidance on where to go and what to see. For a self-propelled tour of New Bern's waterfront, join **Stand Up Outfitters** (244 Craven St., 252/514-0404, www.standupoutfitters.com, lessons from $45, tours from $60, rentals from $35 per day) on their Historic New Bern Tour. This 1.5-2 hour tour will give you a workout and unique views of this beautiful town.

Golfers visiting New Bern will want to check out **Harbour Pointe Golf Club** (1105 Barkentine Dr., 252/638-5338, www.

harbourpointegolfclub.com, 18 holes, par 72, greens fees $38 for 18 holes, $25 for 9 holes, $28 midday, $15 twilight, $25 military, fees include cart). The course presents challenges but gives you plenty of opportunities to take strokes back. And the must-see hole is number 14, where the green's sweeping view of Broad Creek and the Neuse River can even take the sting out of a double bogey. The **Emerald Golf Club** (5000 Clubhouse Dr., 252/633-4440, www.emeraldgc.com, 18 holes, par 72, greens fees $56 for 18 holes, $34 for 9 holes, $40 after 11am, rates include cart) is a pretty course with wide fairways flanked by trees, bunkers, and water.

At **Carolina Colours Golf Club** (3300 Waterscape Way, 252/772-7022, www.carolinacoloursgolfclub.com, 18 holes, par 72, Tues.-Sun., greens fees $49 for 18 holes, $28 for 9 holes), the course winds through some heavily wooded terrain to reveal beautiful fairways that invite seasoned golfers to challenge bunker placements and shoot aggressively for the green, while allowing recreational golfers to play at a pace and level they're accustomed to. This is one of the prettiest public courses in the area.

ACCOMMODATIONS

The ☾ **Aerie Bed and Breakfast** (509 Pollock St., 800/849-5553, www.aeriebedandbreakfast.com, $129-229) is the current incarnation of the 1880s Street-Ward residence. Each of its seven luxurious guest rooms are decorated with Victorian furniture reflecting the house's earliest era. There is a lovely courtyard for guests to enjoy, and the inn is only one block from Tryon Palace.

Pollock Street is lined with charming 19th-century houses decorated in classic bed-and-breakfast style. The **Harmony House Inn** (215 Pollock St., 800/636-3113, www.harmonyhouseinn.com, $109-175) has seven well-appointed guest rooms and three suites. Two of the suites feature king beds and two-person jetted tubs, while the third is more suited to a group that may want to spread out, with a queen bed and a separate living room that has a queen sleeper sofa.

At the **Hanna House Bed and Breakfast** (218 Pollock St., 252/635-3209 or 866/830-4371, http://hannahousenc.net, no children under age 6, $99-165), expect one of the best breakfasts you can get at a B&B. The owners take pride in their morning spread and offer a selection of dishes ranging from eggs en croûte, a variety of frittatas, and my favorite, stuffed french toast. Hanna House isn't all breakfast; each of the five guest rooms is comfortable and spacious for both single travelers and couples.

Also on Pollock Street, the **Meadows Inn** (212 Pollock St., 877/551-1776, www.meadowsinn-nc.com, $139-179) started as a humble four-room home, but was expanded in the late 19th century. You'll find six guest rooms and a two-bedroom third-floor suite, all furnished with a mix of antiques and modern conveniences. Because of its prime location, make reservations early.

Several motels can be found around New Bern as well, including **Holiday Inn Express** (3455 Martin Luther King Jr. Blvd., 252/638-8266, www.hiexpress.com, from around $100), and **Hampton Inn** (200 Hotel Dr., 252/637-2111, www.hamptoninn.com, from around $125).

Camping

New Bern's **KOA Campground** (1565 B St., 800/562-3341, www.newbernkoa.com, from $35) is on the other side of the Neuse River from town, right on the riverbank. Choices include 20-, 30-, 40-amp RV sites; "Kamping Kabins and Lodges"; and tent sites. Pets are allowed, and there is a dog park on-site. The campground has free wireless Internet access. Stop by the New Bern Convention Center's visitor information center before checking in, and pick up a KOA brochure for some valuable coupons.

FOOD

One of the top restaurants in New Bern also happens to have the best view. At **Persimmons Restaurant** (100 Pollock St., 252/514-0033, www.persimmonsrestaurant.com, lunch 11am-2pm Tues.-Fri., 11am-4pm Sat. and Sun., dinner 5pm-9pm Tues.-Thurs. and Sun., 5pm-9:30pm Fri. and Sat.) you can take in the water views from a seat in the comfortable dining room our outside on the dockside deck. With two separate menus—one focused on fine dining, with walnut and whole-grain mustard-crusted red snapper or pan-roasted duck breast and wild-game sausage (dinner entrées $18-31), and the other on burgers, fish tacos, and other handhelds ($10-13), you'll be able to make your meal as refined or relaxed as you want.

For a down-home breakfast, the **Country Biscuit Restaurant** (809 Broad St., 252/638-5151, http://thecountrybiscuit.com, 5am-2pm Mon.-Fri., 5am-9pm Sat., dinner 4pm-9pm Wed.-Fri., breakfast $2-9, lunch and dinner $5-9), is popular, not surprisingly, for its biscuits. They say they serve "real food for real folks," and indeed, the food is simple, homey, and filling.

Moore's Olde Tyme Barbeque (3711 U.S. 17 S./Martin Luther King Jr. Blvd., 252/638-3937, www.mooresbarbeque.com, 10am-8pm Mon.-Thurs., 10am-8:30pm Fri.-Sat., $2.50-9) is a family business, in operation since 1945. They roast and smoke their own barbecue in a pit on-site, burning the wood that you'll see piled up by the shop. The menu is short and simple—pork barbecue, chicken, shrimp, fish, hush puppies, fries, and slaw—and the prices are lower than many fast-food joints. In addition to making some good 'cue, Moore's is a Guinness World Record holder for making the world's largest open barbecue sandwich with slaw, on July 4, 2010. Weighing in at more than half a ton, it was one big sandwich.

There are lots of good snack stops in New Bern to grab a bite or a cup of coffee before a day of touring on foot or on the water. The **Trent River Coffee Company** (208 Craven St., 252/514-2030, 7:30am-5pm Mon.-Fri., 8am-5pm Sat., 10am-5pm Sun.) is a casual coffee shop with good coffee in a cool old downtown storefront. It's sometimes patronized by well-behaved local dogs that lie patiently under the tables while their owners read the newspaper. This is a nice meeting place, and a shaded oasis in the summer heat.

Bear Towne Java (323 Middle St., 252/633-7900, www.beartownejava.com, 7am-6:30pm Mon.-Thurs., 7am-8pm Fri.-Sat., 7am-8pm Sun., meals $9) serves a robust cup of coffee, carries the traditional array of coffee-shop confections, and even serves a respectable lunch and dinner. Try The Florence Panini; it comes with smoked turkey, provolone, and a cherry pepper relish that's just the right balance of sweet and hot.

The **Cow Café** (319 Middle St., 252/672-9269, www.cowcafenewbern.com, 10am-7pm Mon.-Thurs., 10am-9pm Fri.-Sat., 11:30am-5pm Sun., around $7) is a pleasant downtown creamery and snack shop with some unusual and classic homemade ice cream flavors you can't find anywhere else in town. The fun logo and outrageous Holstein cow decor makes it hard to miss from a visual standpoint, and the ice cream makes it hard to miss flavor-wise.

The small but popular **247 Craven** (247 Craven St., 252/635-1879, www.247craven.com, 11am-2:30pm, 5pm-late Tues.-Sat., 11am-2:30pm Sun., lunch around $9, dinner $18-25, brunch around $9) makes one of the best burgers in New Bern, although the lunchtime fried green tomato BLT is a must. For dinner, the seared scallops Fra Diavolo is a crowd pleaser. They focus on local and seasonal ingredients, so the menu varies a little, but no matter the season it's worth a visit.

Sea Glass Café and Bakery (1803 S. Glenburnie Rd., 252/634-2327, http://seaglasscafe.com, 7:30am-3pm Mon.-Sun., around $8) is a local favorite for their pecan cranberry toast made with bread baked on-site and their scones. Open for breakfast and lunch, they put out food ranging from scrambled eggs to chicken salad on pecan cranberry bread to seared ahi tuna over salad. The place is small, but the food is worth the wait if there are no tables free when you arrive.

Croatan National Forest and Vicinity

A huge swath of swampy wilderness, the Croatan National Forest is all the land bounded by the Neuse, Trent, and White Oak Rivers and Bogue Sound, from New Bern to Morehead City and almost all the way to Jacksonville. Despite its size, Croatan is one of the lesser-known and least developed federal preserves in the state. All three nearby towns in Jones County, population just over 10,000, enjoy a similar atmosphere of sequestration, where barely traveled roads lead to dark expanses of forest and swamp as well as narrow old village streets.

CROATAN NATIONAL FOREST

Headquartered just off U.S. 70 south of New Bern, the **Croatan National Forest** (141 E. Fisher Ave., New Bern, 252/638-5628, www.fs.usda.gov) has few established amenities for visitors but has plenty of land and water trails to explore.

Hiking

The main hiking route is the **Neusiok Trail,** which begins at the Newport River Parking area and ends at the Pinecliff Recreation Area on the Neuse River. It traverses 20 miles of beach, salt marsh, swamp, pocosin, and pinewoods. The 1.4-mile **Cedar Point Tideland Trail** covers estuary marshes and woods, starting at the Cedar Point boat ramp near Cape Carteret. The 0.5-mile **Island Creek Forest Walk** passes through virgin hardwood forests and marl (compacted prehistoric shell) outcroppings.

Boating

The spectacular **Saltwater Adventure Trail** is a newly designated water route, roughly 100 miles in length, that starts at Brice's Creek, south of New Bern, and winds north to the Neuse River; it follows the Neuse all the way to the crook at Harlowe, where it threads through

JOHN LAWSON ON ALLIGATORS

Explorer John Lawson, in *A New Voyage to Carolina*, describes a 1709 encounter with an alligator on the Neuse River.

The Allegator is the same, as the Crocodile, and differs only in Name. They frequent the sides of Rivers, in the Banks of which they make their Dwellings a great way under Ground...Here it is, that this amphibious Monster dwells all the Winter, sleeping away his time till the Spring appears, when he comes from his Cave, and daily swims up and down the Streams...This Animal, in these Parts, sometimes exceeds seventeen Foot long. It is impossible to kill them with a Gun, unless you chance to hit them about the Eyes, which is a much softer Place, than the rest of their impenetrable Armour. They roar, and make a hideous Noise against bad Weather, and before they come out of their Dens in the Spring. I was pretty much frightened with one of these once, which happened thus: I had built a House about half a Mile from an Indian Town, on the Fork of the Neus-River, where I dwelt by my self, excepting a young Indian Fellow, and a Bull-Dog, that I had along with me. I had not then been so long a Sojourner in America, as to be thoroughly acquainted with this Creature. One of them had got his Nest directly under my House, which stood on pretty high Land, and by a Creek-side, in whose Banks his Entringplace was, his Den reaching the Ground directly on which my House stood. I was sitting alone by the Fire-side (about nine a Clock at Night, some time in March) the Indian Fellow being gone to Town, to see his Relations; so that there was no body in the House but my self and my Dog; when, all of a sudden, this illfavour'd Neighbour of mine, set up such a Roaring, that he made the House shake about my Ears, and so continued, like a Bittern (but a hundred times louder, if possible), for four or five times. The Dog stared, as if he was frightened out of his Senses; nor indeed, could I imagine what it was, having never heard one of them before. Immediately I had another Lesson; and so a third. Being at that time amongst none but Savages, I began to suspect, that they were working some Piece of Conjuration under my House, to get away with my Goods.... At last, my Man came in, to whom when I had told the Story, he laugh'd at me, and presently undeceiv'd me, by telling me what it was that made that Noise.

the Harlowe Canal. The route then leads down to Beaufort and all the way through Bogue Sound, turning back inland on the White Oak River, and ending at Haywood Landing north of Swansboro. If you're up for the challenge, it's an incredible trip.

For boat rentals, not many outfitters serve the national forest. **White Oak River Outfitters** (U.S. 17, 1 mile south of Maysville, 910/743-2744, www.whiteoakrivercampground.com, single kayaks $30 half-day, $40 full-day, double kayaks $40 half-day, $50 full-day, canoes $40 half-day, $50 full-day) rents out canoes and kayaks, has a shuttle service that makes trips a lot easier, and offers guided tours on the White Oak River and other waters in the area.

Great Lake is a popular spot to explore via canoe, kayak, or small flat-bottomed boat. Surrounded by centuries-old cypress trees, it's easy to feel like you're in another world or another time. A handful of campsites lets you extend your stay, or just enjoy the day paddling

BEAUFORT

© JASON FRYE

Waterways offer countless opportunities to get outdoors.

around or fishing for crappie, perch, and bullhead, all easy catches.

The **Oyster Point Campground,** which is also the trailhead for the Neusiok Trail, offers a boat launch suitable for both motorized and paddle watercraft. It's easy to explore the marshy fringes of the forest from here, or head into one of the tributaries or winding marsh creeks nearby.

Camping

There are three developed campsites in the Croatan Forest. **Neuse River** (also called Flanners Beach, $10-15) has 41 sites with showers and flush toilets. **Cedar Point** ($15) has 40 campsites with electricity, showers, and flush toilets. **Fisher's Landing** (free) has nine sites and no facilities other than vault toilets. Primitive camping areas are at Great Lake, Catfish Lake, and Long Point.

TRENTON

A little way outside Croatan National Forest is the pretty village of Trenton. The Jones County seat's tiny historic business district is an appropriate focal point for this bucolic area. A Revolutionary-era millpond, presided over by a large wooden mill, is a good picnic spot. **Trenton Red and White** (372 NC Hwy. 52 N, 252/448-1134, 6am-10pm daily, under $10) is a grocery store with a great little deli where you can get all sorts of sandwiches, from your standard ham and cheese or turkey and cheese to thick-sliced bologna or even olive loaf.

KINSTON

In years past you wouldn't find Kinston on many must-see lists, but this formerly prosperous tobacco town has made quite a turnaround in recent years. A couple of locals have spearheaded renewal, opening a renowned restaurant and a brewery with a growing reputation for great craft beer and changing the face of downtown. Add to that a top-of-the-line museum dedicated to the town's Civil War history and a community that's passionate about preserving its past.

KINSTON'S MUSICAL LEGACY

Music has always been a big deal here, and African American Kinstonians have made huge contributions to American jazz, R&B, funk, soul, and gospel. In the heyday of jazz, the top musicians—North Carolinians Thelonious Monk and John Coltrane, along with Louie Armstrong and others—would stop in Kinston and play for mixed crowds. It really wasn't until 1964 that Kinston was put on the music map, when James Brown met and hired a promising young drummer and college student, Melvin Parker, a native of Kinston, to play in his band. Melvin agreed, but only if James hired his brother, saxophonist Maceo Parker. The Parkers weren't the only Kinstonians to tour with Brown; bandleader Nat Jones, trombonist Levi Raspberry, trumpeter Dick Knight, and a number of other young musicians from the area made names for themselves and helped create the groundbreaking sound of funk. In fact, Maceo Parker joined Parliament-Funkadelic, the band of George Clinton, another North Carolina native, to further explore funk and influence generations of musicians.

In 2013, a groundbreaking for the African American Music Trail was held. The trail is the result of a partnership among the North Carolina Department of Cultural Resources, Kinston's Community Council for the Arts, and other local entities who have done a lot of hard work. It recognizes the contributions of African American musicians in Kinston and other points along the proposed trail. Construction is underway on the African American Music Trail Gateway Park in downtown Kinston, with plans for it to be a gathering spot for live music as well as a place honoring the depth of African American music in the state.

Sights

Like many towns that were once prosperous and suddenly experienced a downturn, Kinston is an architectural time capsule. Driving, or better, walking the several downtown blocks of **Queen Street,** the town's main artery, is an education in early-20th-century commercial architecture. The Hotel Kinston is the town's tallest building, an 11-story structure with a ground level that's a crazy blend of art deco and Moorish motifs. The 1914 post office is a big heavy beaux-arts beauty, and the Queen Street Methodist Church is turreted to within an inch of its life. The People's Bank building testifies to the heyday of early-20th-century African American commerce. With its many strange and daring experiments in building styles, Queen Street is a crazy quilt, but the buildings are beautifully complementary in their diversity. In the Herritage Street neighborhood, near the bend of the river, block after block of grand old houses stand in threadbare glory. On the other side of town are shotgun houses, the icon of Southern folk housing, lining the alleys of the old working-class neighborhood. Shotgun houses are narrow, at most 12 feet wide, with a door at either end, and usually closely spaced.

◖ CSS *NEUSE* INTERPRETIVE CENTER

The remains of the Confederate ironclad gunboat CSS *Neuse* are on display in Kinston in a museum located near the spot where she was scuttled in 1865 to keep her out of the hands of the advancing Union Army. All that remains is the core of the 158- by 34-foot hull, but even in such deteriorated condition the *Neuse* is a striking feat of boatbuilding. At the **CSS *Neuse* Interpretive Center** (100 N. Queen St., 252/522-2107, 9am-5pm Tues.-Sat., free) you can see what remains of the hull, which sat in the river for more than 100 years before it was salvaged, first for profit, then for preservation. If you're lucky, one of the volunteers will be a Kinston old-timer who can tell you stories about using the *Neuse* as a diving board for summer swims. On display are artifacts recovered from the *Neuse,* including the ironclad's bell, cannonballs and shells, coal rakes, and other small items. Wall plaques tell the story of the ship's construction, demise, and

BATTLE FOR KINSTON AND THE CSS *NEUSE*

In early December 1862, Confederate forces in Kinston manned the earthen fortifications that ringed the city in anticipation of an attack by advancing Union forces. General John G. Foster was leading nearly 10,000 infantry, 640 cavalry, and 40 pieces of artillery with the intention of taking the city and controlling traffic on the Neuse River. Despite being grossly outnumbered—the Confederates numbered somewhere around 2,400—the Confederates mounted an effective, but unimpressive, resistance against probing Union forces. On the second and final day of the battle, the Union soldiers swarmed Confederate positions, overwhelming them and driving them back across the river. Retreating troops, acting on order, burned the bridge across the Neuse and, in the confusion of retreat and burning, left some 400 of their comrades on the Union side of the river. To make matters worse, Confederate artillery began shelling Union positions, including their own trapped troops. By the next day, the Union had secured what remained of the bridge, looted the town, and captured some 400 shell-shocked Confederate soldiers.

That wasn't the end of Kinston's role in the Civil War. In 1863 the CSS *Neuse*, an ironclad gunboat 158 feet long, 34 feet wide, and armored in eight inches of oak and iron plate, was launched with the intention of controlling the river and the lands around it. It was an impressive sight at its launch, but the inexperienced men on board quickly ran it aground, where it sat mired in river mud for nearly a month before it could be refloated. By then, the ground-support troops assigned to it had been reallocated, and the ironclad stayed in Kinston, acting more as a floating fortification and gun emplacement than a proper naval weapon. In March 1865, Union forces were once again attacking Kinston and were once more successful. Confederate troops packed the *Neuse* with explosives, set it on fire, and fled. The ensuing explosion breeched the hull, and the fire burned to the waterline. The wreck stayed in the river for almost 100 years before being raised for historic preservation, and many residents of Kinston remember fishing around the hull or climbing on the deck to dive off into the river.

BEAUFORT

eventual salvage, but the centerpiece is the overhead view of the ironclad's hull. Now outfitted with a ghostly shape showing the original form of the ship, it's an impressive sight.

For a full-scale look at the CSS *Neuse,* the **CSS Neuse II** (Herritage St. and Gordon St., 252/560-2150, www.cssneuseii.org, 9am-2pm Mon.-Fri., 9am-5pm Sat., 1pm-5pm Sun., free), a 158-foot facsimile of the gunboat. Climb aboard to feel how tight the quarters were and peer out the gun ports, then imagine sleeping, eating, and fighting on board.

MOTHER EARTH BREWING

Founded by a father-in-law, son-in-law duo, **Mother Earth Brewing** (311 N. Herritage St., 252/208-2437, www.motherearthbrewing.com, brewery tours on the hour 9am-4pm Tues.-Fri., noon-7pm Sat., free, tap room 4pm-10pm Wed.-Fri., 1pm-9pm Sat.) has been making

craft beer in Kinston since 2008. Since then they've added a popular Christmas seasonal beer, the Silent Night series, and explored new flavors. They've pushed into craft spirits and have a small production still in the brewery, but the focus is beer. Brewery tours are free, but as it is a working brewery, some days the tours may be crowded, limited to certain areas, or canceled altogether. Tours start and end in the **Mother Earth Brewing Tap Room,** solar-powered and serving up the best Mother Earth brews. A mix of original art, exposed brick walls, sleek modern lines, and contemporary lighting make this room one of a kind. Cozy up to the bar or grab a pint to take to a nearby table or to the patio out back. No matter where you chose to enjoy the beer, enjoy it you will. I'm fond of the Dark Cloud Dunkel and Old Neighborhood Oatmeal Porter, but the *kölsch, witbier,* and IPA are popular.

© JASON FRYE

Mother Earth Brewing is a big brewery for a small town.

Entertainment and Events

Kinston is fortunate to have a great local arts engine, the **Kinston Community Council for the Arts** (KCCA, 400 N. Queen St., 252/527-2517, www.kinstoncca.com, 10am-6pm Tues.-Fri., 10am-2pm Sat.), which has the kind of energy and artistic vision one would expect to find in a much larger city. It occupies an old storefront on Queen Street, remodeled into a gorgeous gallery and studio space. In addition to the many community events hosted here, KCCA has consistently innovative exhibits in the main gallery, including avant-garde photography and collage art and a recent exhibition of dozens of custom motorcycles.

Every spring, typically the last weekend in April, barbecue enthusiasts flock to Kinston for the **BBQ Festival on the Neuse** (252/560-2693, www.bbqfestivalontheneuse.com). This four-day festival features competitions pitting barbecue teams against one another in categories such as showmanship, quality, and sauce. During the festival, downtown hosts fair food, smoke from a dozen barbecue cookers, carnival rides, concerts, a wine garden, and beer from Mother Earth Brewing. Many artists come for the opening day's Plein Air Paint Out, a competitive painting event whose winner is the image for next year's festival poster. The Art Fest event invites artists and nonartists alike to make some art inspired by the festival; it's a hit with kids as well as adults who shake off their artistic inhibitions. With concerts, fireworks, and heaping plates of 'cue, there's plenty to do, see, and eat.

Sports and Recreation

In 2013 a new water park, **Lions Water Adventure** (2602 W. Vernon Ave., 252/939-1330, www.lionswateradventure.com, 11:30am-5:30pm Mon.-Sat., 12:30pm-5:30pm Sun., $10 pp, $54 for 6), opened in Kinston, with three three-story high slides—the zebra slide, a twisty tube ride; the lion slide, a straightforward waterslide with a decent drop at the end; and the low-splash slide. There's a 5,000-square-foot kiddie lagoon, a lazy river longer than a football field, a lap pool, and a heated therapeutic pool. They serve food, mainly kid-friendly bites and snacks, but the water park is close enough to town that you can head out for a real meal with little effort.

In Kinston you can enjoy disc golf or a traditional round. At the **Barnet Disc Golf Course** (100 Sand Clay Rd., 252/939-3332, http://kinstondiscgolf.com, dawn-dusk daily, 18 holes, par 67, free), you'll need to bring your own discs, but this fun course layout rewards aggressive but accurate players. For a traditional day on the course, **Falling Creek Country Club** (2359 Falling Creek Rd., 252/522-1828, www.fallingcreekgolf.com, 18 holes, par 71, greens fees $18 Mon.-Fri., $23 Sat.-Sun. and holidays, cart fee $15) is a good option for all skill levels. The course features some narrow fairways, a handful of crooked doglegs, and long par-3s, but it's forgiving enough on other holes to make up for missing the green a time or two.

Accommodations

There's only one bed-and-breakfast in town, but you'll find several chain motels just outside the downtown area. **The Bentley** (117 W. Capitola Ave., 252/523-2337, www.bentleybedandbreakfast.com, $139-159) has four beautiful guest rooms and 13 acres of gardens, lawns, and woods to walk. The house and grounds are large enough to host lavish events like weddings and receptions but has a luxe homey feel you don't find in many places. As for hotels, the **Hampton Inn** (1382 U.S. 258 S., 252/523-1400, www.hamptoninn.com, around $110) is convenient and comfortable, and the staff are especially nice.

Food

Kinston's reputation as a food town has been on the rise lately, thanks in large part to a trio of locals—chef Vivian Howard Knight and brewery owners Stephen Hill and Trent Mooring. They collectively opened a renowned restaurant, a top-notch brewery and tap room, and an oyster bar. And though they may be the best known, they're not the only food options in town.

Chef and the Farmer (120 W. Gordon St., 252/208-2433, www.chefandthefarmer.com, 5:30pm-9:30pm Tues.-Thurs., 5:30pm-10:30pm Fri.-Sat., entrées $12-30), from chef-owner Vivian Howard Knight, elevates the simple Southern food she grew up eating on a farm not far from here into true fine-dining dishes that have been recognized by the James Beard Foundation. The menu changes with the local crops and catch, but a few staples remain, including the wood-fired-oven pizzas, massive burgers, and Pimp My Grits menu (where you can get your grits topped with a variety of interesting cheeses, meats, and veggies). Whether you're there for a multicourse affair (the desserts are fantastic) or just a burger at the kitchen counter, you'll leave full and happy.

Queen Street Deli (117 S. Queen St., 252/527-1900, www.queenstreetdeli.com, 7:30am-4pm Mon.-Thurs., breakfast from $2, lunch around $8) bakes vegan and non-vegan cookies and makes great sandwiches for breakfast and lunch. The Queen's Chicken Salad comes with toasted pecans and cranberries and is a filling sandwich. Their take on the BLT is called Prides Pimento, another good option made with pimento cheese, sliced tomatoes, and bacon.

The entrepreneurial owners of Mother Earth Brewing and Chef and the Farmer have opened **The Boiler Room** (108 W. North St., 252/208-2433, 4:30pm-midnight Tues.-Sat., around $12), an oyster bar, raw bar, and gourmet burger joint so named because of the massive boiler standing in the dining room. The Boiler Room represents the efforts of lifelong-locals Vivian Howard Knight and Stephen Hill to revitalize downtown by leveraging the popularity of their other businesses and serving up some delicious seafood and burgers.

Ginger 108 (108 W. North St., 252/208-2663, www.ginger108.com, 11am-2pm, 5pm-midnight Tues.-Fri., 1pm-midnight Sat., entrées around $22) brings fine Asian Fusion dining to Kinston. The chef uses Taiwanese flair but leaves no ingredient—global or local—unexplored. The miso-butter poached sea bass, or any fish special, for that matter, is a must.

BEAUFORT

BEAUFORT

© JASON FRYE

North Carolina, the Cradle of 'Cue

I'd be remiss if I didn't mention that the North Carolina Barbecue Trail's eastern terminus is in Ayden, just a short drive from Kinston. Here the world-famous **Skylight Inn** (4618 S. Lee St., Ayden, 252/746-4113, www.skylightinnbbq.com, 10am-7pm Mon.-Sat., under $10) serves eastern North Carolina-style barbecue done up in the traditional manner: chopped and served with a vinegary sauce that brings out the flavor in the pork like no other sauce can. This family has been cooking 'cue since 1830, so they know their way around a hog; their current location has been here since 1947.

SEVEN SPRINGS

Seven Springs is an attractive historic little town about 30 minutes' drive southwest of Kinston. It's the site of **Cliffs of the Neuse State Park** (240 Park Entrance Rd., 919/778-6234, http://ncparks.gov, office 8am-5pm Mon.-Fri., park 8am-6pm daily Nov.-Feb., 8am-8pm daily Apr.-May, 8am-9pm daily June-Aug., 8am-8pm daily Sept.-Oct.), a highly unusual blend of environments, including high red bluffs overlooking the Neuse River, hardwood and pine forests, and cypress swamps. Hiking trails follow the cliff line through Spanish moss-draped forests. Boating and swimming (10am-5:45pm daily late May-early Sept.) are permitted at the park's artificial lake during the summer; swimming is allowed only when a lifeguard is on duty. Boats must be rented—no private watercraft are permitted.

Family camping ($20/night) is available year-round. There is a washhouse with hot showers and electricity, and several water stations are located in the campsite. Note that unless you have a medical emergency, when you're camping you must stay inside the park from the time the gates close until 8am the next morning—so no slipping out for a late supper.

Beaufort and Vicinity

The small waterside town of Beaufort has unusual problems stemming from its geography—there's also a Beaufort in South Carolina—and the idiosyncrasies of regional Southern dialects, in that it's also pronounced differently. This Beaufort is pronounced in the French way, "BO-fert," while the name of town in South Carolina is pronounced "BYEW-fert." Pronunciation notwithstanding, Beaufort is a beautiful little town. The third-oldest colonial settlement in North Carolina, it matches its elders, Bath and New Bern, in the charm department. Once North Carolina's window to the world, Beaufort was a surprisingly cosmopolitan place that would often receive news from London or Barbados sooner than from other colonies. Today, you'll find the streets crowded with old homes, many built in that double-porch, steep-sided roof style that shows off the early cultural ties to the Caribbean.

It was long rumored that the pirate Blackbeard ran his ship aground in the inlet here, which is plausible because he did frequent Beaufort, and his pirate base at Ocracoke Island isn't far away. In the late 1990s the rumor was proved to be true: In Beaufort Inlet the *Queen Anne's Revenge,* the French slave ship that Blackbeard captured in 1717 and made into the flagship of his dreaded fleet, sat mired in nearly three centuries of silt. Blackbeard had increased his ship's arsenal to 40 cannons, a fact that helped confirm the identity of the wreck. A few months after he ran his flagship aground, Blackbeard himself was killed at Ocracoke after putting up a tremendous fight with privateers (pirate hunters) sent from Virginia. In the intervening time between the shipwreck and its discovery, incredible artifacts from the *Queen Anne's Revenge* washed up on the shores here, a number of which are on display at the North Carolina Maritime Museum.

From the Maritime Museum, a short walk leads to Beaufort's cafés, boutiques, antiques shops, restaurants, and dock. Across the waterway you can see Carrot Island, home to a herd of wild horses, one of the few remaining in eastern North Carolina. You can also catch a ride on a ferry or tour boat to Cape Lookout National Seashore, where the stunning Cape Lookout Lighthouse has guarded the coast for more than 150 years. Or simply tour the marshes for a close-up glimpse of the area's wildlife.

SIGHTS
C North Carolina Maritime Museum

The **North Carolina Maritime Museum at Beaufort** (315 Front St., 252/728-7317, www.ncmaritimemuseums.com, 9am-5pm Mon.-Fri., 10am-5pm Sat., 1pm-5pm Sun., free) is among the best museums in the state and one three state maritime museums; the others are in Southport and on Roanoke Island. Even if you don't think you're interested in boatbuilding or maritime history, you'll get caught up in the exhibits here. Historic watercraft, reconstructions, and models of boats are on display, well presented in rich historical and cultural context. The display of artifacts and weapons recovered from Blackbeard's *Queen Anne's Revenge* wows visitors. There's also a lot about the state's fishing history, including related occupations, such as the highly complex skill of net-hanging. Far from being limited to the few species caught by today's fisheries, early North Carolinians did big business hunting sea turtles, porpoises, and whales.

Across the street from the museum's main building, perched on the dock, is the **Harvey W. Smith Watercraft Center.** For many generations North Carolina mariners had an international reputation as expert shipbuilders, and even today some builders continue to construct large seaworthy vessels in their own backyards. This has always been done "by the rack of the eye," as locals say, meaning that builders use traditional knowledge handed down through the generations rather than modern industrial

BEAUFORT

BEAUFORT

Spanish moss drips from the trees in Beaufort.

methods. Their exceptional expertise is beautifully demonstrated by the craft in the museum and by boats still working the waters today. At the Watercraft Center is a workspace for builders of full-size and model boats, and it teaches a vast array of classes in both traditional skills and mechanized boatbuilding methods.

🄲 Old Burying Ground

One of the most beautiful places in North Carolina is Beaufort's **Old Burying Ground** (Anne St., daily dawn-dusk), a picturesque cemetery that's quite small by the standards of some old Carolina towns and crowded with 18th- and 19th-century headstones. Huge old live oaks, Spanish moss, wisteria, and resurrection ferns, which unfurl and turn green after a rainstorm, give the Burying Ground an irresistibly Gothic feel. Many of the headstones reflect the maritime heritage of the town, including a sea captain whose epitaph reads,

The form that fills this silent grave
Once tossed on ocean's rolling wave

But in a port securely fast
He's dropped his anchor here at last.

Captain Otway Burns, an early privateer who spent much time in Beaufort, is buried here; his grave is easy to spot as it is topped by a canon from his ship, the *Snap Dragon*. Nearby is another of the graveyard's famous burials, the "Little Girl Buried in a Barrel of Rum." This unfortunate waif is said to have died at sea and been placed in a cask of rum to preserve her body for burial on land. Visitors often bring toys and trinkets to leave on her grave, which is marked by a simple wooden plank. Though hers is the most gaudily festooned, you'll see evidence of this old tradition of funerary gifts on other graves here as well—in this cemetery, most often coins and shells. This is a tradition found throughout the coastal South and the Caribbean, with roots tracing back to Africa. Feel free to add to her haul of goodies, but beliefs hold that it's not karmically advisable to tamper with those already here.

Beaufort Historic Site

The **Beaufort Historic Site** (130 Turner St., 252/728-5225, www.beauforthistoricsite.org, 9:30am-5pm Mon.-Sat. Mar.-Nov., 10am-4pm Mon.-Sat. Dec.-Feb., $8 adults, $4 children) recreates life in late-18th- and early-19th-century Beaufort in several restored historic buildings. The 1770s "jump and a half" (1.5-story) Leffers Cottage reflects middle-class life in its day; a merchant, whaler, or, as in this case, a schoolmaster would have lived it. The Josiah Bell and John Manson Houses, both from the 1820s, reflect the graceful Caribbean-influenced architecture so prevalent in the early days of the coastal South. A restored apothecary shop, a 1790s wooden courthouse, and a haunted 1820s jail that was used into the 1950s are among the other important structures. There are tours led by costumed interpreters as well as driving tours of the old town in double-decker buses.

BLACKBEARD AND BONNET: THE BOYS OF 1718

In the 18th century the Carolina coast was crawling with the vermin of the high seas: pirates. For the most part they hung out around South Carolina's Charleston Harbor, like a bunch of rowdies on a frat-house balcony causing headaches for passersby. Some liked to venture up the coast into the inlets and sounds of North Carolina. The most famous pirate visitors were **Blackbeard,** whose real name was Edward Teach, and **Stede Bonnet,** the so-called "Gentleman Pirate." They did most of their misbehaving here in 1718 and enjoyed a short-lived but spectacular rise to notoriety.

Blackbeard is said never to have killed anyone except in self-defense, but clearly he didn't need to kill to reinforce his reputation. He was a huge man with a beard that covered most of his face, and his hair is usually depicted as twisted into ferocious dreadlocks. He wore a bright red coat and festooned himself with every weapon he could carry; as if all that didn't make him scary enough, he liked to wear burning cannon fuses tucked under the brim of his hat and even in his beard. He caused trouble from the Bahamas to Virginia, taking ships, treasure, and child brides at will.

Poor Stede Bonnet. With a name like that, he should have known better than to try to make a living intimidating people. He is said to have been something of a fancy-pants, a man with wealth, education, and a nagging wife. To get away from his spouse, he bought a ship, hired a crew, and set sail for a life of crime. Though never quite as tough as Blackbeard, with whom he was briefly partners, Bonnet caused enough trouble along the Southern coast that the leaders of Charleston saw to it that he was captured and hanged. Meanwhile, Virginia's leaders had also had it with Blackbeard's interference in coastal commerce, and Governor Spottswood dispatched a team to kill him. This they did at Ocracoke, but it wasn't easy; even after they shot, stabbed, and beheaded Blackbeard, his body is said to have taunted them by swimming laps around the ship before finally giving up the ghost.

In recent years, Blackbeard has surfaced again. In 1996, a ship was found off the North Carolina coast that was identified as Blackbeard's flagship, *Queen Anne's Revenge.* All manner of intriguing artifacts have been brought up from the ocean floor: cannons and blunderbuss parts, early hand grenades, even a penis syringe supposed to have been used by syphilitic pirates to inject themselves with mercury. During one standoff in Charleston Harbor, Blackbeard and his men took hostages to ransom for medical supplies; perhaps this explains why they were so desperate. To view artifacts and learn more about Blackbeard, Stede Bonnet, and their low-down ways, visit the North Carolina Maritime Museum in Beaufort, where you'll find relics from the *Queen Anne's Revenge.* A number of underwater archaeological expeditions have been mounted and are ongoing to recover artifacts from the wreck. In early 2013 two cannons were raised and are undergoing preservation treatment. Keep up with the status of the digs and research into the wreck at the **Queen Anne's Revenge Project** (www.qaronline.org).

SPORTS AND RECREATION
Diving

North Carolina's coast is a surprisingly good place for scuba diving. The **Discovery Diving Company** (414 Orange St., 252/728-2265, www.discoverydiving.com, $65-110 per excursion) leads half-day and full-day scuba trips to explore the reefs and dozens of fascinating shipwrecks near Beaufort.

Cruises and Tours

Coastal Ecology Tours (252/241-6866, www.goodfortunesails.com) runs tours of the Cape Lookout National Seashore and other island locations in the area on the *Good Fortune*, as well as a variety of half-day, full-day, overnight, and short trips to snorkel, shell, kayak, and bird-watch, along with cruises to Morehead City restaurants and other educational and fun trips. Prices range from $180 pp for a 2.5-hour dolphin-watching tour to $600 plus meals for an off-season overnight boat rental.

Island Ferry Adventures (610 Front St., 252/728-7555, www.islandferryadventures.com, $13-18 adults, $5-8 children) runs dolphin-watching tours, trips to collect shells at Cape Lookout, and trips to see the wild ponies of Shackleford Banks. **Lookout Cruises** (600 Front St., 252/504-7245, www.lookoutcruises.com, $25-70 adults, $15-30 under age 13) carries sightseers on lovely catamaran rides in the Beaufort and Core Sound region, out to Cape Lookout, and on morning dolphin-watching trips.

Port City Tour Company leads a **Beaufort Ghost Walk** (601 Front St., 252/772-9925, http://pctourco.com, $15) through town. Highlights include supposedly haunted homes, tales of Blackbeard and other ghost pirates, ghost ships, mysterious murders, and more. Many people report taking photos in the cemetery and seeing ghostly figures, orbs, and other unexplained phenomena in the resulting images.

Take a **Wild Horse and Shelling Safari** (610 Front St., 252/772-9925, http://pctourco.com, $25 adults, $15 children) with Port City Tour Company. On the safari you'll make the journey over to Shackelford, a medium-size barrier island home to wild horses, crabs, and not much more. The shelling is incredible and the beaches pristine, but the real treat is the horses. The herd here is small, but they're active and for the most part easy to spot. Be careful around the horses as they are feral; listen to your safari guide, who knows how to stay safe with them.

ACCOMMODATIONS

Outer Banks Houseboats (324 Front St., 252/728-4129, www.outerbankshouseboats.com) will rent you your own floating vacation home, drive it to a scenic spot for you, anchor it, and then come and check in on you every day during your stay. You'll have a skiff for your own use, but you may just want to lie on the deck all day and soak up the peacefulness. Rates run from $1,200 per weekend for the smaller houseboat to $3,000 per week for the luxury boat, with plenty of rental options in between.

The **Beaufort Inn** (101 Ann St., 252/728-2600, www.beaufort-inn.com, $119-279 summer) is a large hotel on Gallants Channel, along one side of the colonial district. It's an easy walk to the main downtown attractions, and the hotel's outdoor hot tub and balconies have great views, making it tempting to stay in as well. The **Pecan Tree Inn** (116 Queen St., 800/728-7871, www.pecantree.com, $130-189 summer) is such a grand establishment that the town threw a parade in honor of the laying of its cornerstone in 1866. The house is still splendid, as are the 5,000-square-foot gardens. The **Inlet Inn** (601 Front St., 800/554-5466, www.inlet-inn.com, $130-170 summer) has one of the best locations in town, right on the water, near the docks where many of the ferry and tour boats land. If you're planning to go dolphin-watching or hop the ferry to Cape Lookout, you can get ready at a leisurely pace and just step outside to the docks. Even in high season, prices are quite reasonable.

Catty-corner to the Old Burying Grounds is

the **Langdon House Bed and Breakfast** (135 Craven St., 252/728-5499, www.langdonhouse. com, $137-238). One of the oldest buildings in town, this gorgeous house was built in the 1730s on a foundation of English ballast stones, creating a unique look. Unlike most other B&Bs, Langdon House allows guests to customize their breakfast (and overall room rate) by selecting from options that range from coffee and tea only to the two-course Hallmark Breakfast, which includes fresh fruit, waffles, French toast, omelets, and more; it's quite a production.

FOOD

For generations, local families have plied the waters off Beaufort to earn a living and catch fish for their families. To ensure residents and visitors dine at eateries utilizing locally caught seafood when possible, Carteret Catch (http:// carteretcatch.org) provides a list of such restaurants. Not only does this help the local fishing industry, it allows chefs to provide the best and freshest seafood possible, meaning your dinner tastes even better.

Among the Beaufort eateries certified by Carteret Catch is the **Blue Moon Bistro** (119 Queen St., 252/728-5800, www.bluemoonbistro.biz, 5:30pm-late Tues.-Sat., $13-29). Blue Moon Bistro makes what they'd like to eat themselves. To that end, you'll find lasagna and *udon* noodle bowls on the menu alongside local shrimp risotto and steak. The wine list is a little short on wines by the glass, and the plating is always interesting. You'll find the dining room warm and inviting, a good place to spend your dinner hour.

Clawson's 1905 Restaurant (425 Front St., 252/728-2133, www.clawsonsrestaurant.com, 11:30am-9pm Mon.-Sat., noon-8pm Sun., $15-30) was a grocery store long before it was a restaurant. Starting in 1905, Clawson's sold canned goods, fresh produce, and freshly baked bread until the Great Depression forced it to close in 1934. Now a restaurant, it serves everything from burgers to ribs, but the specialty is seafood. It's hard to beat their lump crab cakes or fried seafood plate, but one standout dish is

the mahimahi, grilled and served over tortellini with sweet peas and a champagne dill sauce.

Aqua Restaurant (114 Middle Lane, 252/728-7777, www.aquaexperience.com, dinner 6pm Tues.-Sat., small plates $8-14, big plates $23-28) uses local seafood in a number of their dishes, including a fresh catch tostada, shrimp and grits, and bouillabaisse. Along with local seafood, they also use locally and regionally sourced produce and meats. The menu changes frequently, but structurally it's always tapas, small plates, salads, and big plates. With a number of vegetarian and gluten-free items, the menu is amenable to most dietary needs.

If you're traveling with a cooler and want to buy some local seafood to take home, try the **Fishtowne Seafood Center** (100 Wellons Dr., 252/728-6644, www.fishtowneseafood.com, 9am-6pm Mon.-Sat.). Fresh fish selections include flounder, grouper, speckled trout, red snapper, trigger fish, redfish (or drum), spots, tuna, and black bass. Include in that mix the fresh shrimp, clams, oysters (in season), and crabs and you have a great mix of seafood. The website lists what is seasonally available.

Beaufort Grocery (117 Queen St., 252/728-3899, www.beaufortgrocery.com, lunch and dinner Wed.-Mon., brunch Sun., $23-33), despite its humble name, is a sophisticated little eatery. At lunch it serves salads and crusty sandwiches along with Damn Good Gumbo and specialty soups. In the evening the café atmosphere gives way to that of a more formal gourmet dining room. For starters, the ahi tuna napoleon is both beautiful and delicious, and Aunt Marion's Apple and Onion Salad makes an interesting plate to share. Some of the best entrées include Thai chicken curry; duck two ways (seared and leg confit); and whole rack of lamb, served with a chèvre and mint *gremolata*. Try the cheesecake for dessert.

The waterfront **Front Street Grill** (300 Front St., 252/728-4956, www.frontstreetgrilatstillwater.com, 11:30am-2:30pm, 5:30pm-9:30pm Tues.-Sat., brunch 1130am-2:30pm Sun., lunch $9-16, dinner $15-25, brunch $10-17) is popular with boaters drifting through

BEAUFORT

THE CHANGING FISHING INDUSTRY

Despite its more than 300 miles of coastline and 300 years of fishing traditions, North Carolina's fishing industry has been on a steady decline for the last 50 years. At one time you couldn't find anything but local seafood in supermarkets and restaurants, but today, it's rare to see "local catch" posted outside a handful of small fishmongers up and down the coast. Ask people in the fishing industry what the problem is, and they'll tell you it's overregulation and the imposition of unrealistic catch limits. Ask environmentalists, and they'll tell you it's overfishing and decades of poor harvest practices. The truth probably lies somewhere in between, but whatever the reason, you can sit in a dockside restaurant in North Carolina, watch a fishing boat unload its catch, and dine on shrimp raised in Thailand or fish caught in South America. Like the textile industry, which was big business in the state for a long while but fell off as globalization became the norm, North Carolina's commercial fisheries have suffered tremendous losses at the hands of globalized trade. There are groups dedicated to promoting the interests of local fisheries before it's too late to recover and enjoy anything caught commercially in North Carolina. **Carteret Catch** (in Carteret County, www.carteretcatch.org), **Brunswick Catch** (in Brunswick County), and a number of other groups promote local fishing and the

restaurants that serve locally caught seafood. While visiting the Crystal Coast, take a look at the Carteret Catch website to find local restaurants and fish markets that buy local seafood from people who live and work in the community rather than from international wholesalers.

As recently as 15 years ago, the shores and riverbanks of eastern North Carolina were dotted with fish houses. Often these were small family-run operations and were the best place in the world for seafood lovers. These ramshackle restaurants bought the catch right off the boat and cleaned, cooked, and served it within minutes. Today, things are different; the old-fashioned seafood house is in danger of extinction. Declines in popular fish and shellfish populations have hit North Carolina's fishing business hard, and at the same time, coastal real estate values have skyrocketed, making property taxes unaffordable for generations-old restaurants or worth more to a developer as a waterfront lot. Either way, it's a death knell.

This book will steer you toward some of the few remaining fish houses and seafood restaurants that serve catches fresh from the local docks. Traditional seafood houses may serve dishes you're unfamiliar with, but give them a try—you may love what you find, and paying a visit to one of these mom-and-pops helps support a way of life that's critically endangered.

---

the area as well as diners who arrive by land. The emphasis is on seafood and fresh regional ingredients, and the fried oysters are a must. Front Street Grill's wine list is not extensive but is well stocked, and they have repeatedly won *Wine Spectator* magazine's Award of Excellence. If you're looking for a place where you can sit overlooking the water while you enjoy a fine glass of wine and some excellent food, this is it.

MOREHEAD CITY

Giovanni da Verrazzano may have been the first European to set foot in present-day Morehead City when he sailed into Bogue Inlet. It wasn't until the mid-19th century that the town came

into being, built as the terminus of the North Carolina Railroad to connect the state's overland commerce to the sea. Despite its late start, Morehead City has been a busy place. During the Civil War it was the site of major encampments by both armies. A series of horrible hurricanes in the 1890s, culminating in 1899's San Ciriaco Hurricane, brought hundreds of refugees from the towns along what is now the Cape Lookout National Seashore. They settled in a neighborhood that they called Promise Land, and many of their descendants are still here. The Atlantic and North Carolina Railroad operated a large hotel here in the 1880s, ushering in Morehead's role as a tourism spot, and the

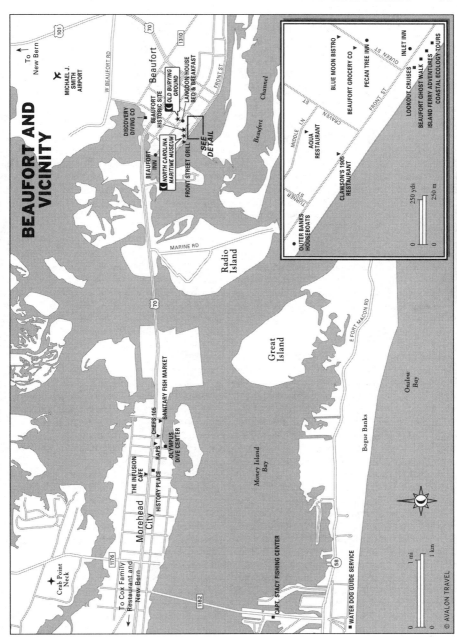

BEAUFORT AND VICINITY

BEAUFORT

To New Bern

101

70

1310

MICHAEL J. SMITH AIRPORT

W BEAUFORT RD

Beaufort

DISCOVERY DIVING CO

BEAUFORT HISTORIC SITE

OLD BURYING GROUND

LANGDON HOUSE BED & BREAKFAST

FRONT ST

BEAUFORT INN

NORTH CAROLINA MARITIME MUSEUM

FRONT STREET GRILL

SEE DETAIL

Beaufort Channel

SEE DETAIL

BLUE MOON BISTRO

BEAUFORT GROCERY CO

PECAN TREE INN

INLET INN

QUEEN ST

FRONT ST

LOOKOUT CRUISES

BEAUFORT GHOST WALK

ISLAND FERRY ADVENTURES

COASTAL ECOLOGY TOURS

CRAVEN ST

MIDDLE LN

AQUA RESTAURANT

CLAWSON'S 1905 RESTAURANT

TURNER ST

OUTER BANKS HOUSEBOATS

250 yds

250 m

0

0

MARINE RD

Radio Island

70

Great Island

Onslow Bay

E FORT MACON RD

Bogue Banks

SANITARY FISH MARKET

CHEFS 105

RAPS

OLYMPUS DIVE CENTER

THE INFUSION CAFE

HISTORY PLACE

Morehead City

Money Island Bay

Crab Point Neck

1176

To Cox Family Restaurant and New Bern

1182

CAPT. STACY FISHING CENTER

WATER DOG GUIDE SERVICE

58

1 mi

1 km

0

0

© AVALON TRAVEL

bridge to the Bogue Banks a few decades later increased holiday traffic considerably.

Morehead is also an official state port, one of the best deepwater harbors on the Atlantic Coast. This mixture of tourism and gritty commerce gives Morehead City a likeable, real-life feel missing in many coastal towns today.

Sights

Morehead City's history is on display at **The History Place** (1008 Arendell St., 252/247-7533, www.thehistoryplace.org, 10am-4pm Tues.-Sat.). There are many interesting and eye-catching historical artifacts on display, but the most striking exhibit is that of a carriage, clothes, and other items pertaining to Morehead City's Emeline Piggott, considered a heroine by the Confederacy. She was a busy woman all through the Civil War, working as a nurse, a spy, and a smuggler. The day she was captured, they found 30 pounds of contraband hidden in her skirts, including Union troop movement plans, a collection of gloves, several dozen skeins of silk, needles, toothbrushes, a pair of boots, and five pounds of candy.

Entertainment and Events

Seafood is a serious art in Morehead City. The enormous **North Carolina Seafood Festival** (252/726-6273, www.ncseafoodfestival.org), the state's second-largest, takes place here every October. The city's streets shut down and some 150,000 visitors descend on the waterfront. Festivities kick off with a blessing of the fleet, followed by music, fireworks, competitions such as the flounder toss, and, of course, loads of food.

If you're in the area on the right weekend in November, you'll not want to deprive yourself of the gluttonous splendor of the **Mill Creek Oyster Festival** (Mill Creek Volunteer Fire Department, 2370 Mill Creek Rd., Mill Creek, 252/247-4777). Food is the focus of this small-town fete, a benefit for the local volunteer fire department, and the meals are cooked by local experts. Choose from all-you-can-eat roasted oysters, fried shrimp, and fried spot (a local fish considered a delicacy by locals and a cult

classic by foodies), all in mass quantities. Many of the oysters may not be local these days, but the cooking is very local—an authentic taste of one of North Carolina's best culinary traditions. You'll find Mill Creek and this extraordinary gastronomic event northwest of Morehead City on the Newport River.

Sports and Recreation

Many of this region's most important historic and natural sites are underwater. From Morehead City's **Olympus Dive Center** (713 Shepard St., 252/726-9432, www.olympus-diving.com, 6am-8pm daily June-Sept., 9am-6pm Mon.-Sat. Oct.-May, lessons from $340, charters from $70), scuba divers of all levels of experience can take charter trips to dozens of natural and artificial reefs that teem with fish, including the ferocious-looking but not terribly dangerous eight-foot-long sand tiger shark. This is the Graveyard of the Atlantic, so there are at least as many shipwrecks to choose from, including an 18th-century schooner, a luxury liner, a German U-boat, and many Allied commercial and military ships that fell victim to the U-boats that infested this coast during World War II.

Anglers love this part of the coast for its inshore and offshore fishing; find an up-to-date list of Morehead City charter boats at www.downtownmoreheadcity.com. Just over the bridge from Morehead City, **Captain Stacy Fishing Center** (416 Atlantic Beach Causeway, Atlantic Beach, 252/247-7501 or 800/533-9417, www.captstacy.com, from $55 adults, $45 children) has been hauling in big fish off the coast for decades. Charter options include a night-time shark fishing expedition where they regularly catch tiger, sand, and black-tip sharks. Full-day and half-day bottom-fishing excursions take you offshore into deep water where you can expect to catch black sea bass, spot-tail porgies, triggerfish, red snapper, and other good eating fish. Serious anglers may want to join one of the overnighters April to November; these trips include a two-day bag limit and have a reputation for bringing in loads of fish. Captain Stacy's can accommodate private charters as well, and most importantly they can point you to the fish.

Inshore fishing has its own fans, and **Water Dog Guide Service** (252/728-7907 or 919/423-6310, www.waterdogguideservice.com, tours from $325) knows where to find the fish, including speckled trout, flounder, and red drum, in the sounds, marshes, and creeks. They also fish at near-shore wrecks and reefs for bluefish, mahimahi, and Spanish mackerel. Check their website to see what's biting and plan a trip around the red drum spawn, when red drum invade the marsh in huge numbers. Or try something different and join them for a duck hunt.

Crystal Coast Ecotours (252/808-3354, www.crystalcoastecotours.com, $100 per hour, $275 half-day, $375 full-day) is run by a marine biologist with a passion for introducing people to the world of the marshes, creeks, barrier islands, and waterways where she makes her home. Tours lead you to secluded barrier islands, the Cape Lookout National Seashore, and even into near-ocean waters so you can explore the area by birding, dolphin watching, shelling, snorkeling, and watching wild horses.

Food

The **C Sanitary Fish Market** (501 Evans St., 252/247-3111, www.sanitaryfishmarket.com, from 11:30am daily, $13-31) is not only the most widely known eatery in Morehead City, it's probably its best-known institution. The rather odd name reflects its 1930s origins as a seafood market that was bound by its lease and its fastidious landlord to be kept as clean as possible. Today, it's a huge family seafood restaurant. Long lines in season and on weekends demonstrate its popularity. Of particular note are its famous hush puppies, which have a well-deserved reputation as some of the best in the state, and the monstrous Famous Deluxe Shore Dinner—soup, fried fish, shrimp, oysters, scallops, soft shelled crab, fries, and, of course, hush puppies. Be sure to buy a Sanitary T-shirt on the way out; it'll help you blend in elsewhere in the state.

Chefs 105 (105 S. 7th St., 252/240-1105, www.chefs105.com.com, 5pm Wed.-Fri., 11am Sat.-Sun., $10-35) sits on the Morehead City waterfront and serves everything from burgers to Steak Oskar. Their seafood is largely fried, but they have a steam bar where you can get clams, shrimp, crab legs, and oysters by the dozen, pound, cluster, or peck. They don't take reservations, so if you want dinner, expect a little wait during summer, or get here early.

El's Drive-In (3706 Arendell St., 252/726-3002, 10:30am-10pm daily, around $7), a tiny place across from Carteret Community College, seems like it has been around almost as long as the town. It's most famous for its shrimp burgers but serves all sorts of fried delights. It's a hit among locals and road-food fans, but most everyone agrees that the shakes are great, as are the onion rings. Be forewarned: It's car-side service and the place is mobbed with gulls at times; they'll swoop down and grab a French fry before you can get it in the car. As fun as they are to watch, it's not a good idea to feed the birds.

The **Bistro-by-the-Sea** (4031 Arendell St., 252/247-2777, www.bistro-by-the-sea.com, 5pm-9:30pm Tues.-Thurs., 5pm-10pm Fri.-Sat., entrées $10-25) participates in Carteret Catch, a program that ensures that fresh locally caught seafood graces the tables of Carteret County. They serve a number of seafood dishes, but don't just stick to the sea; they also serve steaks, prime rib, and even fresh calf liver. Most interesting, though, are the small plates, with items such as a half-slab of baby back ribs, baked oysters, or a Japanese bento box.

For an old-fashioned luncheon or afternoon tea, visit the tiny five-table tearoom at **The Infusion Café** (1012 Arendell St., 252/240-2800,, 10am-5pm Tues.-Thurs., 10am-9pm Fri., 11am-3pm Sat., under $10). In addition to the many teas, you can order scones, desserts, dainty quiches, and sandwiches. They serve a formal tea 2pm-4pm Monday-Friday, with reservations required at least a day in advance.

C Cox Family Restaurant (4109 Arendell St., 252/726-6961, 6am-9pm Mon.-Sat., 6am-8pm Sun., around $8) also has served down-home cooking for many years and is known for its friendly staff and coterie of local regulars. The food here is simple—it is home cooking, after all—but well done. At breakfast, no matter what you get, order a side of home fries; you won't be disappointed.

Raps Grill and Bar (709 Arendell St., 252/240-1213, www.rapsgrillandbar.com, 11am-10pm Mon.-Thurs., 11am-10:30pm Fri.-Sat., bar open later, $10-20) serves a lot of what you'd expect—wings, mozzarella sticks, loaded cheese fries—but then expands into unexpected territory with fried pickles, crab cakes, and fried green tomatoes—and that's just the appetizers. Like other restaurants along the Crystal Coast, they serve version of fried seafood, but they like to bring in a Tex-Mex influence, serving fajitas, iron skillets (think fajitas without the tortillas), and fish tacos.

HARKERS ISLAND

The Core Sound region stretches east-northeast from Beaufort, many miles up to the Pamlico Sound. Filled with birds and boats and not much else, it's a hauntingly beautiful landscape. Like much of the North Carolina coast, the marshes and pocosins serve as way stations for countless flocks of migratory birds as they migrate, regularly adding greatly to the year-round bird population. Fishing has always been a way of life here, but so has hunting, particularly hunting waterfowl. In earlier generations, and to a lesser extent today, men who earned a living fishing most of the year had sideline businesses hunting birds. They ate the birds they shot, sold the feathers for women's hats, trained bird dogs, and worked as birding outfitters to visiting hunters. Consequentially, many Down Easterners became expert decoy carvers. The beautifully carved decoys started as functional pieces, but today most are produced as art for art's sake; either way, the tradition survives.

Woodworking on a much grander scale has defined the culture of the people of Harkers Island, as it is home to generations of boat builders whose creations are as elegant as they are reliable. Keep an eye out as you drive through; you may see boats under construction in backyards and garages—not canoes or dinghies, but full-size fishing boats.

To get to Harkers Island, follow U.S. 70 east from Beaufort around the dogleg that skirts the North River. East of the town of Otway, you'll see Harkers Island Road; go right and head south toward Straits. Straits Road will take you through the town of Straits, and then across a bridge over the Straits themselves, finally ending up on Harkers Island.

◖ Core Sound Waterfowl Museum

The **Core Sound Waterfowl Museum** (1785 Island Rd., 252/728-1500, www.coresound. com, 10am-5pm Mon.-Sat., 2pm-5pm Sun., $5), which occupies a beautiful modern building on Shell Point next to the Cape Lookout National Seashore headquarters, is a community-wide labor of love. The museum is home to exhibits crafted by members of the communities it represents, depicting the Down East maritime life through decoys, nets, and other tools of the trades as well as everyday household objects, beautiful quilts, and other utilitarian folk arts. This is a sophisticated modern institution, but its community roots are evident in touching details like the index-card labels, written in the careful script of elderly women, explaining what certain objects are, what they were used for, and who made them. For instance, just as Piedmont textile workers made and treasured their loom hooks, folks down here took pride in the hooks that they made to assist in the perennial off-season work of hanging nets. Baseball uniforms on display represent an era when one town's team might have to travel by ferry to its opponent's field. The museum hosts Core Sound Community Nights on the second Tuesday of every month. These get-togethers are a taste of the old home days when families and long-lost friends reunite over home-cooked food to reminisce about community history and talk about their hopes and concerns for the future.

The museum's gift shop has a nice selection

of books and other items related to Down East culture. Be sure to pick up a copy of *Island Born and Bred: A Collection of Harkers Island Food, Fun, Fact and Fiction* by the Harkers Island United Methodist Women. This cookbook has become a regional classic for its wonderful blend of authentic family recipes and community stories. You might also be able to find a Core Sound Christmas Tree, made by Harvey and Sons in nearby Davis. This old family fishery has made a hit in recent years manufacturing small Christmas trees out of recycled crab pots. It's a fun, playful item, but it carries significant messages about the past and future of the Core Sound region.

Core Sound Decoy Carvers Guild

Twenty years ago, over a pot of stewed clams, some decoy-carving friends Down East decided to found the **Core Sound Decoy Carvers Guild** (1575 Harkers Island Rd., 252/838-8818, www.decoyguild.com, call for hours). The guild is open to the public and gives demonstrations, competitions, and classes for grownups and children; the museum shop is a nice place to browse.

Events

The Core Sound Decoy Carvers Guild also hosts the **Core Sound Decoy Festival,** usually held in the early winter. Several thousand people come to this annual event—more than the number of permanent residents on Harkers Island—to buy, swap, and teach the art of making decoys.

Food

Captain's Choice Restaurant (977 Island Rd., 252/728-7122, 10am-9pm Tues.-Thurs., 7am-9pm Fri.-Sun., closed Mon., breakfast $2-10, lunch and dinner $6-25) is a great place to try traditional Down East chowder. Usually made of clams but sometimes with other shellfish or fish, chowder in Carteret County is a point of pride. The point is the flavor of the seafood itself, which must be extremely fresh and not hidden behind lots of milk and spices.

Captain's Choice serves chowder in the old-time way—with dumplings.

Fish Hook Grill (980 Island Rd., 252/728-1790, www.fishhookgrill.com, 11am-9pm Mon.-Sat., 11am-3pm Sun., $6-26) is a small-town restaurant serving big portions of seafood, burgers, and more. They're known locally for their chowder, crab cakes, potato salad, hush-puppies, fried oysters, coleslaw, and, well, just about everything on the menu. Check to see if Miss Faye, the owner and operator, is here when you visit; if she is, stop by and say hello. She's as friendly as the food is good.

VILLAGE OF CEDAR ISLAND

For a beautiful afternoon's drive, head back to the mainland and follow U.S. 70 north. You'll go through some tiny communities—Williston, Davis, Stacy—and if you keep bearing north on Highway 12 when U.S. 70 heads south to the town of Atlantic, you'll eventually reach the tip of the peninsula and the village of Cedar Island. This little fishing town has the amazing ambience of being at the end of the earth. From the peninsula's shore you can barely see land across the sounds. The ferry to Ocracoke departs from Cedar Island, a two-hour-plus ride across Pamlico Sound to get there. The beach here is absolutely gorgeous, and horses roam on it; they're not the famous wild horses of the Outer Banks, but they move around freely as if they were.

A spectacular location for bird-watching is the **Cedar Island National Wildlife Refuge** (U.S. 70, east of Atlantic, 252/926-4021, www.fws.gov/cedarisland). Nearly all of its 14,500 acres are brackish marshland, and it's often visited in season by redhead ducks, buffleheads, surf scoters, and many other species. While there are trails for hiking and cycling, this refuge is primarily intended as a haven for the birds.

Accommodations and Food

◀ **The Driftwood Motel** (3575 Cedar Island Rd., 252/225-4861, www.clis.com, $85) is a simple motel in an incredible location, and

BEAUFORT

since the ferry leaves from its parking lot, it's the place to stay if you're coming from or going to Ocracoke. There's also camping (tents $25, RVs $30) here with electricity, water, and sewer hookups.

The Driftwood's **Pirate's Chest Restaurant** (3575 Cedar Island Rd., 252/225-4861, 5pm-8:30pm Thurs., 5pm-9:30pm Fri. and Sat., noon-8pm Sun., around $18) is the only restaurant on Cedar Island, so it's a good thing that it's a good one. Local seafood is the specialty, and many dishes can be adapted for vegetarians. Their Cream of Crab Soup is an interesting take on the she-crab soup you'll find served in Virginia and Maryland.

GETTING THERE AND AROUND
By Car
One of the state's main east-west routes, U.S. 70 provides easy access to most of the destinations in this chapter. From Raleigh to Beaufort is a little over 150 miles, but keep in mind that long stretches of the highway are in commercial areas with plenty of traffic and red lights. U.S. 70 continues past Beaufort, snaking up along Core Sound through little Down East towns like Otway and Davis, finally ending in the town of Atlantic. At Sea Level, Highway 12 branches to the north, across the Cedar Island Wildlife Refuge and ending at the Cedar Island-Ocracoke Ferry.

Down south, to reach the Bogue Banks (Atlantic Beach, Emerald Isle, and neighboring beaches) by road, bridges cross Bogue Sound on Highway 58 at both Morehead City and Cedar Point (not to be confused with Cedar Island).

By Ferry
Inland, a 20-minute free passenger and vehicle ferry (800/339-9156, pets allowed) crosses the Neuse River between Cherry Branch (near Cherry Point) and Minesott Beach in Pamlico County every 30 minutes.

Lower Outer Banks

The southern stretch of the Outer Banks of North Carolina contain some of the region's most diverse destinations. Core and Shackleford Banks lie within Cape Lookout National Seashore, the fifth national seashore established in the country and the second in North Carolina (Cape Hatteras National Seashore to the north was the first in the country). It's a wild place, a maritime environment populated by birds, herds of wild horses, and not a single human. The towns of Bogue Banks—Atlantic Beach, Salter Path, Pine Knoll Shores, Indian Beach, and Emerald Isle—are classic beach towns with clusters of motels and restaurants and even a few towel shops and miniature golf courses. Both areas are great fun; Cape Lookout especially so for ecotours and history, and Bogue Banks for those looking for a day on the beach followed by an evening chowing down on good fried seafood.

◖ CAPE LOOKOUT NATIONAL SEASHORE
Cape Lookout National Seashore (1800 Islands Rd., Harkers Island, 252/728-2250, www.nps.gov/calo) is an otherworldly place: 56 miles of beach stretched out across four barrier islands, a long tape of sand seemingly so vulnerable to nature that it's hard to believe there were ever any towns on its banks. There were: Cape Lookout was settled in the early 1700s, and people in the towns of the south Core Banks made their living in fisheries that might seem brutal to today's seafood eaters—whaling and catching dolphins and sea turtles, among the more mundane species. Portsmouth, at the north end of the park across the water from Ocracoke, was a busy port of great importance to the early economy of North Carolina. Portsmouth declined slowly, but catastrophe rained down all at once on the people of the southerly Shackleford Banks, who were driven out of their own long-established

communities to start new lives on the mainland when a series of terrible hurricanes decimated the islands in the 1890s.

Islands often support unique ecosystems. Among the dunes, small patches of maritime forest fight for each drop of fresh water, while ghost forests of trees that were defeated by advancing saltwater look on resignedly. Along the endless beach, loggerhead turtles come ashore to lay their eggs, and in the waters just off the strand, three other species of sea turtles are sometimes seen. Wild horses roam the beaches and dunes, and dolphins frequent both the ocean and sound sides of the islands. Other mammals, though, are all of the small and scrappy variety: raccoons, rodents, otters, and rabbits. Like all of coastal North Carolina, it's a great place for bird-watching as it's located in a heavily traveled migratory flyway. Pets are allowed if they're on a leash. The wild ponies on Shackleford Banks can pose a threat to dogs that get among them, and the dogs can frighten the horses, so be careful not to let them mingle.

Portsmouth Village

Portsmouth Village, at the northern tip of the Cape Lookout National Seashore, is a peaceful but eerie place. The village looks much as it did 100 years ago, the handsome houses and churches all tidy and in good repair, but with the exception of caretakers and summer volunteers, no one has lived here in nearly 50 years. In 1970 the last two residents moved away from what had once been a town of 700 people and one of the most important shipping ports in North Carolina. Founded before the Revolution, Portsmouth was a lightering station, a port where huge seagoing ships that had traveled across the ocean would stop and have their cargo removed for transport across the shallow sounds in smaller boats. There is a visitors center located at Portsmouth, open varying hours April-October, where you can learn about the village before embarking on a stroll to explore the quiet streets.

In its busy history, Portsmouth was captured by the British during the War of 1812 and by Union troops in the Civil War, underscoring its

strategic importance. By the time of the Civil War, though, its utility as a way station was already declining. An 1846 hurricane opened a new inlet at Hatteras, which quickly became a busy shipping channel. After abolition, the town's lightering trade was no longer profitable without enslaved people to perform much of the labor. The fishing and lifesaving businesses kept the town afloat for a few more generations, but Portsmouth was never the same.

Once a year, an unusual thing happens when boatloads of people arrive on shore, the church bell rings, and the sound of hymns being sung comes through the open church doors. At the Portsmouth Homecoming, descendants of the people who lived here come from all over the state and the rest of the country to pay tribute to their ancestral home. They have an old-time dinner on the grounds and then tour the little village together. It's like a family reunion with the town itself the matriarch. The rest of the year, Portsmouth receives visitors and National Park Service caretakers, but one senses that it's already looking forward to the next spring when its children will come home again.

Shackleford Banks

The once-busy villages of Diamond City and Shackleford Banks are like Portsmouth in that, although they have not been occupied for many years, the descendants of the people who lived here retain a profound attachment to their ancestors' homes. Diamond City and nearby communities met a spectacular end. The hurricane season of 1899 culminated in the San Ciriaco Hurricane, a disastrous storm that destroyed homes and forests, killed livestock, flooded gardens with saltwater, and washed the Shackleford dead out of their graves. The Bankers saw the writing on the wall and moved to the mainland en masse, carrying as much of their property as would fit on boats. Some actually floated their houses across Core Sound. Harkers Island absorbed most of the refugee population, and many also went to Morehead City; their traditions are still an important part of Down East culture. Daily and weekly programs held at the Light Station Pavilion and

BEAUFORT

the porch of the Keepers Quarters during the summer months teach visitors about the natural and human history of Cape Lookout, including what day-to-day life was like for the keeper of the lighthouse and the keeper's family.

Descendants of the Bankers feel a deep spiritual bond to their ancestors' home, and for many years they would return frequently, occupying fish camps that they constructed along the beach. When the federal government bought the Banks, it was made known that the fish camps would soon be off-limits to their deedless owners. The outcry and bitterness that ensued reflected the depth of the Core Sounders' love of their ancestral grounds. The National Park Service may have thought that the fish camps were ephemeral and purely recreational structures, but to the campers, the Banks was still home, even if they had been born on the mainland and had never lived here for longer than a fishing season. Retaining their sense of righteous, if not legal, ownership, many burned down their own fish camps rather than let the government take them down.

Cape Lookout Lighthouse

By the time you arrive at the 1859 **Cape Lookout Lighthouse** (252/728-2250, www. nps.gov/calo, visitors center and Keeper's Quarters Museum 9am-5pm daily Apr.-Nov., lighthouse climbs 10am-3:45pm Wed.-Sat. early May-mid-Sept., $8 adults, $4 seniors and under age 13), you will have seen it portrayed on dozens of brochures, menus, signs, and souvenirs. With its striking diamond pattern, it looks like a rattlesnake standing at attention. This 163-foot-tall lighthouse was first lit in 1859. Like the other lighthouses along the coast, it's built of brick. At its base, the walls are nine feet thick, narrowing to two feet at the top. The present lighthouse isn't the first to guard this section of the coast; originally a lighthouse was built only a few yards away, but it was plagued with problems and replaced by the current structure.

Accommodations

There are cabins to rent on Cape Lookout, but you must reserve well in advance to obtain one. On **Long Point, Great Island, and Morris Marina** (877/444-6777, www.nps.gov/calo, reservations www.recreation.gov, Apr.-Nov. $73-170) you can rent cabins with hot and cold water, gas stoves, and furniture, but in some cases visitors must bring their own generators for lighting as well as linens and utensils. Rentals are not available December-March, and before you make a reservation, remember that with no air-conditioning, it can get quite hot in these cabins; fall or spring are more comfortable than summer.

CAMPING

Camping is permitted within Cape Lookout National Seashore. There are no designated campsites or camping amenities, and everything you bring must be carried back out when you leave. Campers can stay for up to 14 days, and large groups (25 or more campers) require special permits. The National Park Service website for Cape Lookout (www.nps.gov/calo) has full details on camping regulations and permits.

Getting There

Except for the visitors center at Harkers Island, Cape Lookout National Seashore can only be reached by ferry. Portsmouth, at the northern end of the park, is a short ferry ride from Ocracoke, but Ocracoke is a very long ferry ride from Cedar Island. The **Cedar Island-Ocracoke Ferry** (800/293-3779) is part of the state ferry system, and costs $15 one-way for regular-size vehicles (pets allowed). It takes 2.25 hours to cross Pamlico Sound, but the ride is fun, and embarking from Cedar Island feels like sailing off the edge of the earth. The **Ocracoke-Portsmouth Ferry** is a passenger-only commercial route, licensed to Captain Rudy Austin of **Austin Boat Tours** (252/928-4361 or 252/928-5431, www.portsmouthnc.com, $20 pp, 3-person minimum, daily as weather permits). Call to ensure a seat. Most ferries operate April-November, with some exceptions.

Commercial ferries cross every day from mainland Carteret County to the southern parts of the national seashore. There is generally a ferry route between Davis and Great Island, but service can be variable; check the Cape Lookout National Seashore website (www.nps.gov/calo) for updates.

From Harkers Island, passenger ferries to Cape Lookout Lighthouse and Shackleford Banks include **Harkers Island Fishing Center** (252/728-3907, http://harkersmarina.com, $15 adults, $10 children, $6 pets) and **Local Yokel** (516 Island Rd., 252/728-2759, www.tourcapelookout.com, $15 adults, $10 children).

From Beaufort, passenger ferries include **Outer Banks Ferry Service** (326 Front St., 252/728-4129, www.outerbanksferry.com, $15 adults, $8 children), which goes to both Shackleford Banks and to Cape Lookout Lighthouse; **Island Ferry Adventures at Barbour's Marina** (610 Front St., 252/728-6181, www.islandferryadventures.com, $15 adults, $8 children) does as well. Morehead City's passenger-only **Waterfront Ferry Service** (201 S. 6th St., 252/503-1955, www.crystalcoastferry.com, $15 adults, $8 children) goes to Shackleford Banks too. On-leash pets are generally allowed, but call ahead to confirm with the ferry operator.

BOGUE BANKS

The beaches of Bogue Banks are popular, but they have a typically North Carolinian laid-back feel, a quieter atmosphere than the fun-fun-fun neon jungles of beaches elsewhere. The major attractions, Fort Macon State Park and the North Carolina Aquarium at Pine Knoll Shores, are a bit more cerebral than, say, amusement parks and bikini contests. In the surfing, boating, bars, and restaurants, and the beach itself, there's also a bustle of activity to keep things hopping. Bogue, by the way, rhymes with "rogue."

◖ North Carolina Aquarium

The **North Carolina Aquarium at Pine Knoll Shores** (1 Roosevelt Blvd., Pine Knoll Shores, 800/832-3474, www.ncaquariums.com, 9am-5pm daily, 9am-9pm Thurs. July, $8 adults, $7 seniors and under age 13, free under age 3)

is one of the state's three great coastal aquariums. Here at Pine Knoll Shores, exhibit highlights include a 300,000-gallon aquarium in which sharks and other aquatic beasts go about their business in and around a replica German U-Boat (plenty of originals lie right off the coast and form homes for reef creatures); a "jelly gallery" (they really can be beautiful); a tank filled with the beautiful but dangerous nonnative lionfish; a pair of river otters; and many other wonderful animals and habitats.

Trails from the parking lot lead into the maritime forests of the 568-acre **Theodore Roosevelt Natural Area** (1 Roosevelt Dr., Atlantic Beach, 252/726-3775), where network of trails takes your through secluded marshes, on a high dune ridge, and under a coastal forest canopy, providing plenty of opportunities for bird-watching and wildlife viewing. The trails close at 4:30pm, so get an early start.

Fort Macon State Park

At the eastern tip of Atlantic Beach is **Fort Macon State Park** (2300 E. Fort Macon Rd., 252/726-3775, http://ncparks.gov, visitors center 9am-6pm daily, fort 9am-5:30pm daily, bathhouse area 8am-5:30pm Nov.-Feb., 8am-8pm Mar.-Oct., swimming area 10am-5:45pm daily May-Sept. as staffing allows). The central feature of the park is Fort Macon, an 1820s federal fort that was a Confederate garrison for one year during the Civil War. Guided tours are offered, and there are exhibits inside the casemates. For such a stern and martial building, some of the interior spaces are surprisingly pretty. The park has 1.5 miles of beach, perfect for fishing, swimming, sunbathing, or simply strolling. At different times throughout the year, the park is filled with costumed Civil War reenactors.

Sports and Recreation

The ocean side of Bogue Banks offers plenty of public beach access. In each of the towns—Atlantic Beach, Pine Knoll Shores, Salter Path, Indian Beach, and Emerald Isle—are parking lots, some free and some paid. The beach at **Fort Macon** is bounded by the ocean, Bogue

Sound, and Beaufort Inlet. Because there's a Coast Guard station on the Sound side and a jetty along the Inlet, swimming is permitted only along one stretch of the ocean beach. A concession stand and bathhouse are located at the swimming beach.

Atlantic Beach Surf Shop (515 W. Fort Macon Rd., Atlantic Beach, 252/646-4944, www.absurfshop.com) gives individual ($50 per hour) and group ($40 per hour, call for reservations) surfing lessons on the beach at Pine Knoll Shores in the morning and early afternoon. This is a great place to learn because the south-facing beach catches some big long-riding swells, especially when the wind's right.

Barrier Island Kayaks (160 Cedar Point Rd., Swansboro, 252/393-6457, www.barrier-islandkayaks.com) offers custom trips, excursions to Bear Island at the southern edge of this region, eco-adventures focused on wandering marsh creeks and viewing wildlife up close, and trips out to the Cape Lookout National Seashore. They also rent out kayaks and stand-up paddleboards ($30 for 2 hours, $40 half-day, $55 full-day, $35 additional days).

Lookout Adventures (208 Arendell St., 252/515-0356, http://lookoutadventures.com) has a long list of boat charters ($195-675), including a private dolphin cruise, sunset fishing excursions, and daylong fishing or sightseeing trips to Cape Lookout and surrounding islands. Their combo-day package brings together the best of fishing (a half-day in their personal fishing hot spots) and sightseeing as you cruise the marshes and waterways and learn about the ecology of the Cape Lookout area.

Reef Gander Tours (Atlantic Beach, 252/725-4444, www.reefgandertours.com, call for rates) has been exploring the waters around Carteret County, Cape Lookout, and Atlantic Beach for more than 25 years. Customized tours include hitting the best fishing spots, exploring the barrier islands or marsh creeks, shelling, and swimming on one of the barrier islands.

At **Dragonfly Parasail** (Anchorage Marina, 571 E. Fort Macon Rd., 252/422-5500, www.dragonflyparasail.com, $65-75, observers

$10-20), you can join the 100,000 other people who've taken a flight over the beautiful waters off Atlantic Beach. Decide before you go up if you want to get wet; if you do, they'll slow the boat and let you drift down from more than 400 feet until you touch the water, and then pull you back into the air. It's kid-friendly and provides spectacular views.

If fishing's your thing, **Pelagic Sportfishing** (212 Smith St., 252/904-3361, www.pelagicsportfishing.com, fishing $400-1,700, cruising $100 per hour) has 31-foot and 61-foot boats at Atlantic Beach for half-day and full-day charters for tuna, mahimahi, and redfish. Sunset cruises and sightseeing tours are also offered.

Accommodations

The **Atlantis Lodge** (123 Salter Path Rd., Atlantic Beach, 252/726-5168 or 800/682-7057, www.atlantislodge.com, $55-280) is an old established family-run motel. It has simple and reasonably priced efficiencies in a great beachfront location; the hotel's private board-walk puts you on the beach in two minutes. Well-behaved pets are welcome for an additional fee. The **Clamdigger Inn** (511 Salter Path Rd., Atlantic Beach, 252/247-4155 or 800/338-1533, http://clamdiggerinn.com, $49-255) is another reliable option with all-oceanfront guest rooms. You'll find beach chairs and umbrellas to use as well as a game room, a poolside bar, and wireless Internet access. Pets are not allowed. The **Windjammer Inn** (103 Salter Path Rd., Atlantic Beach, 252/247-7123 or 800/233-6466, www.windjammerinn.com, $169-205) is another simple, comfortable motel with decent rates through the high season and great rates (under $100) in the off-season.

Food

The **Channel Marker** (718 Atlantic Beach Causeway, Atlantic Beach, 252/247-2344, 11am-late daily, $14-37) is a fancier alternative to some of the old-timey fried seafood joints on Bogue Banks. They offer shrimp nine ways, including with grits (classic), steamed (peel and eat—classic), blackened, panned in butter, scampi, fried calabash-style, and broiled in garlic-herb butter. Channel Marker gives you a break from the ubiquitous fried seafood with a selection of broiled seafood; the flounder is especially good broiled, as are the bay scallops. Try the crab cakes with mango chutney, or the Greek shrimp salad. The extensive wine list has wines from the Biltmore Estate in Asheville.

White Swan Bar-B-Q and Chicken (2500-A W. Fort Macon Rd., Atlantic Beach, 252/726-9607, www.whiteswanbarbeque. com, 7am-2pm Mon.-Sat., around $8) has been serving the Carolina trinity of barbecue, coleslaw, and hush puppies since 1960, using a 70-year-old top-secret recipe. This is a "whole hog" barbecue joint, meaning they cook whole hogs, not just shoulders or butts, giving it a richer flavor and providing the pit master and assistants plenty of meat, bark (that crispy outer rind of good barbecue), and juices to work with when assembling your plate. They also flip a mean egg for breakfast.

The **Big Oak Drive-In and Bar-B-Q** (1167 Salter Path Rd., 252/247-2588, www.bigoakdrivein.com, 11am-3pm Tues.-Thurs. and Sun., 11am-8pm Fri. and Sat., around $6) is a classic beach drive-in: a little red, white, and blue-striped building with a walk-up counter and drive-up spaces. They're best known for their shrimp burgers ($5), a fried affair slathered with Big Oak's signature red sauce, coleslaw, and tartar sauce. Then there are the scallop burgers, oyster burgers, clam burgers, hamburgers, and barbecue, all cheap and made for snacking on the beach.

Frost Seafood House (1300 Salter Path Rd., Salter Path, 252/247-3202, www.frostseafoodhouse.com, 4:30pm-9:30pm Mon.-Thurs., 7am-9pm Fri. and Sat., breakfast around $7, dinner around $22) began in 1954 as a gas station and quickly became the restaurant that it is today. The Frost family catches its own shrimp and buys much of its other seafood locally. Be sure to request a taste of the "ching-a-ling" sauce. Another community institution is the **Crab Shack** (140 Shore Dr., Salter Path, 252/247-3444, www.thecrabshacksalterpath.com, daily from 11am, $16-38), behind the Methodist Church in Salter Path. Operated by the Guthries—a family name that dates back to the early colonists in this area—the restaurant was wiped out in 2005 by Hurricane Ophelia but has since been rebuilt.

BEAUFORT

WILMINGTON AND THE CAPE FEAR REGION

In 1524, Giovanni da Verrazzano, the first known European explorer to arrive in the Cape Fear Region, wrote in a letter to the king of France that the land was "as pleasant and delectable to behold as is possible to imagine." With barrier islands that contain the largest intact piece of maritime forest in the state, beautiful beaches, miles of river, marsh, and creek to explore, and the rising Sandhills and hardwood forests inland, the southeastern corner of North Carolina is a natural beauty.

As enthusiasm for the New World built in Europe, the influence of England, Spain, and France profoundly changed the cultural and physical landscapes of the Caribbean and the southern Atlantic coast of North America. Towns and forts sprung up where Native Americans once lived among the trees, built by enslaved Africans for their European masters. Wilmington shares this legacy with other cities in the Atlantic-Caribbean region such as Havana, Nassau, New Orleans, Savannah, and Charleston. The architecture of these cities shows European influence, and the culture—language, food, and folkways—shows the influence of Africans.

The Lumbee people, Native Americans historically and spiritually tied to the blackwater Lumber River, now make their home in Pembroke. They are the largest indigenous community east of the Mississippi River, though their name is not widely known. This is due in part to the fact that they've been denied federal status, a complex and contentious issue that continues to cast a shadow for members of the community. They don't have a reservation,

© JASON FRYE

HIGHLIGHTS

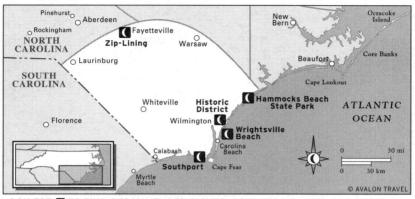

© AVALON TRAVEL

LOOK FOR **[C** TO FIND RECOMMENDED SIGHTS, ACTIVITIES, DINING, AND LODGING.

[C Wilmington's Historic District: Downtown reflects its glory days of commerce and high society in the state's largest 19th-century historic district, a gorgeous collection of antebellum and late-Victorian townhouses and commercial buildings, including many beautiful Southern iterations of the Italianate craze that preceded the Civil War (page 114).

[C Wrightsville Beach: North Carolina has many wonderful beaches, but few can compare with Wrightsville for its pretty strand, easy public access, clear waters, and overall beauty (page 117).

[C Hammocks Beach State Park: One of the wildest and least disturbed Atlantic coast beaches, accessible only by boat, Bear Island is a popular stopover for migrating waterfowl and turtles (page 133).

[C Southport: From this picturesque fishing town you can see the oldest and newest lighthouses in North Carolina, enjoy dinner on the water with the locals, and celebrate your independence at the state's official Fourth of July celebration (page 137).

[C Zip-Lining: Soaring through the trees at ZipQuest in Fayetteville provides thrills and an unusual look at pine and hardwood forests (page 151).

and for centuries have lived a rural existence with deeply rooted Christianity. Their little-known history can be explored in and around Pembroke.

Between Wilmington and Lumberton the landscape of the state's southeast corner becomes a waterscape comprising blackwater creeks and seductive, even eerie swamps, bays, marshes, and rivers. It's the world's only native habitat of the Venus flytrap. Many visitors wrinkle their noses at the marsh's distinctive smell as the tide recedes and the mudflats are exposed, but to locals the mingled scent of marsh and salt water is the scent of home. The cypress knees, tannic creeks, marsh birds, and occasional alligator make this region pleasant and delectable to behold, an experience that is enhanced by staying a little longer.

The greatest draw is the water: the beautiful beaches of Brunswick, New Hanover, Pender, and Onslow Counties and the well-known Wrightsville and Topsail beaches as

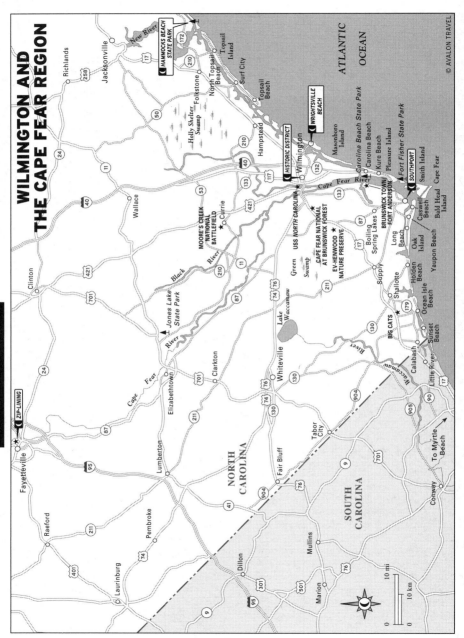

WILMINGTON AND THE CAPE FEAR REGION

© AVALON TRAVEL

well as other hidden gems just north of bustling Myrtle Beach, South Carolina. You can find the same mini golf and beach-towel vendors peppering the beach towns of North Carolina, but the state's coast mostly seems downright bucolic compared to its southern neighbor.

Inland, the landscape changes but the water is no less important. At the edge of this region is Fayetteville, with a long history that includes Revolutionary War standoffs, Civil War battles, and links to the Cape Fear River. At Fayetteville the marshes give way to rolling hills with a mix of pines and hardwoods. Home to Fort Bragg, Fayetteville has a large military presence and history, dating to the colonial era when immigrant Scots called these hills home.

PLANNING YOUR TIME

There's a lot to do in the Cape Fear region, and depending on your interests, a wide range of choices for a home base. Wilmington is the obvious choice: Centrally located on the coast, it's minutes from Wrightsville, Kure, and Carolina Beaches and only a little farther from Topsail and the beaches of Brunswick County. Fayetteville and Raleigh are only a couple of hours away, making day trips a possibility. The town of Wilmington is full of activities and sights, and you'll want a day or two to explore this historic river city. For inland adventures in the region, Fayetteville offers a good selection of motels, and it's still a reasonable drive to the coast for a day at the beach.

HISTORY

Giovanni da Verrazzano's 1524 visit started a land race that took two centuries to take off. Lucas Vásquez de Ayllón and his crew, which possibly included the first enslaved Africans brought to what is now the United States, walked the shores here in 1526 scouting for resources and settlement sites before their shipwreck in South Carolina. In the 1660s explores from the Massachusetts Bay Colony visited and either didn't like what they found or wanted others to think it was undesirable land; at the end of their short trip they left a sign at the end of the cape that read, in essence, "Don't bother; nothing to see here."

The next summer a settlement appeared on the banks of the river, but it failed as colonists, citing the humidity, hurricanes, and bugs, among other things, abandoned it. It wasn't until 1726 that European settlement took hold in the region. Maurice Moore and his brother Roger established their family's domain at Brunswick Town and Orton Plantation, 0.5 miles north. Today, only ruins remain at Brunswick Town in the form of ballast-stone house foundations and the brick walls of an Anglican church, but Orton Plantation still stands and is once again owned by Moore descendants. The machinations of the Moores and Brunswick Town residents led to the demise of the indigenous Cape Fear people. Many of them were driven off, and the remainder were rounded up and later murdered.

Brunswick Town was an important port, as the only inland deepwater access on the river, but it was soon eclipsed by Wilmington to the north once dredging technology allowed the shoals between the two towns to be cleared. As Brunswick Town declined, the Revolution heated up, and the small port town played important roles in defying George III's taxes and harrying General Cornwallis and his troops as they raided the area. At the same time, the large population of Scottish immigrants around Fayetteville grew even larger, making their living in the forests preparing tar, pitch, and turpentine for naval stores.

In the lower Cape Fear Region, especially present-day Brunswick, New Hanover, Bladen, and Onslow Counties, the concentration of enslaved laborers was significantly larger than in many other parts of the state. The naval stores industry demanded workers, as did the large rice and indigo plantations, including Orton, that once dominated the local agricultural industry. The same was true along the coasts of South Carolina, Georgia, and parts of northern Florida, where many of the slaves had been taken from the same part of Africa. These large communities of African-born and first-generation American-born people shared ideas, memories, and culture, which became what is known today as Gullah or Geechee culture. Most prominent around Charleston and Savannah, the Gullah dialect and cultural influence still exist in and around Wilmington. The dialect is reminiscent of English as spoken in the Caribbean, and cultural traditions still in evidence include the cuisine, heavy with gumbo, peanuts, and okra; and folklore, in which houses are painted bright blue to keep bad luck away, and bottle trees are used to capture evil spirits.

Another cultural group in the Cape Fear region is the indigenous Lumbee people. Also called the Croatan Indians, Pembroke Indians, and Indians of Robeson County, they're they largest indigenous community in the eastern United States. During the time of slavery and the Civil War they were called "free people of color," and they had no right to vote or to bear arms. The Lumbee people have a long history of resistance and defending their land. Most famously, in the 19th century Henry Lowry (sometimes spelled Lowrie) Band of outlaws defined the Lumbee cause for future generations. Another transformative moment in Lumbee history was a 1958 armed conflict near Maxton. Ku Klux Klan grand wizard "Catfish" Cole and about 40 other armed Klansmen held a rally at Hayes Pond. Fed up with a recent wave of vicious intimidation at the hands of the Klan, 1,500 armed Lumbee people showed up at the rally and shot out the lone electric light. No one was killed in the exchange of gunfire, and the Klansmen fled. The confrontation was reported around the country, energizing the cause of Native American civil rights.

In the late 20th and early 21st century, southeastern North Carolina's role as a military center expanded. Fort Bragg in Fayetteville is one of the country's largest Army installations and home to thousands of the soldiers who were stationed in Iraq and Afghanistan; the base continues to grow. Nearby Pope Air Field is the home of the 440th Airlift Wing, and there is a major Marine Corps presence nearby at Camp Lejeune in Jacksonville. Numerous museums in Fayetteville and Jacksonville tell the history of the military in southeastern North Carolina.

Perhaps most important in the region's recent history is the booming film industry. Wilmington is the center of cinematography in North Carolina, as evidenced by a 50-acre studio lot, the largest outside Los Angeles. Productions such as *Iron Man 3, Dawson's Creek,* and innumerable TV pilots and independent features have been filmed in the region, along with production offices and set pieces for productions like *The Hunger Games* and *Homeland.*

INFORMATION AND SERVICES

Area hospitals include two in Wilmington, **Cape Fear Hospital** (5301 Wrightsville Ave., Wilmington, 910/452-8100, www.nhrmc. org) and the **New Hanover Regional Medical Center** (2131 S. 17th St., Wilmington, 910/343-7000, www.nhrmc.org); two in Brunswick County, **Brunswick Novant Medical Center** (240 Hospital Dr. NE, Lockwoods Folly, 910/721-1000, www.brunswicknovant.org) and **Dosher Memorial Hospital** (924 N. Howe St., Southport, 910/457-3800, www.dosher.org); in Onslow County, **Onslow Memorial Hospital** (317 Western Blvd., Jacksonville, 910/577-2345, www.onslow.org); in Pender County, **Pender Memorial Hospital** (507 E. Fremont St., Burgaw, 910/259-5451, www.nhrmc.org); and Fayetteville's **Cape Fear Valley Medical Center** (1638 Owen Dr., Fayetteville, 910/615-4000, www.capefearvalley.com). Myrtle Beach, South Carolina, has the **Grand Strand Regional Medical Center** (809 82nd Pkwy., Myrtle Beach, SC, 843/692-1000, www.grand-strandmed.com), not far from the southernmost communities in Brunswick County. In an emergency, of course, call 911.

More information on dining, attractions, and lodging is available through local convention and visitors bureaus: the **Wilmington and Beaches CVB** (505 Nutt St., Unit A, Wilmington, 877/406-2356, www.wilmingtonandbeaches.com, 8:30am-5pm Mon.-Fri., 9am-4pm Sat., 1pm-4pm Sun.), **Brunswick**

County Tourism Development Authority (20 Referendum Dr., Bldg. G, 800/795-7263, www.ncbrunswick.com), and the **Fayetteville**

Area CVB (245 Person St., Fayetteville, 800/255-8217, www.visitfayettevillenc.com, 8am-5pm Mon.-Fri.).

Wilmington

In some ways, Wilmington is a town where time has stood still. During the Civil War, General Sherman's fiery march that razed so many Southern towns missed Wilmington. For most of the 20th century the economy moved in fits and starts with long slumps, standstills, and short boom periods. Surviving the Civil War combined with a slow economy provided Wilmington's architecture with an unexpected benefit: historic preservation. Much of the downtown remains a museum of beautiful buildings dating to the town's first heyday, and that historic appeal accounts for much of its popularity as a destination today.

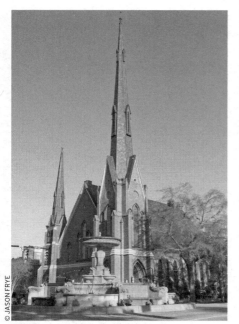

Wilmington's historic district

Things are looking up for Wilmington economically, in part because of the burgeoning film industry. It's not uncommon to see film crews at downtown locations or to run into film stars at local eateries.

HISTORY

Founded in the early 1730s, Wilmington went through a short identity crisis as New Carthage, New Liverpool, and New Town before settling on Wilmington in 1739. Early on it was a deepwater port and quickly became a bustling shipping center for the export of lumber, rice, and naval stores, including turpentine and tar tapped from longleaf pine trees and lumber for ships' keels and ribbing from live oak branches. Wilmington's reputation and commerce grew. By 1769 the town had grown from a collection of wharves, warehouses, and homes into a respectable colonial city, included on a map drawn by acclaimed French cartographer C. J. Sauthier. By 1840 the city was booming, one of the largest in the state, and positioned as the southern terminus of the Wilmington and Weldon Railroad (the 161-mile track was the longest in the world at the time).

During the Civil War the Wilmington and Weldon Railroad line was an essential Confederate artery for trade and troop transport. The Union navy attempted a blockade of the Cape Fear River and inlets up and down the coast, but Wilmington's port was a hive of blockade runners bringing in arms, food, medicine, and materials from Europe and the Caribbean. In January 1865 the Union took nearby Fort Fisher, the key gun emplacement guarding the river's mouth, and Wilmington soon fell. It was a crushing blow to the failing Confederacy. Continued commerce at the port allowed Wilmington to thrive during the

© JASON FRYE

WILMINGTON AND CAPE FEAR

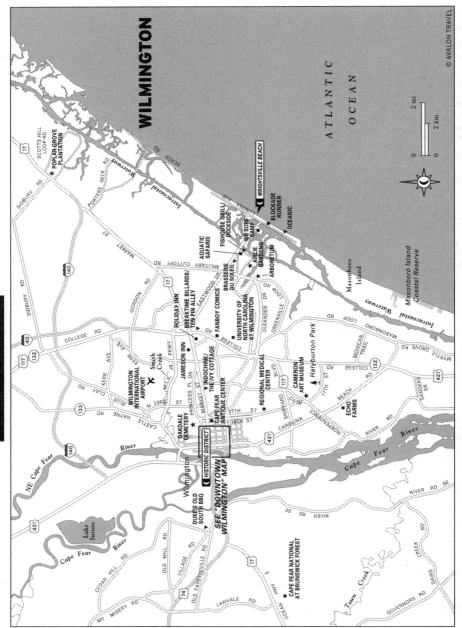

WELCOME TO "HOLLYWOOD EAST"

It all started with a little girl who played with fire. From the ashes of the 1984 feature film *Firestarter*, an adaptation of Stephen King's novel of the same name, Wilmington's film industry grew and North Carolina became a film-friendly state. Wilmington is known as "Hollywood East" for good reason: since that first film, hundreds of films, television programs, reality shows, and music videos have been shot here, and EUE/ScreenGems Studios maintains 10 soundstages on a 50-acre studio lot, the largest outside Los Angeles. Some of the most notable films and television shows shot in Wilmington include:

- *Firestarter*
- *Blue Velvet*
- *Maximum Overdrive*
- *Trick or Treat*
- *Weekend at Bernie's*
- *Teenage Mutant Ninja Turtles*
- *Super Mario Brothers*
- *Billy Bathgate*
- *The Crow*
- *I Know What You Did Last Summer*
- *Summer Catch*

- *Domestic Disturbance*
- *Divine Secrets of the Ya-Ya Sisterhood*
- *Safe Haven*
- *Iron Man 3*
- *Dawson's Creek*
- *One Tree Hill*
- *Eastbound and Down*
- *Revolution*
- *Under the Dome*

Filmed elsewhere in the state, you may have seen:

- *Bull Durham*
- *Cold Mountain*
- *Days of Thunder*
- *The Last of the Mohicans*
- *The Hunger Games*
- *Hannibal*
- *The Green Mile*
- *Evil Dead II*
- *Homeland*
- *Banshee*

Civil War and Reconstruction, unlike many towns in the South; by 1890 the population hit 20,000, making it the largest city in North Carolina.

Political tensions ran high during Reconstruction, and there were conflicts between whites and blacks, Democrats and Republicans, and staunch Confederate supporters and carpetbaggers (Northerners who came to South for economic opportunities) and copperheads (their Southern supporters). In 1898 the only successful coup d'état on American soil took place in the Wilmington Race Riot. White Democrats loyal to the long-dead Confederacy threatened to overthrow the city government if their candidate lost. He did,

and two days after the election, a mob of white Democrats and their supporters overthrew the city's Republican government, destroyed the city's African American newspaper, the *Daily Record,* and killed at least 22 African American citizens.

In the early 20th century, North Carolina's power center shifted from the agriculture and shipping at coastal towns like Wilmington to the textile mills and manufacturing of the Piedmont region. Charlotte surpassed Wilmington in population, interstate highways joined larger cities to the rest of the nation, and economically Wilmington stood still. In 1960 the Atlantic Coast Line Railroad relocated its headquarters to Florida, and the city

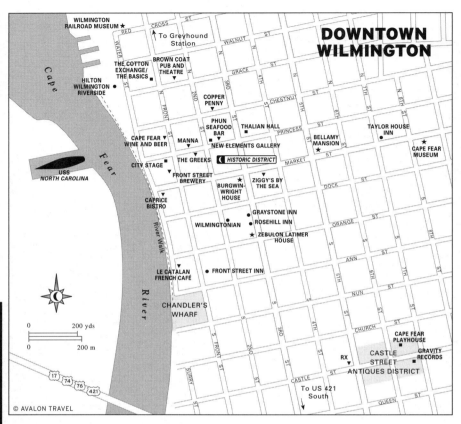

DOWNTOWN WILMINGTON

© AVALON TRAVEL

experienced several decades of decline. After I-40 was completed, connecting Wilmington to the rest of the country, the tourism industry began to rise. Wilmington and surrounding towns had a real estate boom in the late 1990s that lasted for several years. At the same time, the film industry grew, boosting the local economy and influencing local culture. Like most of the country, Wilmington was hit hard by the end of the real estate bubble in 2006, and the city is still climbing out from under the wreckage of that widespread economic collapse. There are signs of growth, however, thanks to the University of North Carolina, the tourism and film industries, and the resilience of the people.

SIGHTS
◖ Historic District

Comprising more than 200 blocks, Wilmington's historic district is among the largest in North Carolina. You'll find shady tree-lined streets and a gorgeous collection of antebellum and late Victorian homes, mansions, and commercial buildings. Wilmington is home to the state's largest 19th-century historic district, which includes beautiful examples of pre-Civil War Italianate architecture as well as influences from the French and English Caribbean. Until 1910, Wilmington was the state's most populous city; the earlier boom and subsequent decline are reflected in the

© JASON FRYE

Bellamy Mansion

architecture, as the city lacks the fine examples of early-20th-century buildings found in cities like Asheville and Charlotte.

The **Bellamy Mansion** (503 Market St., 910/251-3700, www.bellamymansion.org, tours hourly 10am-5pm Tues.-Sat., 1pm-5pm Sun., $10 adults, $4 under age 12) is a superb example of Wilmington's late-antebellum mansions. This porticoed, four-story, 22-room home shows both Greek Revival and Italianate architectural influences and stands as one of the most beautiful Southern city homes of its era. Just two months before North Carolina seceded from the Union in 1861, planter and physician John Bellamy and his family moved into their city home, where they lived until the fall of Fort Fisher and the ensuing fall of Wilmington to the Union. After the war, Bellamy traveled to Washington to ask President Andrew Johnson, a fellow North Carolinian, for a pardon, and used his pardon to recover the home from federal ownership.

In addition to the mansion, another significant building stands on the property: the slave quarters. This two-story brick building is a rare surviving example of urban dwellings for enslaved people, and the interior, which remained largely unchanged through the years, is an important part of the historical record of slavery in the South.

The **Burgwin-Wright House** (224 Market St., 910/762-0570, www.burgwinwrighthouse. com, tours 10am-4pm Tues.-Sat. Feb.-Dec., $10 adults, $5 ages 5-12) is older than the Bellamy Mansion by nearly a century, but it has an oddly similar history. John Burgwin ("ber-GWIN"), a planter and treasurer of the North Carolina colony, built the home in 1770 atop the city's early jail. Soon after, British forces commandeered the home as their headquarters during the Revolutionary War. In 1781, General Cornwallis, then on the last leg of his campaign before falling into George Washington's trap that signaled the end of British occupation, took the house as his headquarters. Joshua Grainger Wright purchased the house in 1799, and it served as a residence until 1937, when the National Society of the Colonial Dames of America purchased the home because of its historic significance.

Like the Bellamy Mansion, the Burgwin-Wright House is a version of the classic white-columned, magnolia-shaded Southern home of the wealthy merchant-planter class, but it's not overly ostentatious. Seven terraced gardens filled with native plants and those grown in the 18th century surround the house; through the years, restoration efforts have helped preserve many original garden structures, including walls, paths, steps, and gates.

Another beautiful home in Wilmington's historic district is the **Zebulon Latimer House** (126 S. 3rd St., 910/762-0492, www.hslcf.org, tours 10am and 3pm Mon.-Fri., hourly 10am-3pm Sat., $10 adults, $5 ages 5-12). Merchant Zebulon Latimer built this home in 1852, and it housed three generations of Latimers, until 1963 when it became a museum and the headquarters of the Lower Cape Fear Historical Society. In its day the Latimer House was a little more fashion-forward, architecturally speaking, than its neighbors; delicate cast-iron cornices and porch railings speak to both the Italianate and emerging Victorian influences. Also located on the grounds are a two-story brick dwelling for slaves and gardens planted with period-authentic plants.

A **three-house ticket** ($24) to tour the Bellamy Mansion, the Latimer House, and the Burgwin-Wright House is available at the first house you visit; it will save you several dollars if you plan to spend the day touring the historic district. Join the **Historic Wilmington Guided Walking Tour** (910/762-0492, 10am Sat., reservations recommended, $10), departing from the Latimer House.

Just three blocks from the Latimer House is the **Wilmington Riverwalk,** a mile-long riverside promenade that stretches the length of downtown Wilmington, overlooking the Cape Fear River and the battleship USS *North Carolina.* Most of the boutiques, dining, and nightlife in Wilmington are on the Riverwalk or a block from it. A **Visitors Information**

Wilmington Riverwalk

Booth (Market St.) or friendly locals can steer you in the right direction.

Wrightsville Beach

A few miles east of Wilmington is one of the nicest beaches on the Carolina coast: **Wrightsville Beach.** Wide and easily accessible, it is one of the most visitor- and family-friendly beaches you'll find. Wrightsville benefits from the proximity of the Gulf Stream; here the warm ocean current sweeping up the Atlantic seaboard lies only 30-40 miles offshore, which means warmer waters that are colored more like the Caribbean.

A number of lodging and rental choices along the beach make it an easy place to stay, and numerous public beach access points (www.towb.org), some of which are disabled-accessible, and some with showers or restrooms, line Lumina Avenue. The largest public parking lot, with 99 spaces, disabled access, showers, and restrooms, is a Beach Access 4 (2398 N. Lumina Ave.). Beach Access 36 (650 S. Lumina Ave.) has 86 parking spaces, disabled access, showers, and restrooms. On busy days the parking lots can fill up, but trekking from one access point to the next will often yield a spot. To avoid the rush, plan to park before 9am, when you'll be able to grab a spot in most of the lots or on the street.

Historic Sights Around Wilmington
POPLAR GROVE PLANTATION

North of the city, about halfway between Wilmington and Topsail Island, is **Poplar Grove Plantation** (10200 U.S. 17 N., 910/686-9518, www.poplargrove.com, 9am-5pm Mon.-Sat., noon-5pm Sun., $10 adults, $9 seniors and military, $5 ages 6-15, $7 self-guided tour). This antebellum peanut plantation preserves the homestead of a successful farming family, including the beautiful main house, a restored tenant farmer's cabin, a blacksmith's shop, and a barn. A 67-acre nature preserve with an extensive network of hiking trails winds through coastal forests and wetlands, and a **Farmers Market** (8am-1pm

© JASON FRYE

Wrightsville Beach

Wed. Apr.-Nov.) shows off the bounty of the area's agriculture.

MOORE'S CREEK NATIONAL BATTLEFIELD

In Wilmington and the surrounding area are a number of significant military sites, most dating to the Revolutionary War and the Civil War. About 20 miles northwest of Wilmington, outside the town of Currie, near Burgaw, is the **Moore's Creek National Battlefield** (40 Patriots Hall Dr., Currie, 910/283-5591, www.nps.gov/mocr, 9am-5pm daily, closed Thanksgiving, Dec. 25, and Jan. 1). The site commemorates the brief but bloody battle of February 1776 between Loyalist Scottish highlanders, kilted and piping and brandishing broadswords, and Patriot colonists. The Patriots fired on the Scotsmen with cannons and muskets as they crossed a bridge over Moore's Creek. Some 30 Loyalists died in the attack, and the remainder scattered into the surrounding swamps and woods. The battle marked an important moment in the Revolutionary War, as the Scottish Loyalists were unable to join General Cornwallis's army in Southport and mount an attack on Patriots nearby. It also marks an important moment in Scottish military history, as the battle was the last major broadsword charge in Scottish history, led by the last Scottish clan army.

USS *NORTH CAROLINA*

Don't be alarmed if you notice a battleship across the Cape Fear River from Wilmington; it's the **USS *North Carolina*** (1 Battleship Rd., Eagles Island, 910/251-5797, www.battleshipnc.com, 8am-8pm daily late May-early Sept., 8am-5pm daily early Sept.-late May, $12 adults, $10 seniors and active or retired military, $6 ages 6-11, free under 5), a decommissioned World War II warship that now serves as a museum and memorial to North Carolinians who died in World War II. This hulking gray colossus participated in every major naval offensive in the Pacific, earning 15 battle stars, and was falsely reported to have sunk six times.

Tours are self-guided and start with a short film providing an overview of the museum, then proceed onto the one-acre deck of the battleship. Nine levels of the battleship are open to explore, including the 16-inch gun turrets on the deck, the bridge, crew quarters, ship's hospital, kitchens, and the magazine, where munitions were stored. It gets tight belowdecks and stairways are quite steep, so visitors prone to claustrophobia and those unable to traverse steep steps may want to stay topside. The hallways and quarters below are dark, narrow, and surprisingly deep; from the heart of the ship, it takes more than a few minutes to find your way back to the deck. Crowds can make this more constricting, but nothing like it would have been in the balmy Pacific with 2,000 sailors aboard.

The USS *North Carolina* is also one of North Carolina's most famous haunted houses—reputedly home to several ghosts, seen and heard by staff and visitors alike. The SyFy Channel has featured the ship on various ghost-hunting and paranormal shows, and it has been the subject of extensive investigations. Check out **Haunted NC** (www.hauntednc.com) to hear some chilling and unexplained voices recorded by investigators.

OAKDALE CEMETERY

By the mid-19th century, Wilmington was experiencing growing pains as the bustling shipping and railroad center of North Carolina. The city's old cemeteries were becoming overcrowded with former residents, and **Oakdale Cemetery** (520 N. 15th St., 910/762-5682, www.oakdalecemetery.org, 8am-5pm daily year-round) was founded some distance from downtown to ease the graveyard congestion. Designed in the parklike style of graveyards popular at the time, it was soon filled with superb examples of funerary art—weeping angels, obelisks, willow trees—set off against the natural beauty of the place. Separate sections were reserved for Jewish burials and for victims of the 1862 yellow fever epidemic. Oakdale's website has an interesting guide to Victorian grave art symbolism.

ANOLES OF CAROLINA

© JASON FRYE

WILMINGTON AND CAPE FEAR

anole, dewlap extended

While you're in the Wilmington area, you'll almost certainly run across a few anoles. These tiny bright-green lizards skitter up and down trees and walls and dash along railings–impossibly fast and improbably green. You may hear locals call them "chameleons" because anoles can change their color from bright green to dirt brown as a way to camouflage themselves against the background and guard against predators. If you watch them long enough, you'll see a fascinating courtship and territorial dominance ritual: a male anole will spread his forelegs wide and do several "push-ups," then puff out his little crescent-shaped dewlap, the scarlet pouch beneath the chin. When you see one do this, keep still and keep watching; they often repeat the act several times.

Explorer John Lawson was quite taken with them, as he describes in his 1709 *A New Voyage to Carolina:*

Green lizards are very harmless and beautiful, having a little Bladder under their Throat, which they fill with Wind, and evacuate the same at Pleasure. They are of a most glorious Green, and very tame. They resort to the Walls of Houses in the Summer Season, and stand gazing on a Man, without any Concern or Fear. There are several other Colours of these Lizards, but none so beautiful as the green ones are.

Museums

CAPE FEAR MUSEUM

The **Cape Fear Museum** (814 Market St., 910/798-4350, www.capefearmuseum.com, 9am-5pm Tues.-Sat., 1pm-5pm Sun., $7 adults, $6 seniors, military, and college students, $4 ages 3-17) has exhibits showing the history and ecology of Wilmington and the region, including locally important historical perspectives and the fossil skeleton of a giant ground sloth unearthed in town.

CAMERON ART MUSEUM

The **Cameron Art Museum** (3201 S. 17th St., 910/395-5999, www.cameronartmuseum.com, 10am-5pm Tues.-Wed. and Fri.-Sun., 10am-9pm Thurs., closed July 4, Thanksgiving, Dec. 25, and Jan. 1, $8 adults, $5 seniors, military, and students, $3 ages 2-12) is one of the major art museums in North Carolina. This 42,000-square-foot facility includes a permanent collection of art in a range of styles and media, with an emphasis on North Carolina artists. Artists represented include masters like Mary Cassatt and Utagawa Hiroshige, and North Carolina artists like Claude Howell and Minnie Evans. Special exhibits change throughout the year.

WILMINGTON RAILROAD MUSEUM

The **Wilmington Railroad Museum** (505 Nutt St., 910/763-2634, www.wilmingtonrailroadmuseum.org, hours vary, generally 10am-4pm Mon.-Sat., $8.50 adults, $7.50 seniors and military, $4.50 ages 2-12) sheds light on a largely forgotten part of Wilmington's history: its role as a railroad town. In 1840, Wilmington became the southern terminus for the world's longest continuous rail line, The Wilmington and Weldon (W&W) Railroad, which was an important supply line during the Civil War and one of the reasons Wilmington became a priority target for federal troops. In 1900 the Atlantic Coast Line Railroad absorbed W&W and kept its headquarters in Wilmington until the 1960s, when it moved its offices and employees to Florida, devastating the city's economy for years. On display at the museum are a number of railroad artifacts, including timetables, tools, and locomotives. A classic locomotive, steam engine number 250, has been lovingly restored and maintained and now greets visitors as they enter the museum.

Gardens and Parks

AIRLIE GARDENS

Airlie Gardens (300 Airlie Rd., 910/798-7700, www.airliegardens.org, 9am-5pm daily, closed Thanksgiving Day, Dec. 24-25, Jan. 1, $5 adults, $3 ages 6-12), a formal garden park dating to 1901, features more than 50,000 azaleas, several miles of walking trails, and grassy areas perfect for picnics and park concerts, including the Summer Concert Series (1st and 3rd Fri. May-Sept., call for hours). Highlights of Airlie Gardens include the Airlie Oak, a massive live oak believed to be 500 years old, and the Minnie Evans Sculpture Garden and Bottle Chapel. Evans, a visionary African American artist whose mystical work is among the best examples of outsider art, was the gatekeeper here for 25 of her 95 years; examples of her work can also be seen at the Cameron Art Museum. Most of the paths and walkways comply with federal disabled-access rules, but for visitors not mobile enough to walk the gardens, trams are available; the tram schedule is listed on the website.

BLUETHENTHAL WILDFLOWER PRESERVE

On the campus of the University of North Carolina Wilmington, you'll find the **Bluethenthal Wildflower Preserve** (601 S. College Rd., University of North Carolina Wilmington campus, located behind the Fisher University Union on Price Dr., 910/962-3000, http://uncw.edu/physicalplant/arboretum/bluethenthal.htm, dawn-dusk daily, free), a small nature preserve with a rich bed of wildflowers and, more importantly, carnivorous plants like the venus fly trap. It's a lovely walk any time of year, though a little buggy if the wind is still. You'll bump into a number of professors and contemplative students.

HALYBURTON PARK

There are a number of parks in and around Wilmington, but many visitors stop by **Halyburton Park** (4099 S. 17th St., 910/341-0075, www.halyburtonpark.com, grounds dawn-dusk daily, nature center 9am-5pm Mon.-Sat.) for the natural landscape made for walking and biking. A 1.3-mile disabled-accessible trail encircles the 58-acre park, while the interior is a spiderweb of trails, both of which provide a glimpse of the Sandhills, Carolina bays (elliptical, often boggy, depressions in the ground), and longleaf pine and oak forest that once dominated the area's landscape.

NEW HANOVER COUNTY ARBORETUM

The **New Hanover County Arboretum** (6206 Oleander Dr., 910/798-7660, dawn-dusk daily) is another popular spot for a stroll or a picnic. The five-acre gardens are also home to a Cooperative Extension horticulture laboratory. Most of the gardens comprise native plants and showcase the floral variety of the area.

ENTERTAINMENT AND EVENTS
Performing Arts

Thalian Hall (310 Chestnut St., 800/523-2820, www.thalianhall.com), the only surviving theater designed by prominent architect John Montague Trimble, has been in near-continuous operation since it opened in 1858. Once serving as the city hall, a library, and an opera house, at the time of its construction it could seat one-tenth of the population of Wilmington, North Carolina's largest city. In its heyday, Thalian Hall was an important stop for theater troupes, productions, and artists touring the country, and today it serves as a major arts venue in the region, hosting a variety of musical acts, ballet, children's theater, and art-house and limited-release films. The resident theatre company, the **Thalian Association** (910/251-1788, www.thalian.org), can trace its roots back to 1788 and is North Carolina's official community theater company.

A number of other theater groups call Thalian Hall home. In 2015 the **Opera House**

© JASON FRYE

Thalian Hall

Theatre Company (910/762-4234, www.op-erahousetheatrecompany.net) will celebrate its 30th anniversary. Opera House has produced annual big-name musicals and dramas as well as works by important North Carolinians and other Southern playwrights at Thalian Hall. **Stageworks Youth Theatre** (910/538-8378, www.stageworksyouth.org), a community company comprising actors ages 10 to 17, also calls Thalian Hall home. Stageworks puts on serious dramas, comedies, and musicals and regularly partners with **Cape Fear Shakespeare on the Green** (910/399-2878, www.capefearshakespeare.org) to put on plays by the Bard at Thalian Hall and at Greenfield Lake Amphitheatre.

Being an artsy town with a flair for stage and screen performances, it's no surprise to learn that a lot of theater is produced "off Thalian," as it were. **Big Dawg Productions** (910/367-5237, www.bigdawgproductions.org) puts on several plays each year at their 50-seat Cape Fear Playhouse (613 Castle St.). Plays range from classical to contemporary works. They also host the **New Play Festival** each year, a celebration of first-time productions authored by playwrights under the age of 18. The festival is approaching its 20th anniversary and has seen many works that premiered here go on to wider audiences and acclaim.

City Stage (21 N. Front St., 5th Fl., 910/264-2602, www.citystagenc.com), puts on a number of performances, ranging from edgy musicals like *Hedwig and the Angry Inch* and *The Rocky Horror Picture Show* to comedies and dramas, in a building once owned by Dennis Hopper. Nearby, **Brown Coat Pub and Theatre** (111 Grace St., 910/341-0001, www.browncoattheatre.com, 10pm-2am Mon.-Wed., 7pm-2am Thurs.-Sat., 4pm-2am Sun.) stages all sorts of productions, including musical comedies, Shakespeare, and contemporary plays. They also host a number of other live performance events, including poetry nights, independent and local film screenings, and a live weekly sitcom.

Festivals

Wilmington plays host to a number of small festivals throughout the year, but the crown jewel is the **Azalea Festival** (910/794-4650, www.ncazaleafestival.org), held at venues around the city each April, hopefully coinciding with the blooming of the namesake flowering shrubs. Tours of azalea-laden historic and contemporary homes and gardens draw many visitors, but the street fair, which takes over much of Water Street and a good portion of Front Street, draws many more. With over 200 arts and crafts vendors, countless food vendors, a dedicated children's area, and four stages of entertainment from national and local acts, the street fair is quite a party. Garden tours and the street fair only scratch the surface of what the Azalea Festival has to offer; a parade, a circus, dance competitions, gospel concerts, boxing matches, and fireworks round out Azalea Festival events. And like any self-respecting Southern town, it crowns royalty—in this case, the North Carolina Azalea Festival Queen, a Princess, the Queen's Court, a phalanx of cadets from The Citadel, and 100 Azalea Belles. The Azalea Festival draws more than 300,000 visitors annually, so book accommodations and make dinner reservations well in advance. If you decide to visit the area on a weekend trip in early April, be prepared to find Wilmington far more bustling than normal.

Each October, **Riverfest** (910/452-6862, www.wilmingtonriverfest.com) takes over part of downtown for a street fair that includes art shows; art, crafts, and food vendors; and car shows. It's smaller than the Azalea Festival, but many downtown venues coordinate concerts and events with Riverfest, making downtown more vibrant for the weekend.

What would a film town be without a film festival? The **Cucalorus Film Festival** (910/343-5995, www.cucalorus.org) celebrates independent films and filmmakers each November. About 150 films from national and international indie filmmakers are shown, along with panels featuring filmmakers, writers, and actors, at Thalian Hall and other

© JASON FRYE

The Azalea Festival in Wilmington draws more than 300,000 visitors annually.

venues around town. In a short time Cucalorus has garnered the attention of major film-industry publications and has been called "one of the 25 coolest film festivals."

In the town of Hampstead, between Wilmington and Topsail Island, the annual **North Carolina Spot Festival** (www.ncspotfestival.com) celebrates the spot, a small fish that's a traditional staple of coastal Carolina. For more than 50 years, hundreds of people have gathered here at the end of September to deep-fry and gobble up spot. The festival features art and crafts vendors, a pageant, concerts, and fireworks, but the fun is in eating spot.

Burgaw, a tiny town 30 minutes north of Wilmington, is home to the **North Carolina Blueberry Festival** (www.ncblueberryfestival.com) each June. Live music, food vendors, and loads of products featuring blueberries—soap, barbecue sauce, ice cream, muffins—make up this festival. Along with the Spot Festival, the Blueberry Festival is a great small-town festival experience.

Nightlife

Ziggy's By The Sea (208 Market St., 910/769-4096, http://ziggysbythesea.com, box office noon-5pm Mon.-Fri., doors generally open around 8 p.m. with shows starting shortly thereafter, cash only, credit card users should purchase online) hosts live music in a renovated building in the historic district.

Craft beer fans will want to pull up a barstool at **Cape Fear Wine and Beer** (139 N. Front St., 910/763-3377, www.capefearwineandbeer.net, 4pm-2am Mon.-Wed., 1pm-2am Thurs.-Sun.), a spot that's more punk than trendy, but one that welcomes beer lovers of any ilk. The bartenders know their brews and can guide you to one you like from their vast collection of bottled and draft beers. You'll find rare microbrews, meads, and barley wines from around the world, but you'll also find a strong emphasis on the best North Carolina beers. Throughout the week, Cape Fear Wine and Beer runs specials on beer flights, chair massages, and North Carolina beer, among others. Get here early and spend a little time talking to the bartender to find your perfect brew. Don't be shy about asking for a sample pour of a draft beer if you're unsure.

Just down the street, **Front Street Brewery** (9 N. Front St., 910/251-1935, www.frontstreet-brewery.com, 11:30am-midnight daily) serves lunch and dinner, and as good as the pulled-chicken nachos are, the best part about Front Street Brewery is the *kölsch*, IPA, pilsner, and seasonal beers brewed on-site; you can tour the brewery and get a sample to wet your whistle 3pm-5pm every afternoon.

On the other end of town, **Satellite Bar and Lounge** (120 Greenfield St., www.satel-litebarandlounge.com, 4pm-2am Mon.-Sat., 2pm-2am Sun.) draws a diverse hip crowd to this former industrial space. The rustic decor matches the large selection of bottled and canned beer, and an outdoor seating area allows the bar, which can get crowded, to breathe. Local food trucks swing by on a rotating basis to serve grub to the late-night crowd, and on Sunday, the Satellite Bluegrass Band treats patrons to an extended and lively bluegrass jam session. Satellite is on the outskirts of Wilmington, bordering some less than savory neighborhoods, so it's best to call a cab or bring a designated driver.

Breaktime Billiards/Ten Pin Alley (127 S. College Rd., 910/452-5455, www.breaktime-tenpin.com, billiards and bowling 11am-2am daily, lounge 6pm-2am Mon.-Fri., 11am-2am Sat.-Sun.) is a 30,000-square-foot entertainment palace, with 24 billiard tables and one regulation-size snooker table, 24 bowling lanes and skee-ball, and between them the Lucky Strike Lounge, a full bar and snack shop with all manner of video games and which hosts soft-tip dart and foosball tournaments. Put in an order for a meal and a beer or cocktail, and the staff will bring it to you if you're in the middle of a game.

SHOPPING
Shopping Centers
The group of buildings known as **The Cotton Exchange** (Front St. and Grace St., 910/343-9896, www.shopcottonexchange.com,

10am-5:30pm Mon.-Sat., noon-4pm Sun.) has housed a variety of businesses in 150 years of continuous operation: the largest flour and hominy mill in the south, a printing company, a Chinese laundry, a "mariners saloon" (where they served more refreshment than just beer), and, of course, a cotton exchange. Today, dozens of boutiques and restaurants call these historic buildings home. **Caravan Beads** (O'Brien Building, 910/343-3000) has an impressive selection of beads and beading materials; **Down to Earth** (O'Brien Building, 910/251-0041) carries essential oils and will make custom blends in-house for you; and **Occasions—Just Write** (O'Brien Building, 910/343-9033) is a great shop for writers and stationery lovers.

Near Wrightsville Beach, the boutique shops and restaurants of **Lumina Station** (1900 Eastwood Rd., 910/256-0900, www.lu-minastation.com, 10am-6pm Mon.-Sat.) can keep shoppers busy for an afternoon. Some of Wilmington's nicest boutiques call Lumina Station home, including **Island Passage** (Suite 8, 910/256-0407, www.islandpassage-clothing.com), specializing in women's wear; **Ziabird** (Suite 9, 910/208-9650, www.ziabird.com), which carries beautiful jewelry and accessories from local designers; and **Airlie Moon** (1908 Eastwood Rd., 910/256-0655, www.air-liemoon.com), a purveyor of chic coastal home goods.

Mayfaire Town Center (6861 Main St., 910/256-5131, www.mayfairetown.com, 10am-9pm Mon.-Sat., noon-6 Sun.) is a Main Street-meets-the mall shopping center, with a familiar range of shops, but one of my favorites is **Brilliant Sky Toys** (910/509-3353, www.wilmingtontoystores.com), a store packed with toys, games, and puzzles for kids. The 16-screen movie theater, wide selection of shops to browse, and numerous restaurants in Mayfaire make it an easy place to spend part of a day shopping, dining, and taking in a movie, alone or in a group.

Antiques and Consignment Stores
On Castle Street, along the southern edge

of the historic district, an expanding group of antiques shops, restaurants, and stores, all clustered in a three- or four-block stretch, have emerged in recent years. **Michael Moore Antiques** (539 Castle St., 910/763-0300, 10am-6pm Mon.-Sat. 1pm-6pm Sun.) carries a collection of pristine furniture, as do many of the antiques stores in the area. Be sure to stop in **Maggy's Antiques and Collectibles** (507 Castle St., 910/343-5200, 10am-5pm Tues.-Sat., 1pm-5pm Sun.), which occupies an old church building, and **Castle Corner Antiques** (555 Castle St., 910/815-6788, 10am-5pm Mon.-Sat., 1pm-5pm Sun.).

In the riverfront area, **Silk Road Antiques** (103 S. Front St., 910/343-1718, 10:30am-5pm Mon.-Sat., 10:30am-4pm Sun.) and **Antiques of Old Wilmington** (25 S. Front St., 910/763-6011, 10am-6pm daily in summer, 10am-5pm daily in winter) are only a block apart, one block from the Riverwalk, and surrounded by great restaurants and coffee shops.

On Market Street, heading away from downtown, you'll find **Cape Fear Antique Center** (1606 Market St., 910/763-1837, 10am-5:30pm Mon.-Sat., noon-5pm Sun.), an antiques shop that specializes in vintage home furnishings, from bedroom and dining room furniture to desks and armoires. They also have a nice selection of antique jewelry.

A little farther up Market Street, **The Ivy Cottage** (3020, 3030, 3100 Market St., 910/815-0907, www.threecottages.com, 10am-5pm Mon.-Fri., 10am-6pm Sat., 12am-5pm Sun.) occupies a trio of buildings and an overflow warehouse, all filled with antiques and consignment furniture. In Cottage 2, you'll find antique jewelry as well as an extensive collection of crystal stemware and decanters; I found my favorite decanter in Cottage 2. At Cottage 3, you'll find more beachy, shabby-chic furniture and home goods, while Cottage 1 carries more armoires, dressers, and knick-knacks. It's worth a stop to snoop and explore; you never know what you'll find.

Books and Comics

Wilmington has an active and vibrant literary culture. The University of North Carolina Wilmington is home to a creative writing program of growing renown, and the town several good bookstores. **McAllister & Solomon** (4402-1 Wrightsville Ave., 910/350-0189, www.mcallisterandsolomon.com, 10am-6pm Mon.-Sat.) stocks over 20,000 used and rare books and is quite a treat to explore if you're a bibliophile. Nearby, **Pomegranate Books** (4418 Park Ave., 910/452-1107, www.pombooks.net, 10am-6pm Mon.-Sat.) hosts readings by local writers and boasts a good selection of literary work by local and regional authors. **Two Sisters Bookery** (318 Nutt St., Cotton Exchange, 910/762-4444, www.twosistersbookery.com, 10am-5:30pm Mon.-Sat., noon-4pm Sun.) carries books covering all genres and subject matters and is a great place to pick up a best-seller. **Old Books on Front Street** (249 N. Front St., 910/762-6657, www.oldbooksonfrontst.com, 9am-9pm Mon.-Sat., noon-9pm Sun.) is a used bookstore with nearly two miles of books on their floor-to-ceiling shelves. Knowledgeable staff and extensive selection make this a must-stop for book lovers.

Fanboy Comics (419 S. College Rd., University Landing, 910/452-7828, www.fanboycomics.biz, 11am-7pm Mon.-Tues., 10am-9pm Wed., 11am-7pm Thurs.-Sat.) specializes in buying and selling Silver and Bronze Age super-hero comics, a period beginning in the 1950s and ending, at least in terms of Fanboy's stock, around 1977. The owner and staff know their comics and can point out the finer details of this era's stories and art, such as the character development of the heroes and various stylistic innovations. There are also contemporary comics and books about comic-book characters, art, and storytelling.

Galleries and Art Studios

New Elements Art Gallery (201 Princess St., 910/343-8997, www.newelementsgallery.com, 11am-6pm Tues.-Sat.) has been showcasing works by local and regional artists since 1985. Featuring contemporary art in a wide range of styles and media, New Elements remains an influential gallery today, and openings are well attended. With art that includes the avant-garde, classical plein air oil paintings, and wire or ceramic sculptures, they always have something you'll want to take home.

Between Wilmington and Wrightsville is **The Gallery at Racine** (203 Racine Dr., 910/452-2073, www.galleryatracine.com, 11am-5pm Tues.-Fri., 10am-5pm Sat.-Sun.), a huge gallery with works ranging in price from $8 to $150,000 and ranging in style from folk art to fine blown glass. The gallery features only local and regional artists and is an excellent way to get a feel for a broad spectrum of the area's arts scene.

Perhaps the most interesting art studio in Wilmington is **Acme Art Studios** (711 N. 5th Ave., 910/232-0027, www.acme-art-studios.com). This shared space is home to a dozen or more artists working in media such as oils, tintype photography, sculpture, and printmaking. Open to the public only for Wilmington's Fourth Friday Gallery Crawl (910/343-0998, http://artscouncilofwilmington.org, 6pm-9pm fourth Friday of each month) and exhibit openings, the work coming out of Acme is some of the best in the region.

Barouke (119 S. Water St. in the Old City Market, 910/762-4999, www.barouke.com, 10am-6pm Sun.-Thurs., 10am-9pm Fri. and Sat.) carries handcrafted works by master woodworkers, including hand-turned pens and vases, clocks, decorative bowls, boxes, games, kitchen accessories, and more. Most everything is finished in such a way as to allow the wood's natural beauty to show through.

River to Sea Gallery (225 S. Water St., in Chandler's Wharf, 910/763-3380, www.rivertoseagallery.com, 10am-5pm Mon.-Sat., 1pm-4pm Sun.) carries works from around three dozen local artists. You'll find serious art photography and plein air paintings alongside whimsical ceramic and knit pieces and illustrative art.

Music

With the advent of digital music, most of Wilmington's music stores are gone, but

Gravity Records (612 Castle St., 910/343-1000, 9am-6pm Mon.-Sat., noon-6pm Sun.), has held on, carving out a niche for itself by stocking LPs and CDs by the most relevant contemporary artists. If you want to know what to listen to next, the staff at Gravity Records can turn you on to it. They've got a huge stock of vinyl as well as an impressive selection of new and used CDs.

SPORTS AND RECREATION
Masonboro Island

Just a few minutes' boat ride or a 30-minute paddleboard or kayak ride from Wrightsville Beach brings you to Masonboro Island. Masonboro is an 8.5-mile-long undeveloped barrier island that is fantastic for shelling, birding, surfing, and camping. Get here via your own boat, kayak, or paddleboard, or catch a lift with **Wrightsville Beach Scenic Tours** (275 Waynick Blvd., Wrightsville Beach, 910/200-4002, www.wrightsvillebeachscenictours.com, water taxi $20), docking across the street from the Blockade Runner and offering a shuttle to and from the island three times daily Monday-Saturday during summer. The boat leaves Wrightsville Beach at 9am, 12:30pm, and 2pm, and departs Masonboro at 11:30am, 2:30pm, and 5pm. If you go over, you'll be there for a while, so pack a cooler with plenty of water, and remember your sunscreen. Wrightsville Beach Scenic Tours also offers a number of other tours for adults and for families, including birding tours ($35) in and around Masonboro Island, shelling tours, pirate tours ($30 adults, $20 kids), and sunset tours ($25).

In Wilmington you can tour the Cape Fear River with **Wilmington Water Tours** (212 S. Water St., Cape Fear Riverwalk, 910/338-3134, www.wilmingtonwatertours.net, $10-35 adults, $5-16.50 kids). From the comfort of the 46-foot catamaran *Wilmington* you can learn more about the Cape Fear River, its tributaries, and the history of the surrounding land. Bring your binoculars and a zoom lens for your camera because you'll spot ospreys, eagles, and other birds on your trip.

Surfing

East Coast surfers love Wrightsville Beach because the waves are consistent and the surf is fun year-round. If you've never tried hanging 10, join one of the many surf camps in the area and they'll have you in the water and riding a wave in no time. **WB Surf Camp** (222 Causeway Dr., 910/256-7873, www.wbsurfcamp.com, camps from $200-600, more for overnight or travel camps) is one of the largest surfing schools in the area, with a large number of classes, including one-day, week-long, kids-only, teens-only, women-only, and family camps. **Crystal South Surf Camp** (Public Access 39, Wrightsville Beach, 910/465-9638, www.crystalsouthsurfcamp.com) offers individual five-day instruction for all ages ($265).

Kayaking and Stand-Up Paddleboarding

With miles of winding marsh creeks around Masonboro Island and lining the shores of the Intracoastal Waterway, there's no shortage of areas to explore by kayak or stand-up paddleboard. Several outfitters lead tours, provide lessons, and rent out all the gear you'll need to get on the water. **Hook, Line and Paddle** (435 Eastwood Rd., 910/792-6945; 275 Waynick Blvd., 910/685-1983, www.hooklineandpaddle.com, fishing kayaks $50 half day to $155 weekly, single kayaks $40 half day to $130 weekly, double kayaks $60 half day to $160 weekly, tours $45-75, fishing guide $175 for 5 hours) leads group tours around Wrightsville Beach and Masonboro Island and has a variety of kayaks for rent, including fishing kayaks, sit-in and sit-on kayaks, and double kayaks. **Mahanaim Adventures** (910/547-8252, www.mahanaimadventures.com, from $55 for half day and $90 for full day, $150 and up for overnight trips) offers kayak trips on the rivers and in the swamps and creeks inland from the area's beaches. **Town Creek, Three Sisters Swamp,** and **Black River** expeditions are fun and take you into parts of the coastal landscape you'd otherwise never see.

For a different type of paddling experience, try stand-up paddleboarding. Stand-up

© JASON FRYE

Blackwater creeks like Town Creek are great for kayaking.

paddleboards resemble oversize surfboards that you propel with a long paddle, and they can take you anywhere a kayak can go. **Wrightsville SUP** (275 Waynick Blvd., 910/378-9283, www. wrightsvillesup.com, lessons $80 for two hour instructional tour, $20/hour rentals, $15/hour for return customers) rents out paddleboards and provides lessons, as does Hook, Line and Paddle (rentals $60/half day to $160/week). It looks difficult at first, but once you get the hang of it, you'll gain confidence quickly.

Diving

The warm, clear water along North Carolina's coast beckons divers from the world over, and the abundance of shipwrecks, ledges, and natural formations off the coast of Wrightsville Beach make it an ideal location for diving. **Aquatic Safaris** (7220 Wrightsville Ave., Suite A, 910/392-4386, www.aquaticsafaris. com, 9am-7pm Mon.-Fri., 6:30am-6pm Sat., 6:30am-5pm Sun. summer, 10am-6pm Mon.-Fri., 10am-5pm Sat., noon-4pm Sun. off-season, beginner open water classes $295, rental gear $10-50, charters $50-145) has been getting divers in the water since 1988, visiting sites from 3 to 59 miles offshore in water as shallow as 25 feet or as deep as 130 feet. They rent out gear, give classes that will have beginners in open water in as few as three days, and provide charter services to two dozen offshore sites.

Evolve Freediving (910/358-4300, www. evolvefreediving.com, introductory freediving $350) offers an entirely different undersea experience. In free diving, all you have is a mask, fins, a wetsuit, and a deep breath, because you dive without an air tank. Husband and wife duo Ren and Ashley Chapman (she holds multiple world records for free dives, including diving 266 and 269 feet deep on a single breath) teach courses that will have novices holding their breath for more than two minutes and diving up to 66 feet in a couple of days. This is not a sport for the faint of heart, but it is exciting and challenging.

Golf

One of the best things about the Wilmington region is the weather, perfect for both the beach and the golf course. In the winter the weather is mild enough to play anytime, and in the summer the courses are immaculate, and it doesn't get all that hot on the greens. Hit the links at **Beau Rivage** (649 Rivage Promenade, 910/392-9021, www.beaurivagegolf.com, 18 holes, par 72, greens fees $20-60), just south of Wilmington, halfway to Kure Beach; it's a lovely and reasonably priced course with challenging holes. Risk-taking players will enjoy taking shots over water hazards on several holes, including one par 3 that will put your ball in the drink if you don't land it just right.

Echo Farms (4114 Echo Farms Rd., 910/791-9318, www.echofarmsnc.com, 18 holes, par 72, greens fees $19-40), also south of Wilmington, is another fun fast-paced course. The Donald Ross-designed **Wilmington Municipal Golf Course** (311 S. Wallace Ave., 910/791-0558, 18 holes, par 71, greens fees $7-26) features forgiving fairways and on more than one hole raises the classic question "Can I carry that bunker?" North of Wilmington, **Castle Bay** (107 Links Court, 910/270-1978, www.castlebaycc.com, 18 holes, par 72, greens fees $35-39 Mon.-Thurs., $42-48 Fri.-Sun., includes cart) offers a different round of golf. As a Scottish links-style course, it's level, open, and full of deep bunkers, water, and waste areas. The wind can be a factor here, but it's a beautiful course where you can play a round unlike any other in the area.

Spectator Sports

Wilmington has its own professional basketball team, the **Wilmington Sea Dawgs** (910/791-6523, www.goseadawgs.com), part of the Tobacco Road Basketball League. They play downtown in the Schwartz Center at Cape Fear Community College (601 N. Front St.). In baseball, the **Wilmington Sharks** (910/343-5621, www.wilmingtonsharks.com, reserved seats $8 adults, $7 seniors, military, and ages 1-12, general admission $6 adults, $5 seniors, military, and ages 6-12, free under age 6) play in the Coastal Plain League. Home games are played at Legion Sports Complex

(2131 Carolina Beach Rd.). Also playing at the Legion Sports Complex are the **Wilmington Hammerheads** (910/777-2111, www.wilmingtonhammerheads.com, $12 adults, $10 seniors, $8 children), a professional soccer team in the United Soccer Leagues Pro division.

Each summer in early July, rugby teams from around the world descend on Wilmington for the **Cape Fear Sevens Tournament** (http://fear7s.com), a stripped-down, fast-paced form of rugby that showcases the best in speed, tackles, and ball handling, it's a fun, free event that serves to introduce newcomers to the sport and give rugby fans a charge. In the past it has been held at Ogden Park (7069 Market St.), but check the website for the date and location of this two-day tournament.

ACCOMMODATIONS
Bed-and-Breakfasts
Wilmington's Historic District is large and filled with historic bed-and-breakfasts. Check with the **Wilmington and Beaches Convention and Visitors Bureau** (www.wilmingtonandbeaches.com) for a comprehensive listing of area lodging.

◖ **Front Street Inn** (215 S. Front St., 800/336-8184, www.frontstreetinn.com, $139-239) is a tiny boutique B&B only a block from the Riverwalk and a short stroll to a number of notable restaurants and charming shops. It occupies an old Salvation Army building and offers bright, airy guest rooms in a great location. The **Wilmingtonian** (101 S. 2nd St., 800/525-0909, www.thewilmingtonian.com, $155-175) is a three-building complex closer to the heart of downtown offering beautiful guest rooms and locally roasted coffee with breakfast. The **Rosehill Inn Bed and Breakfast** (114 S. 3rd St., 800/815-0250, www.rosehill.com, $139-199) occupies a gorgeous 1848 home only three blocks from the river. The flowery high-B&B-style decor suits the house.

The **Taylor House Inn** (14 N. 7th St., 800/382-9982, www.taylorhousebb.com, $125-250) is in a newer home that dates to 1905. Despite this relative novelty it's a pretty but not ostentatious building, unlike some of the

homes nearby. The famous **Graystone Inn** (100 S. 3rd St., 888/763-4773, www.graystoneinn.com, $159-379) was built in the same year as the Taylor House Inn but with a very different aesthetic. Solid stone and castle-like, the Graystone has beautiful guest rooms in a beautiful home only blocks from good restaurants, shopping, and nightlife. **Angie's B&B** (1704 Market St., 901/762-5790, www.angiesbandb.com, $139-179) is just out of downtown in a more residential but no less charming section of Wilmington. The home and grounds are owned by local restaurateurs, and the breakfast they deliver is out of this world.

Hotels
An upscale place to stay is the **Hilton Wilmington Riverside** (301 N. Water St., 910/763-5900, www.wilmingtonhilton.com, rooms from $169), located right on the river so that many of the guest rooms have stunning river views; others enjoy a beautiful cityscape. The Riverwalk is right out the door, putting the restaurants and nightlife of downtown Wilmington only a short walk away, along with the on-site Ruth's Chris Steakhouse.

At Wrightsville Beach, it's hard to beat the **Blockade Runner** (275 Waynick Blvd., 800/541-1161, www.blockade-runner.com, $169-479). From the outside it looks like any other 1960s hotel, but inside it's chic, stylish, and comfortable. Every guest room has a great view—the Atlantic Ocean and sunrise on one side, the Intracoastal Waterway and sunsets on the other—and with several adventure outfitters operating in the hotel, recreation options abound. The hotel restaurant, East, is a hidden gem in Wilmington's dining scene.

There are plenty of more affordable options available just a couple of miles out of downtown. The **Holiday Inn** (5032 Market St., 866/893-2703, wilmingtonhi.com, $97) on Market Street is clean, comfortable, close to downtown, and minutes from the beach. The **Jameson Inn** (5102 Dunlea Court, 910/452-5660, www.jamesoninns.com, from $77) is another affordable option, although it can be hard to find. From Market Street, turn onto

New Centre Drive and look for the sign across the street from Target.

FOOD
French
For a town of its size, Wilmington has a surprising number of good restaurants. Downtown, **Caprice Bistro** (10 Market St., 910/815-0810, www.capricebistro.com, 5pm-10pm Sun.-Thurs., 5pm-11pm Fri.-Sat., bar until 2am daily, entrées $14-24) serves some delicious traditional French cuisine and has an extensive wine list. Upstairs, an intimate bar lined with sofas and a scattering of tables serves a limited menu but is one of the more relaxed places to grab a quick bite and a drink downtown. This is one of the best restaurants downtown.

Just a few blocks away on the Riverwalk, **Le Catalan French Café** (224 S. Water St., 910/815-0200, www.lecatalan.com, lunch and dinner from 11:30am Tues.-Sat., $5-15) serves small plates of classic French food such as quiches, cassoulet, and a well-known chocolate mousse. As good as the food is at Le Catalan, the location and the view are even better. Situated right on the Riverwalk, their outdoor seating area is the perfect place to enjoy the sunset and a glass of wine.

One of the best restaurants in Wilmington is **Brasserie du Soleil** (1908 Eastwood Rd., 910/256-2226, www.brasseriedusoleil.com, lunch 11:30am-5pm Mon.-Sat., dinner 5pm-10pm Sun.-Thurs., dinner 5pm-11pm Fri.-Sat., entrées $12-32), a brasserie-style French restaurant that utilizes the best ingredients from local, regional, and small-farm sources to create food that will keep you coming back. Personal favorites include the duck and flounder for dinner, and the burgers—three sliders made of either lamb, short ribs, or salmon—or a build-your-own-salad for lunch. For dessert, the mini chocolate pots de crème (served in a shot glass) is the way to go. When the weather's nice, enjoy your meal at one of the outdoor tables.

Italian
Two good Italian restaurants in Wilmington are **Terrazzo Trattoria** (1319 Military Cutoff Rd., 910/509-9400, www.terrazzatrattoria.com, dinner from 5pm Mon. and Sat., lunch and dinner 11:30am-10pm Tues.-Fri., entrées $10-30) and **Osteria Cicchetti** (1125-K Military Cutoff Rd., 910/256-7476, www.osteria-cicchetti.com, lunch 11:30am-4pm Mon.-Fri., dinner from 5pm daily, entrées $11-21). They're both popular and can get crowded even on weeknights, so reservations are recommended, especially in summer. Terrazzo's veal margherita, linguini filleto de pomodoro, or neapolitan pizza are good choices for dinner. At Osteria Cicchetti, or OC as it's known to regulars, the pizzas are rustic and a perfect starter (try the Soprano or the Parma); for pasta, the linguini with clams or spaghetti cicchetti, with meatballs and sausage, make great meals.

Seafood
Near Wrightsville Beach, **Fishhouse Grill** (1410 Airlie Rd., 910/256-3693, www.thefishhousegrill.com, lunch and dinner from 11:30am daily, entrées $6-18) and **Dockside** (1308 Airlie Rd., 910/256-2752, www.thedockside.com, 11am-9pm daily, entrées $7-24), two restaurants only steps apart on the Intracoastal Waterway, deliver good food and great views. At Fishouse, the food is a little more casual, with a menu that focuses on burgers and sandwiches; Dockside focuses more on seafood, and their elevated deck gives you a bird's-eye view of passing boats while you dine.

On Wrightsville Beach proper, **Oceanic** (703 S. Lumina Ave., 910/256-5551, www.oceanicrestaurant.com, 11am-11pm Mon.-Sat., 10am-10pm Sun., entrées $8-32) serves seafood with fine fusion preparations and stunning ocean views. The restaurant is in an old pier house with a good portion of the restored Crystal Pier jutting out into the ocean. Tables on the pier are ideal when the weather is nice, but they go fast, so make a reservation or come early if you want to dine on the deck.

Southern and Barbecue
Downtown at the Cotton Exchange, **The Basics** (319 N. Front St., 910/343-1050, www.thebasicswilmington.com, 8am-9pm

Mon.-Thurs., 8am-10pm Fri., 10am-10pm Sat., 10am-4pm Sun., entrées $10-18) serves up classic Southern comfort food, including lunch, dinner, and Sunday brunch. If breakfast is what you're craving, look no further than the **Dixie Grill** (116 Market St., 910/762-7280, 8am-3pm Mon.-Sat., 8am-2pm Sun., $4-13). This old-fashioned diner is a fixture for locals and visitors alike, and on the weekend there can be a wait; it's worth it. For gussied-up Southern food, head to **Rx** (421 Castle St., 910/399-3080, www.rxwilmington.com, 11:30am-10pm Tues.-Thurs. and Sun., 11:30am-1am Fri.-Sat., entrées around $25). Their cast iron skillet-fried chicken is hard to beat, and their innovative takes on classic Southern dishes will make you look at the region's cuisine in a new light.

What's a visit to North Carolina without barbecue? Fortunately, two great barbecue restaurants near downtown serve up eastern North Carolina 'cue (a style that relies on a thin, spicy, vinegar-based sauce) and all the fixin's, buffet style. **Casey's Buffet Barbecue and Home Cookin'** (5559 Oleander Dr., 910/798-2913, lunch Tues.-Sat., dinner Wed.-Sun., under $10), in Wilmington, delivers a feast of barbecue, Brunswick stew, fried chicken, okra, collard greens, and more. Adventurous non-Southerners will want to try chitterlings (pronounced "CHIT-lins," but you already knew that) and chicken gizzards; Casey's is a rare opportunity to try these Southern and soul food staples. Just across the Cape Fear River in the town of Leland, **◖ Duke's Old South BBQ** (318 Village Rd., Leland, 910/833-8321, www.dukesoldsouthbbq.com, 11am-9pm Wed.-Sat., 11am-3pm Sun., buffet $9) serves both eastern North Carolina and South Carolina (known for a sweeter, often mustard-based sauce) 'cue, fried chicken, and some great 'nanner pudding. Duke's barbecue is some of the best in the area, take it from me: I'm a certified North Carolina barbecue judge.

Eclectic American

Wilmington native Keith Rhodes, a James Beard Award semifinalist and a *Top Chef* contender, owns two restaurants in Wilmington,

both of which serve his "Viet-South" cuisine, a fusion of Vietnamese flavors and Southern ingredients and techniques. **Catch** (6623 Market St., 910/799-3847, www.catchwilmington.com, lunch 11:30am-2pm Tues.-Fri., dinner from 5:30pm Mon.-Sat., entrées around $28), his flagship restaurant, is more formal than **Phun Seafood Bar** (215 Princess St., 910/762-2841, www.phunrestaurant.com, lunch 11:30am-2:30pm Mon.-Fri., dinner 5pm-10pm Wed.-Sat., entrées around $22), but both restaurants use locally caught seafood and other fresh local ingredients. At Catch, you can't go wrong with anything served alongside Rhodes's grits, and at Phun, the duck noodle bowl is a hit.

Down the street from Phun is **Manna** (123 Princess St., 910/763-5252, www.mannaavenue.com, dinner from 5:30pm Tues.-Sun., entrées around $28), an innovative restaurant that also focuses on local seasonal ingredients. Their menu is playful, with dishes like Snapper John MD and Iron Chef: Bobby Filet, but the food is seriously good. One of the few bars in Wilmington where making a cocktail is treated as an art, this is definitely a restaurant where you'll want to show up early and enjoy a drink at the bar. Reservations are advised.

Across the street from Manna, **◖ The Greeks** (124 Princess St., 910/343-6933, www.the-greeks.com, 10am-3pm Mon., 10am-9pm Tues.-Sun., entrées around $9) offers a completely different dining experience: a diner serving classic Greek dishes. The Authentic, a pork gyro loaded with tomato, onion, french fries, and mustard, is a dish the owner grew up eating in Greece and is a popular choice. But if you love falafel, theirs is the best in town, hands down.

One block over, the **Copper Penny** (109 Chestnut St., 910/762-1373, www.copperpennync.com, lunch and dinner from 11am Mon.-Sat., from noon Sun., entrées $10-15) serves traditional pub grub in a traditional pub atmosphere. It can get crowded and loud, especially on game days, but the food, especially their cheesesteak, chicken wings, and fish-and-chips, make any wait worth it.

Circa 1922 (8 N. Front St., 910/762-1922,

www.circa1922.com, 5pm-10pm Sun.-Thurs., 5pm-11pm Fri.-Sat., brunch 10am-3pm Sun., entrées $13-21, 3-course prix fixe $23), an eclectic restaurant serving tapas-style small plates as well as traditional entrées, has a menu driven by seasonal availability. The small plates naturally encourage sharing, making this a great downtown place to grab an intimate meal with friends.

Flaming Amy's Burrito Barn (4002 Oleander Dr., 910/799-2919, www.flamingamysburritobarn.com, 11am-10pm daily) is, in their own words, "Hot, fast, cheap, and easy." They've got a long menu with 20 specialty burritos (Greek, Philly steak, Thai), eight fresh salsas, and bottled and on-tap beers. It's inexpensive—you can eat well for under $10, drinks included. Frequent special promotions include Tattoo Tuesdays: if you show the cashier your tattoo, they discount your meal by 10 percent.

CAM Café (3201 S. 17th St., 910/777-2363, www.camcafe.org, 11am-3pm Tues.-Sat., dinner 5pm-9pm Thurs., lunch $12 and under, dinner around $15) is one of the best spots in town for lunch. Housed inside the Cameron Art Museum, the CAM Café offers an upscale lunch that features everything from fish tacos to vegetarian and even vegan options. The menu, which changes frequently, is often inspired by the art museum's current special exhibits.

Asian

Where Catch and Phun take Asian cuisine and blend it with Southern food culture, a number of Asian restaurants in Wilmington stay true to their roots. **Indochine** (7 Wayne Dr., at Market St., 910/251-9229, www.indochinewilmington.com, lunch 11am-2pm Tues.-Fri., noon-3pm Sat., dinner 5pm-10pm daily, entrées $11-20) serves an expansive menu of Thai and Vietnamese dishes as well as a number of vegetarian options. Entrées are huge, so sharing is encouraged, but even then, be prepared for leftovers. **Big Thai 2** (1319 Military Cutoff Rd., 910/256-6588, www.bigthaiwilmington.com, lunch 11am-2:30pm Mon.-Sat., dinner 5pm-9:30pm Mon.-Thurs., 5pm-10pm Fri.-Sat., noon-9:30pm Sun., entrées around $14) has delicious and authentic pad thai and massaman curry, and their coconut cake is a great way to end the meal.

Blue Asia (341 S. College Rd., 910/799-0002, www.blueasia.info, 11am-10pm Mon.-Wed., 11am-10:30pm Thurs.-Sat., noon-10pm Sun., entrées around $15) serves pan-Asian cuisine but focuses primarily on Japanese and Chinese dishes. Sushi lovers will appreciate the all-you-can-eat sushi lunch and dinner.

Nikki's Restaurant and Sushi Bar (16 S. Front St., 910/772-9151, www.nikkissushibar.com, 11am-10pm Mon.-Thurs., 11am-11pm Fri. and Sat., noon-10pm Sun., $5-25) is a longtime downtown Wilmington favorite. Serving up sushi, a wide selection of vegetarian dishes, bento boxes and other Asian-inspired plates, Nikki's has built a reputation for good food and cold sake.

NORTH OF WILMINGTON
Topsail Island

If you want to say it like a local, Topsail is pronounced "TOP-sel," so called because legend has it that pirates once hid behind the island and only their topsails were visible to passing ships. There are three towns on Topsail Island—Topsail Beach, North Topsail Beach, and Surf City. All are popular beach destinations and are less commercial than many beach communities but still have enough beach shops and souvenir shacks to keep that beach town charm. A swing bridge spans the Intracoastal Waterway at Surf City, and it opens on the hour for passing ships (expect traffic backups when it opens). At the north end of the island, a tall bridge between Sneads Ferry and North Topsail Beach eliminates the traffic backups from passing ships and provides an unheralded view of the 26-mile-long island and the marshes around it.

Among Topsail's claims to fame is its importance in the conservation of sea turtles. The **Karen Beasley Sea Turtle Rescue and Rehabilitation Center** (822 Carolina Ave., Topsail Beach, www.seaturtlehospital.org, visiting hours 2pm-4pm Mon.-Tues. and Thurs.-Sat. June-Aug.) treats sea turtles that have been injured by sharks or boats, or that have fallen ill or become stranded. Its 24 enormous tubs, which look something like the vats at a brewery, provide safe places for the animals to recover from their injuries and recoup their strength before being released back into the ocean. Hospital staff also patrol the full shoreline of Topsail Island every morning in the summertime, before the crowds arrive, to identify and protect any new clutches of eggs that were laid overnight. Founder Jean Beasley has been featured as a Hero of the Year on the Animal Planet TV channel. Unlike most wildlife rehabilitation centers, this hospital allows visitors.

Topsail has an interesting history of naval warfare, starting with pirates—Blackbeard was known to haunt these waters—through World War II, when the island was a proving ground for Navy missiles. The **Missiles and More Museum** (720 Channel Blvd., 910/328-8663, www.missilesandmoremuseum.org, 2-4pm Mon.-Fri. in Apr., May, Sept., and Oct., 2pm-4pm Mon.-Sat. from the second week of May-first week of Sept., free, donations accepted) commemorates the island's naval history, paying special attention to Operation Bumblebee. Operation Bumblebee led to major advancements in missile technology and the development of jet engines, which were later used in supersonic jet design. The fascinating exhibits include real warheads left over from the tests, including one that washed up on the beach 50 years after it was fired. A rare color film from a 1940s missile test over the island gives visitors a strange look back in this island's history.

One of the best places to eat on the island is the **Beach Shop and Grill** (701 S. Anderson Blvd, 910/328-6501, www.beachshopandgrill.com, 8am-9pm Thurs.-Sat., 8am-2pm Sun., entrées around $22), an island fixture since 1952 when it served burgers and hot dogs as Warren's Soda Shop. Now it serves sophisticated cuisine that plays with local ingredients and Southern food traditions, with some great dishes for breakfast, lunch, and dinner.

Jacksonville

Jacksonville is best known as the home of **Camp Lejeune,** a massive Marine Corps installation that dates to 1941. Lejeune is the home base of the II Marine Expeditionary Force and MARSOC, the Marine Corps division of U.S. Special Operations Command. The base's nearly 250 square miles include extensive beaches where service members receive training in amphibious assault skills.

Camp Johnson, a satellite installation of Camp Lejeune, used to be known as Montford Point and was the home of the famous African American Montford Point Marines, the first African Americans to serve in the United States Marine Corps. Their history, a crucial chapter in the integration of the U.S. Armed Forces, is paid tribute at the **Montford Point Marine Museum** (Bldg. 101, East Wing, Camp Gilbert Johnson, 910/450-1340, www.montfordpointmarines.com, 11am-2pm and 4pm-7pm Tues. and Thurs., 11am-4pm Sat., free, donations accepted).

Hammocks Beach State Park

At the appealing little fishing town of Swansboro you'll find the mainland side of **Hammocks Beach State Park** (1572 Hammocks Beach Rd., 910/326-4881, http://ncparks.gov, 8am-6pm daily Sept.-May, 8am-7pm daily June-Aug.). Most of the park lies on the other side of a maze of marshes on Bear and Huggins Islands. These wild, totally undeveloped islands are important havens for migratory waterfowl and nesting loggerhead sea turtles. Bear Island is 3.5 miles long and less than 1 mile wide, surrounded by the Atlantic Ocean, Intracoastal Waterway, Bogue and Bear Inlets, and wild salt marshes. Much of the island is covered by sandy beaches and dunes. A great place to swim, Bear Island has a bathhouse complex with a snack bar, restrooms, and outdoor showers. Huggins Island, by contrast, is significantly smaller and covered in ecologically significant maritime forest and lowland marshes. Two paddle trails, one just over 2.5 miles long and the other 6 miles long, weave through the marshes that surround the islands.

Camping is permitted on Bear Island in reserved and first-come, first-served sites near the beach and inlet, with restrooms and showers available nearby ($13/day).

A private boat or **passenger ferry** (910/326-4881, http://ncparks.gov, $5 adults, $3 seniors and children) are the only ways to reach the islands. The ferry's schedule varies by the day of the week and the season, but generally departs from the mainland and the islands every 30 to 60 minutes from midmorning until late afternoon; ferries don't run every day in the off-season. Check the website for current ferry times.

GETTING THERE AND AROUND

Wilmington is the eastern terminus of I-40, more than 300 miles east of Asheville and approximately 120 miles south and east of Raleigh. The Cape Fear region is also crossed by a major north-south route, U.S. 17, the old Kings Highway of colonial times. Wilmington is roughly equidistant along U.S. 17 between

Jacksonville to the north and Myrtle Beach, South Carolina, to the south; both cities are about an hour's drive.

Wilmington International Airport (ILM, 1740 Airport Blvd., Wilmington, 910/341-4125, www.flyilm.com) serves the region with flights to and from East Coast cities. For a wider selection of routes, it may be worthwhile to consider flying into Myrtle Beach or Raleigh and renting a car. Driving to Wilmington from the Myrtle Beach airport, add another 30 to 60 minutes to get through Myrtle Beach traffic, particularly in summer, as the airport is on the southern edge of town. Driving from Raleigh-Durham International Airport takes at least 2.25 hours. There is no passenger train service to Wilmington.

Wave Transit (910/343-0106, www.wavetransit.com), Wilmington's public transportation system, operates buses throughout the metropolitan area and trolleys in the historic district. Fares are a low $2 one-way. If you're planning on exploring outside the city, you'll need a car.

The Southern Coast

From the beaches of Brunswick and New Hanover County to the swampy subtropical fringes of land behind the dunes, this little corner of the state is special, one of the most beautiful parts of North Carolina. Extending south from Wrightsville Beach, a series of barrier islands and quiet low-key beaches stretches to the South Carolina border. Starting with Pleasure Island, which comprises Kure and Carolina Beach, and ending with the Brunswick Island, including Oak Island, Holden Beach, Sunset Beach, and Ocean Isle, these beaches are family-friendly places where you're more likely to find rental homes than high-rise hotels.

You'll see some distinctive wildlife here, including the ubiquitous green anole, called "chameleons" by many locals. These tiny lizards, normally bright lime green, are able to

fade to brown. They're everywhere—skittering up porch columns and along balcony railings, peering around corners, and hiding in the fronds of palmetto trees. The males put on a big show by puffing out their strawberry-colored dewlaps. Generations of Lowcountry children have spent thousands of hours trying to catch them, usually with next to no success. If you catch them from the front, they'll bite (albeit harmlessly), and if you catch them from behind, they'll ditch their writhing tails while the rest of them keeps running. From a respectful distance, they're amusing companions on your outdoor sojourns in this region.

This is also the part of the state where you'll find the largest population of alligators. Unlike their tiny cousins, the anoles, which threaten but can't back it up, alligators have the potential to be deadly. All along river and creek banks and in bays and swamps, you'll see their scaly hulks basking in the sun. If you're in a kayak, a canoe, or on a paddleboard, you may mistake them for a log until you see their eyes and nostrils poking out of the water. Be careful and be aware of where you, children, and pets step when hiking, and avoid swimming in fresh water in places where alligators are prone to lurk. All that said, alligators are thrilling to see and generally will vacate the area if you come too close.

If you're in the area during the early part of summer, you could see a sea turtle dragging herself into the dunes to lay a clutch of eggs. Huge loggerhead sea turtles, tiny Kemp's ridley sea turtles, greens, and even the occasional leatherback make their nests along the beaches here. Nesting season runs from mid-May through August, although August nestings are rare, and they hatch between 60 and 90 days later, depending on the species. Organizations such as the **Bald Head Island Conservancy** (700 Federal Rd., Bald Head Island, 910/457-0089, www.bhic.org) on Bald Head Island help protect nests and educate area residents and visitors on issues relevant to protecting sea turtles.

In certain highly specialized environments, mainly in and around Carolina bays, which have both moistness and nutrient-poor soil, the Venus flytrap and other carnivorous plants thrive. The flytrap and some of its cousins are endangered, but in this region—and nowhere else in the world—you'll have plenty of opportunities to see them growing wild.

KURE BEACH

Kure is a two-syllable name, pronounced "KYUR-ee" like the physicist Marie Curie, not like "curry." This is a small beach community without the neon lights and towel shops of larger beaches. Most of the buildings on the island are houses, both rentals for vacationers and the homes of Kure Beach's year-round residents, although a few motels and hotels are scattered through the community. The beach itself, like all North Carolina ocean beaches, is public.

Carolina Beach State Park

Just to the north of Kure is **Carolina Beach State Park** (1010 State Park Rd., off U.S. 421, Carolina Beach, 910/458-8206, http://ncparks.gov, grounds 8am-5pm daily, facility hours vary). Of all the state parks in the coastal region, this may be the one with the greatest ecological diversity. Within its boundaries are coastal pine and oak forests, pocosins between the dunes, saltwater marshes, a 50-foot sand dune known as Sugarloaf Dune, and limesink ponds. Of the limesink ponds, one is a deep cypress swamp, one is a natural garden of water lilies, and one is an ephemeral pond that dries into a swampy field every year, an ideal home for carnivorous plants. You'll see Venus flytraps and their ferocious cousins, but resist the urge to dig them up, pick them, or tempt them with your fingertips. Sort of like stinging insects that die after delivering their payload, the flytraps' traps can wither and fall off once they're sprung.

The park has 83 drive-in and walk-in campsites (year-round except Dec. 24-25, $20, $15 over age 62), each with a grill and a picnic table. Two are wheelchair-accessible, and restrooms and hot showers are nearby.

Fort Fisher State Park

At the southern end of Kure Beach is **Fort Fisher State Park** (1000 Loggerhead Rd., off U.S. 421, 910/458-5798, http://ncparks.gov, 8am-9pm daily June-Aug., 8am-8pm daily Mar.-May and Sept.-Oct., 8am-6pm daily Nov.-Feb.), with six miles of beautiful beach; it's a less crowded and less commercial alternative to the other beaches of the area. A lifeguard is on duty 10am-5:45pm daily late May-early Sept. The park also includes a 1.1-mile hiking trail that winds through marshes and along the sound, ending at an observation deck where visitors can watch wildlife.

Fort Fisher is also a significant historic site, a Civil War earthwork stronghold designed to withstand massive assault. Modeled in part on the Crimean War's Malakhoff Tower, Fort Fisher's construction was an epic saga as hundreds of Confederate soldiers, enslaved

© JASON FRYE

Flip flops pile up like sand dunes at the beach.

African Americans, and conscripted indigenous Lumbee people were brought here to build what became the Confederacy's largest fort. After the fall of Norfolk in 1862, Wilmington became the most important open port in the South, a vital harbor for blockade-runners and military vessels. Fort Fisher held until nearly the end of the war. On December 24, 1864, U.S. General Benjamin "The Beast" Butler attacked the fort with 1,000 troops but was repulsed; his retreat led to him being relieved of his command. A few weeks later, in January 1865, Fort Fisher was finally taken, but it required a Union force of 9,000 troops and 56 ships in what was the largest amphibious assault by Americans until World War II. Without its defenses at Fort Fisher, Wilmington soon fell, hastening the end of the war, which came just three months later. Due to the final assault by the Union forces and 150 years of wind, tides, and hurricanes, not much of the massive earthworks survive, but the remains of this vital Civil War site are preserved in an oddly peaceful and pretty seaside

park that contains a restored gun emplacement and a visitors center with interpretive exhibits.

The **North Carolina Aquarium at Fort Fisher** (900 Loggerhead Rd., 910/458-8257, www.ncaquariums.com, 9am-5pm daily year-round except Thanksgiving, Dec. 24, and Jan. 1, $8 adults, $7 seniors, $6 ages 3-12) is one of three aquariums operated by the state; this is a beautiful facility that shows all manner of marinelife native to North Carolina waters. The aquarium follows the path of the Cape Fear River from its headwaters to the ocean. Along the way you'll meet Luna, an albino alligator; have the opportunity to touch horseshoe crabs, sea stars, and even bamboo sharks; and see a variety of sharks, fish, eels, and rays in a two-story 235,000-gallon aquarium. Dive shows and daily feedings complement the exhibits. It's hard to miss the Megalodon exhibit, dedicated to the huge prehistoric shark—it was bigger than a school bus—with teeth the size of dinner plates and a jaw eight feet across. Fortunately, all that remains are fossil relics of this two-million-year-old animal, many of which are found at dive sites nearby in less than 100 feet of water. Pose for a picture behind the massive set of jaws as proof of the ultimate fish story.

Accommodations

The beaches of the Carolinas used to be lined with boardinghouses, the old-time choice in lodging for generations. They were a precursor to today's bed-and-breakfasts, cozy family homes where visitors dined together with the hosts and were treated like houseguests. Hurricane Hazel razed countless boardinghouses when it pummeled the coast in 1954, ushering in the epoch of the family motel. The **Beacon House** (715 Carolina Beach Ave. N., 877/232-2666, www.beaconhouseinnb-b.com, some pets allowed in cottages, $139 summer) at Carolina Beach, just north of Kure, is a rare survivor. The early-1950s boardinghouse has the typical upstairs and downstairs porches and dark wood paneling indoors, along with nearby cottages. You'll be treated to a lodging experience from a long-gone era.

Food

Seafood is a staple all along Kure and Carolina Beaches. **Shuckin' Shack Oyster Bar** (6a N. Lake Park Blvd., 910/458-7380, www.pleasureislandoysterbar.com, 11am-2am Mon.-Sat., noon-2am Sun., entrées from $10) is a friendly oyster bar that serves fresh seafood, including oysters by the bucket. You can shuck your own (don't be ashamed to ask for a tutorial if you've never used a shucking knife) or enjoy oysters on the half shell, but we recommend shucking your own and enjoying a steamed oyster on a saltine cracker with a dash of hot sauce. **Ocean Grill and Tiki Bar** (1211 S. Lake Park Blvd., 910/458-2000, www.oceangrilltiki.com, 5pm-9pm Mon.-Thurs., 11am-9pm Fri.-Sun., entrées $10-24) serves fried, grilled, and steamed seafood and has great views from the dining room and outdoor tiki bar, where you can hear live music on weekends throughout the summer. **Freddie's Restaurant** (111 K Ave., Kure Beach, 910/458-5979, www.freddiesrestaurant.com, from 5pm daily, entrées $12-25) in Kure

Beach has a big menu and serves even bigger portions. With seafood, pasta, and a good specialty pork chop menu, it's not hard to find something to eat. Watch the tables around you for guidance about whether you want individual entrées or to share. **Pop's Diner** (104 N. Lake Park Blvd., 910/458-7377, 11am-10pm Sun.-Thurs., 11am-3am Fri. and Sat., $1-10) serves classic diner food in a 1950s-style diner. With checkerboard tiles, a stainless steel front, and red vinyl booths, they help keep a piece of the golden age of beach towns alive. If you're lucky, you may see the owner in one of his Elvis Presley jumpsuits.

After dinner, stop by **Britt's Donuts** (11 Boardwalk), a Carolina Beach institution since 1939. They use a secret recipe for their doughnut batter, and they come out salty, sweet, airy, crispy, and perfect. Pull up a seat at the bar and order half a dozen to enjoy.

◖ SOUTHPORT

Without a doubt, Southport is one of North Carolina's most picturesque coastal towns. The Cape Fear River, Intracoastal Waterway, and Atlantic Ocean meet here, and the water is almost always crowded with watercraft of all sizes and shapes: sailboats, shrimpers, anglers out for the day, huge cargo ships headed upriver to Wilmington, yachts, kayaks, and deep sea fishing boats. The town's history is rooted in the water, and there are still several multigenerational fishing and shrimping families around. River pilots who know the shoals and tides like no one else operate out of Southport, heading offshore in speedy boats to the container ships and tankers making their way to Wilmington; they help navigate the cumbersome ships through the currents and the channel and guide them safely to the port and back out to sea, just as people from local families have for 200-plus years. Throughout the town, historic buildings, including Fort Johnson, a British fort built in 1745, line the oak-shaded streets. The Old Smithville Burying Ground, a community cemetery dating to before the founding of the town, is a beautiful spot, and many of the headstones are inscribed with epitaphs for sea captains and their widows. Stop in at the **Fort Johnston-Southport Museum and Visitors Center** (203 E. Bay St., 910/457-7927, 10am-4pm Mon.-Sat., 1pm-4pm Sun., free) for more information on the town, although Southport is small enough to explore and discover on your own. While you're at the visitors center, ask about the history of four of the town's street names: Lord, Howe, Dry, and I Am.

Sights

The **North Carolina Maritime Museum at Southport** (204 E. Moore St., 910/457-0003, www.ncmaritimemuseums.com, 9am-5pm Tues.-Sat., free) tells the story of Southport as a maritime town in some detail. The pirate Blackbeard and his compatriot Stede Bonnet prowled these waters, and Stede Bonnet was captured on the river about a mile from the museum, then sent to Charleston, where he was hanged for his crimes. The museum sheds some light on their exploits. Other displays include a 2,000-year-old Native American canoe fragment, information on the blockade of the river during the Civil War, and many artifacts brought up from nearby shipwrecks.

Given the beauty of the town and its proximity to Wilmington, it's no surprise that Southport has been the star, location-wise, of several television shows and films. *Safe Haven,* an adaptation of North Carolina literary son Nicholas Sparks's novel of the same name, takes place here; one reviewer called the movie "an extended infomercial for the lulling charms of Southport." Since the movie's 2012 debut, a steady stream of fans has been touring its locations. **Southport Tours** (910/750-1951, $10) and **Southport Fun Tours** (608/334-0619, www.southportfuntours.com, $10 adults, $5 seniors and under age 12) both offer film and town-history tours.

Festivals

Southport has its share of fairs and festivals throughout the year, but they all pale in comparison to the **North Carolina 4th of July Festival** (800/457-6964, www.nc4thofjuly. com), the official Independence day celebration

for the state. Some 50,000 people attend the parade, the festival park and street fair, and the fireworks in the evening. Launched from a barge on the river, the fireworks are a special treat as they reflect on the water. Perhaps the most moving of the events is the naturalization ceremony for new Americans as they declare their loyalty and enjoy their first 4th of July celebration.

Golf

In the vicinity of Southport, golfers will find several courses that are both challenging and beautiful. On Oak Island, the **Oak Island Golf Club's** (928 Caswell Beach Rd., Oak Island, 800/278-5275, www.oakislandgolf. com, 18 holes, par 72, greens fees from $45) is a 6,720-yard George Cobb-designed course that provides the serenity of a golf course with occasional ocean views and ocean breezes. In Boiling Spring Lakes, you can walk or ride **The Lakes Country Club** (591 S. Shore Dr., Boiling Spring Lakes, 910/845-2625, www.thelakes-countryclub.com, 18 holes, par 72, greens fees from $25), the oldest golf course in Brunswick County.

Shopping

There are a number of cute boutiques, antiques stores, and kid's shops in Southport, but our favorites are **Ocean Outfitters** (121 E. Moore St., 910/457-0433, www.oceanoutfitters.com, 10am-5:30pm Mon.-Fri., 10am-6pm Sat., 11am-4pm Sun. summer, 10am-5pm Mon.-Sat., 11am-4pm Sun. winter), a sportswear outfitter that carries clothing perfect for the local climate, and **Cat on a Whisk** (600-C N. Howe St., 910/454-4451, www.catonawhisk.com, 10am-5pm Mon.-Sat.), a kitchen store with knowledgeable staff, a fantastic selection of gadgets and cookware, and a friendly cat or two.

Accommodations

Lois Jane's Riverview Inn (106 W. Bay St., 910/457-6701, www.loisjanes.com, $120-180) is a Victorian waterfront home built by the innkeeper's grandfather. The guest rooms are comfortably furnished, bright and not froufrou; the Queen Deluxe Street, a cottage behind the inn, has its own kitchen and separate entrance. The front porch of the inn has a wonderful view of the harbor. At the same location the **Riverside Motel** (106 W. Bay St., 910/457-6986, $85-105) has a front porch with a fantastic panorama of the shipping channel. Another affordable option is the **Inn at River Oaks** (512 N. Howe St., 910/457-1100, www.theinnatriveroaks.com, $80-110, lower off-season), a motel-style inn with very simple suites.

At Oak Island, west of Southport, **Captain's Cove Motel** (6401 E. Oak Island Dr., Oak Island, 910/278-6026, www.captainscovemotel.net, $90) is a long-established family motel one block from the beach. The **Island Resort and Inn** (500 Ocean Dr., Oak Island, 910/278-5644, www.islandresortandinn.com, $132-220) is a beachfront property with standard motel rooms and one- and two-bedroom apartment suites. The **Ocean Crest Motel** (1417 E. Beach Dr., Oak Island, 910/278-3333, www.ocean-crest-motel.com, $105-330) is a large condo-style motel, also right on the beach.

One unusual bed-and-breakfast is the **Frying Pan Shoals Light Tower** (offshore, 704/907-0399, www.fptower.com, $300-500). Located some 30 miles offshore at the end of Frying Pan Shoals, this former light tower (think of a lighthouse on an oil derrick) has been converted to a bed-and-breakfast that caters to the adventurous set. You have to take a boat or a helicopter from Southport to reach the B&B, which can be booked when you book your room. The restoration project at Frying Pan Shoals is vast and ongoing, and often the owners will have "working getaways" when guests will pitch in to repair, restore, or reopen some part of the structure. Naturally, every guest room has water views, and deep-sea fishing and diving opportunities are literally right under your feet; the tower stands in 50 feet of water.

Food

For a town this size, Southport has a surprising number of good restaurants. I love to dine on the water at **Yacht Basin Provision Company** (130 Yacht Basin Dr., 910/457-0654, 11am-9pm daily, entrées around $10), shortened to "Provision Company" by locals, to enjoy a plate

WILMINGTON AND CAPE FEAR

© JASON FRYE

Yacht Basin Provision Company in Southport

of peel-and-eat shrimp or a grouper sandwich. **Frying Pan** (319 W. Bay St., 910/363-4382, 4pm-10pm daily, entrées around $18) is a restaurant that serves fried seafood and local delicacies from a dining room elevated 18 feet off the ground, offering commanding water views. Both restaurants get very crowded in summer, with two-hour waits at Provision for lunch around July 4; you can wait for your table at **Old American Fish Factory** (150 Yacht Basin Dr., 910/457-9870, www.oldamericanfish.com), an open-air bar featured in *Safe Haven* and other film and TV shot in Southport. The views are incredible as the deck extends out over the water. During the highest tides, your feet can get wet. Try not to drop anything; it may fall through the cracks in the deck into the river below.

Moore Street Market (130 E. Moore St., 910/363-4208, 7am-4pm daily, $1-10), a small coffee shop and deli, makes a good lunch and serves the best cup of coffee in town. Its central location is steps from antiques shops and historic sites in Southport. Dinner is always good at **Ports of Call Bistro and Market** (116 N. Howe St., 910/457-4544, www.portsofcall-bistro.com, lunch 11:30am-2pm Tues.-Sat., dinner 5pm-9pm Tues.-Sat., brunch 10am-2pm Sun., entrées $17-33), a Mediterranean-inspired restaurant serving both tapas and entrée-size portions. Their menu changes seasonally and always features local seafood.

BALD HEAD ISLAND

Two miles off the coast of Southport is Bald Head Island. From the mainland you can see the most prominent feature, Old Baldy, the oldest lighthouse in North Carolina, standing tall above the trees. Accessible only by a 20-minute ferry ride or private boat, the island is limited to golf carts, bicycles, and pedestrians; the only larger vehicles are emergency services and those for deliveries or construction. Combined with the largest intact section of maritime forest in North Carolina, Bald Head Island seems like it's a world away.

Sights

Old Baldy was commissioned by Thomas Jefferson and built in 1817. You can climb to

early morning on Bald Head Island

© JASON FRYE

the top of the 109-foot lighthouse with admission to the **Smith Island Museum** (101 Lighthouse Wynd, 910/457-7481 www.old-baldy.org, 10am-4pm Tues.-Sat., 11am-4pm Sun., $5 adults, $3 ages 3-12). The museum, housed in the former lighthouse keeper's cottage, tells the story of Old Baldy and the other lighthouses that have stood on the island. The **Old Baldy Foundation** (910/457-5003, tours 10am Mon.-Sat., $57, $47 under 12, price includes ferry passage to and from Bald Head Island) also conducts historic tours that reveal the long and surprising history of the island.

Sports and Recreation

There are 14 miles of beaches to explore on Bald Head Island, several hundred acres of maritime forest with marked trails, miles of creeks that wind through the marsh behind the island, and ample opportunities to explore with one of the island's outfitters. **Riverside Adventure Company** (910/457-4944, www.riversideadventure.webly.com, rentals from $45, tours from $55) conducts guided kayak tours,

nature hikes, sailing cruises, and surfing lessons from their storefront on the harbor. Riverside also runs other tours such as ghost walks and kids camps through the summer. If you want to try stand-up paddleboarding on the marsh or ocean, **Coastal Urge** (12B Maritime Way, 800/383-4443, www.rentals.coastalurge.com) supplies all the gear and lessons you need to get on the water.

The **Bald Head Island Conservancy** (700 Federal Rd., 910/457-0089, www.bhic.org, tours around $50 for off-island guests and $20 for on island guests, off-island ticket includes round trip ferry fare, dates and times vary, call or check the website for weekly schedule), a group dedicated to preserving the flora and fauna of the island, leads kayak tours, birding walks, kids camps, and, in the summer, turtle walks, giving Conservancy members (you can join while you're here) the chance to see a sea turtle make her nest.

Accommodations

Most of the houses on Bald Head Island are rental homes, ranging from one-bedroom

© JASON FRYE

kayaking Bald Head Island's marsh creeks

WILMINGTON AND CAPE FEAR

cottages to massive beachside homes ideal for family reunions. Rentals are available through Bald Head Island Limited (www.baldheadisland.com) and Tiffany's Rentals (www.tiffanysrentals.com); rates range from $2,000 to $12,000 per week. One bed-and-breakfast, **The Marsh Harbour Inn** (21 Keelson Row, 910/454-0451, www.marshharbourinn.com, $275-575), operates here. With beautiful harbor and marsh views, free use of golf carts for guests, and membership privileges to the private Bald Head Island Club, this is a great option for visitors not in a large group.

Food

There are only a few places to eat on the island, but fortunately they're good. In the harbor, **Delphina Family Eatery and Pub** (10 Marina Wynd, 910/457-1222, www.delphinacantina.webs.com, 11am-11pm daily, $6-15) and **Sandpiper Sweets and Ice Cream** (located inside Delphina at 10 Maritime Wynd, 7am-4:30pm Sun.-Thurs., 7am-9:30pm Fri.-Sat., under $10) are great options for families. **Mojo's on the Harbour** (16 Marina Wynd, 910/457-7217, www.mojosontheharbour.com, 11:30am-9pm Sun.-Tues., 11:30am-10pm Wed.-Thurs., 11:30am-11pm Fri.-Sat., $13-32) has harbor-side dining with beautiful sunset views.

The **Maritime Market Café** (8 Maritime Way, 910/457-7450, www.maritimemarketbhi.com, breakfast 8am-10:30am daily, lunch 11am-3pm daily), attached to a full-service grocery store, serves breakfast and lunch that includes standard options and daily specials.

OCEAN ISLE

Ocean Isle is the next-to-most-southerly beach in North Carolina, separated from South Carolina only by Bird Island and the town of Calabash. In October, Ocean Isle is the site of the **North Carolina Oyster Festival** (www.ncoysterfestival.com), a huge event that's been happening for nearly 30 years. In addition to an oyster stew cook-off, a surfing competition, and entertainment, this event features the North Carolina Oyster Shucking Competition. Oyster shucking is not as picayune a skill as it might sound. In the not-that-long-ago days when North Carolina's seafood industry was ascendant, workers—most often African American women—lined up on either side of long work tables in countless oyster houses along the coast and the creeks, opening and cutting out thousands of oysters a day. A complex occupational culture was at work in those factories, with its own vocabulary, stories, and songs. The speed at which these women worked was a source of collective and individual pride, and the fastest shuckers enjoyed quite a bit of prestige among their colleagues. High-speed shucking is a skill that's well remembered by many Carolinians who might now be working at Wal-Mart rather than in the old dockside shacks and warehouses.

SOUTH ALONG U.S. 17

U.S. 17 is an old colonial road; its original name, still used in some places, is the King's Highway. George Washington passed this way on his 1791 Southern tour, staying with the prominent planters in the area and leaving in his wake the proverbial legends about where he lay his head of an evening. Today, the King's Highway, following roughly its original course, is still the main thoroughfare through Brunswick County into South Carolina.

Brunswick Town and Fort Anderson

Near Orton is the **Brunswick Town-Fort Anderson State Historic Site** (8884 St. Philip's Rd. SE, Winnabow, 910/371-6613, www.nchistoricsites.org, 9am-5pm Tues.-Sat., free, donations accepted), the site of what was a bustling little port town in the early and mid-1700s. In its brief life, Brunswick saw quite a bit of action. It was attacked in 1748 by a Spanish ship that, to residents' delight, blew up in the river. One of that ship's cannons was dragged out of the river and is on display. In 1765 the town's refusal to observe royal tax stamps was a successful precursor to the Boston

Tea Party eight years later. But by the end of the Revolutionary War, Brunswick Town was gone, burned by the British but also made obsolete by the growth of Wilmington.

Today, nothing remains of the colonial port except the lovely ruins of the 1754 **St. Philip's Anglican Church** and some building foundations uncovered by archaeologists. During the Civil War, Fort Anderson was built on this site; some of its walls also survive. It was a series of sand earthworks that were part of the crucial defenses of the Cape Fear, protecting the blockade-runners who came and went from Wilmington. A visitors center at the historic site tells the story of this significant stretch of riverbank, and the grounds, with the town's foundations exposed and interpreted, are an intriguing vestige of a forgotten community.

Perhaps the most interesting artifact on display at the visitors center at Brunswick Town is the Fort Anderson battle flag that Confederate soldiers flew over the fort during their final battle. Once the fort fell, the flag was captured by a regiment from Illinois, who gave it to their commander, who gave it to the Illinois governor, who gave it to Abraham Lincoln in a ceremony at the National Hotel, the same National Hotel where John Wilkes Booth lived, that was reportedly witnessed by Booth. A number of Civil War and Lincoln scholars believe that this moment, when Lincoln received the battle flag, was when Booth's plan changed from kidnapping to assassinating the President.

Nature Preserves

The Nature Conservancy's **Green Swamp Preserve** (Hwy. 211, 5.5 miles north of Supply, regional office 910/395-5000, www.nature.org) contains more than 17,000 acres of some of North Carolina's most precious coastal ecosystems, the longleaf pine savanna and evergreen shrub pocosin. Hiking is allowed in the preserve, but the paths are primitive. It's important to stay on the trails and not dive into the wilds because this is an intensely fragile ecosystem. In this preserve are communities of rare carnivorous plants, including the monstrous little pink-mawed Venus flytrap, four kinds of pitcher plant, and sticky-fingered sundew. It's also a habitat for the rare red-cockaded woodpecker, which is partial to diseased old-growth longleaf pines as a place to call home.

The Nature Conservancy maintains another nature preserve nearby, the **Boiling Spring Lakes Preserve** (Hwy. 87, Boiling Spring Lakes, regional office 910/395-5000, www.nature.org), with a trail that begins at the Community Center. Brunswick County contains the state's greatest concentration of rare plant species and the most diverse plant communities anywhere on the East Coast north of Florida. This preserve is owned by the Plant Conservation Program and includes over half the acreage of the town of Boiling Spring Lakes. The ecosystem is made up of Carolina bays, pocosins, and longleaf pine forests. Like the Green Swamp Preserve, many of the species are dependent on periodic fires in order to propagate and survive. The Nature Conservancy does controlled burns at both sites to maintain this rare habitat.

The University of North Carolina Wilmington maintains a 174-acre nature preserve in Brunswick County, the **Ev-Henwood Nature Preserve** (6150 Rock Crek Road NE, near Town Creek, www.uncw.edu, dawn-dusk daily). Ev-Henwood (pronounced like "heaven wood" without the initial "h") is named after the surnames of the former owner's grandparents: Evans and Henry. The property had been owned by the family since 1799 and was the site of turpentine stills, tar kilns, and a working farm. Now several miles of hiking trails wind through the property past barns and home sites, across fields, beside the beautiful and eerie blackwater Town Creek, and through longleaf pine woods. Pick up a trail map at the parking lot and head out for a few hours in the woods. Bring water, bug spray, and your camera; if you're quiet enough, you may see otters playing in Town Creek or deer in the woods at the edge of a field.

WILMINGTON AND CAPE FEAR

© JASON FRYE

Decide on a kayak route — into or out of the marsh?

Golf

Brunswick County is a golf mecca, where more than 30 championship courses appeal to all skill levels and playing styles. The website **Brunswick Islands** (www.ncbrunswick. com) maintains a list of golf courses, among them the notable **Cape Fear National at Brunswick Forest** (1281 Cape Fear National Dr., Brunswick Forest, 910/383-3283, www. capefearnational.com, greens fees from $47), named one of the "Top 18 Course Openings in the World 2010" by *Links* magazine when it opened, the course is beautifully maintained and fun to play from any tee. **Crow Creek** (240 Hickman Rd. NW, Calabash, 910/287-3081, www.crowcreek.com, greens fees from $60), is almost on the South Carolina state line. About 45 minutes south of Wilmington, the **Big Cats** (351 Ocean Ridge Pkwy. SW, 800/233-1801, www.bigcatsgolf.com, greens fees $82-140) is at Ocean Ridge Plantation with five stunning courses—Tiger's Eye, Leopard's Chase, Panther's Run, Lion's Paw and Jaguar's Lair.

Calabash and Vicinity

The tiny fishing village of Calabash, just above the South Carolina state line, was founded in the early 18th century as Pea Landing, a shipping point for the local peanut crop. Local legend holds that calabash gourds were used as dippers in the town drinking water supply, explaining the town's 1873 renaming. Others hold that the crooked marsh creek that leads to the sea inspired the name. Either way, Calabash is home to some world-famous seafood.

In the early 1940s, Lucy High Coleman began frying fish for the local fisheries workers in a kettle of oil by the dock. Later she used a tent, which in turn became a lean-to and eventually a full-fledged restaurant, The Original, which was, well, the original Calabash-style seafood restaurant. Calabash-style seafood is marked by its light crispy batter and the freshness of the seafood, and Coleman's descendants carry on the family tradition at several restaurants in town. Locals like to say that like champagne, which can only come from one region in

France, or bourbon, only distilled in Kentucky, you can only get Calabash seafood in Calabash; everything else is just an imitation. **Coleman's Original Calabash Restaurant** (9931 Nance St., 910/579-6875, 4pm-9pm daily, $10-30) is on the site of the original venue, and its yesteryear kitsch is undeniably charming. Just up the street is **Ella's of Calabash** (1148 River Rd., 910/579-6728, www.ellasofcalabash.com, 11am-9pm daily, entrées around $14); Ella was Lucy's sister. **Beck's Restaurant** (1014 River Road, 910/579-6776, www.becksrestaurant.com, 11am-9pm daily, $5-19) rounds out the offerings of the original three Calabash restaurants.

All of these restaurants are run by descendants of Lucy High Coleman, but that's only part of her seafood legacy. In the 1940s, Calabash was little more than a dot on the map until Jimmy Durante, the comedian, big band leader, and radio personality, spent the night in town. Lucy High Coleman's descendants will tell you that Durante sampled the food

© JASON FRYE
on the dock after a day of fishing

and asked to meet the chef, who introduced herself as "Mrs. Calabash." He was so enamored with her, the food, and the town that he began to sign off his radio program with the famous line "Good night, Mrs. Calabash, wherever you are."

Indigo Farms (1542 Hickman Rd. NW, 910/287-6794, www.indigofarmsmarket.com, 9am-5pm Mon.-Sat., longer hours in summer), three miles north of the South Carolina line in Calabash, is a superb farm market, selling all manner of produce, preserves, and baked goods. They also have corn mazes and farm activities in the fall.

Sunset Beach, the southernmost of the Brunswick County beaches, is a wonderfully small place, a cozy town that until 2008 could only be reached via a one-lane pontoon bridge. One of the area's most popular restaurants is located just on the inland side of the bridge to Sunset Beach: **Twin Lakes Seafood Restaurant** (102 Sunset Blvd., Sunset Beach, 910/579-6373, http://twinlakesseafood.com) was built almost 40 years ago by Clarice and Ronnie Holden, both natives of the area. Clarice was born into a cooking family—she's the daughter of Lucy High Coleman—so she knows her way around a restaurant. Twin Lakes serves fresh, locally caught seafood, fried Calabash-style or broiled. In-season and on weekends, expect long lines.

In the nearby town of Shallotte (pronounced "Shuh-LOTE"), **Holden Brothers Farm Market** (5600 Ocean Hwy. W., 910/579-4500, 8am-6pm daily March-Memorial Day, 8am-7pm daily Memorial Day-Labor Day, 8am-6pm Labor Day-Dec. 25, closed Dec. 26-Mar.) is a popular source for local produce. The peaches in season are wonderful, and the variety of homemade canned goods and pickles are worth the trip.

GETTING THERE AND AROUND

The Brunswick County beaches like Holden, Ocean Isle, and Sunset are easily accessed

WILMINGTON AND CAPE FEAR

on U.S. 17. The beaches and islands along the cape, due south of Wilmington, are not as close to U.S. 17. They can be reached by taking U.S. 76 south from Wilmington, then turning onto Highway 133 (closest to Wilmington), Highway 87, or Highway 211 (closer to the South Carolina border), or by ferry from Southport.

The **Southport-Fort Fisher Ferry** (Ferry Rd. SE, Southport, 800/368-8969 or 800/293-3779, from Southport 5:30am-7:45pm daily summer, 5:30am-6:15pm daily winter, from Fort Fisher 6:15am-8:30pm daily summer, 6:15am-7pm daily winter, $1 pedestrians, $2 bicycles, $3 motorcycles, cars $5, longer vehicles $15) is popular as a sightseeing jaunt as well as a means to get across the river. It's a 30-minute crossing; most departures are 45 minutes apart. Pets are permitted if leashed or in a vehicle, and there are restrooms on all ferries.

A small airport near Oak Island, **Cape Fear Regional Jetport** (4019 Long Beach Rd., Oak Island, 910/457-6534, www.capefearjetport.com), has no scheduled passenger service but is suitable for small private aircraft.

Inland from Wilmington

Driving inland from the Wilmington area, you first pass through a lush world of wetlands distinguished by the peculiar Carolina bays. Not necessarily bodies of water, as the name would suggest, bays are actually ovoid depressions in the earth of unknown and much-debated origin. They are often water-filled, but by definition are fed by rainwater rather than creeks or groundwater. They create unique environments and are often surrounded by bay laurel trees (hence the name), and home to a variety of carnivorous plants.

The next zone, bounded by the Waccamaw and Lumber Rivers, largely comprises farmland and small towns. For generations this was prime tobacco country, and that heritage is still very much evident in towns like Whiteville, where old tobacco warehouses line the railroad tracks. Culturally, this area—mostly in Columbus County and extending into Robeson County to the west and Brunswick County to the east—is linked with Horry, Marion, and Dillon Counties in South Carolina, with many of the same family names still found on both sides of the state line.

The area around the Lumber River, especially in Robeson County, is home to the Lumbee people, Native Americans with a long history of steadfast resistance to oppression and a heritage of devotion to faith and family. If you turn on the radio while driving through the area, you'll hear Lumbee gospel programming and get a sense of the cadences of Lumbee English. The characteristics that distinguish it from the speech of local whites and African Americans are subtle, but idiosyncratic pronunciation and grammar, which include subvariations among different Lumbee families and towns, make it one of the state's most distinctive dialects.

At the edge of the region is Fayetteville. From its early days as the center of Cape Fear Scottish settlement to its current role as one of the most important military communities in the United States, Fayetteville has always been a significant city.

ALONG U.S. 74

A short distance inland from Calabash, the countryside is threaded by the Waccamaw River, a gorgeous dark channel full of cypress knees and dangerous reptiles. The name is pronounced "WAW-cuh-MAW," with more emphasis on the first syllable than on the third. It winds its way down from Lake Waccamaw through a swampy portion of North Carolina and crossing Horry County, South Carolina (unofficial motto: "The *H* is Silent"), before

THE LEGEND OF HENRY BERRY LOWRY

In several pockets across the South, the Civil War didn't end the day General Robert E. Lee surrendered, but instead smoldered on in terrible local violence. One such place was the Lumbee community of Robeson County in the days of the famous Lowry Band.

Then as now, Lowry (also spelled Lowrie) was a prominent name in among the indigenous Lumbee people. During the Civil War, Allen Lowry led a band of men who hid out in the swamps, eluding conscription into the backbreaking corps of slave laborers who were forced to build earthworks to defend Wilmington and nearby gun emplacements. When the war ended, violence against the Lumbees escalated, and the Lowry Band retaliated, attacking the plantations of their wartime persecutors. Allen Lowry and his oldest son were captured in 1865 and killed. The youngest son, Henry Berry Lowry, inherited the mantle of leadership.

For the next several years, long after the end of the Civil War, the Lowry Band, now led by Henry Berry, was pursued relentlessly. Arrested and imprisoned, Lowry and his band escaped incarceration in Lumberton and Wilmington. Between 1868 and 1872 the state and federal governments tried everything from putting a bounty on Lowry's head to sending in a federal artillery battalion in an effort to capture Lowry. After an 11-month campaign of unsuccessful pursuit, the federal soldiers gave up. Soon afterward, the Lowry Band emerged from the swamps, raided Lumberton, and made off with a large amount of money. This was the end of the Lowry Band as one by one its members were killed in 1872—except, perhaps, Henry Berry. It's unknown whether he died, went back into hiding, or left the area altogether. As befits a legend, he seems to have simply disappeared.

Henry Berry Lowry is a source of fierce pride for modern Lumbee people, a symbol of their resistance and resilience. For many years, members of the community performed the outdoor drama *Strike at the Wind*, which tells the story of the Lowry Band. Funding for the play dried up, but the story lives on in oral and written histories and in the 2001 novel *Nowhere Else on Earth* by Josephine Humphreys.

joining the Pee Dee and Lumber Rivers in South Carolina to empty into Winyah Bay at the colonial port of Georgetown. Through the little toenail of North Carolina that the Waccamaw crosses, it parallels the much longer Lumber River, surrounding rural Columbus County and part of Robeson County in an environment of deep subtropical wetlands.

Sights

Pembroke is the principal town of the Lumbee people, and at the center of life here is the University of North Carolina at Pembroke (UNCP). Founded in 1887 as the Indian Normal School, UNCP's population is now only about one-quarter Native American, but it's still an important site in the history of North Carolina's indigenous people. The **Museum of the Native American Resource Center** (Old Main, UNCP, University Rd., Pembroke, 910/521-6282, www.uncp.edu, 8am-5pm Mon.-Sat., free) is on campus, occupying Old Main, a 1923 building that's a source of pride for Pembroke. The Resource Center has a small but very good collection of artifacts and contemporary art by Native Americans from across the country.

Laurinburg's **John Blue House** (13040 X-Way Rd., Laurinburg, 910/276-2495, grounds open daily, house and grounds tours 10am-noon and 1pm-4pm Tues.-Sat., free, donations accepted) is a spectacle of Victorian design, a polygonal house built entirely of heart pine harvested from the surrounding property and done up like a wedding cake with endless decorative devices. John Blue, the builder and original owner, was an inventor of machinery used in the processing of cotton. A pre-Civil

War cotton gin stands on the property, used today for educational demonstrations throughout the year. In October this is the site of the **John Blue Cotton Festival** (www.johnbluecottonfestival.com), which showcases not only the ingenuity of the home's famous resident and the process of ginning cotton, but also lots of local and regional musicians and other artists.

Entertainment and Events

Several of the state's big agricultural festivals are held in this area. If you're in the little town of Fair Bluff in late July, you might be lucky enough to witness the coronation of the newest Watermelon Queen. The **North Carolina Watermelon Festival** (910/949-6845, www.fairbluff.com) began as an annual competition between two friends, local farmers whose watermelons grew to over 100 pounds. The competition expanded into this festival that celebrates watermelon-growing throughout the state; a new court of watermelon royalty is crowned every year.

In Tabor City, there's a famous **Yam Festival** (910/377-3012 www.ncyamfestival.com) in late October, during which the tiny town's population sometimes quadruples. Yam partisans crown their own royal court during this festival. When spring rolls around, Chadbourn holds its annual **Strawberry Festival** (910/654-3518, www.ncstrawberry-festival.com), at which the coronation of the Strawberry Queen takes place. If this seems a strange sort of royalty, bear in mind that across the state line in South Carolina, they have a Little Miss Hell Hole Swamp competition.

Sports and Recreation

Several beautiful state parks line the Waccamaw and Lumber Rivers. **Lake Waccamaw State Park** (1866 State Park Dr., Lake Waccamaw, 910/646-4748, http://ncparks.gov, office 8am-5pm daily, park 8am-6pm daily Nov.-Feb., 8am-8pm daily Mar.-May and Sept.-Oct., 8am-9pm daily June-Aug.) encompasses the 9,000-acre lake. The lake is technically a Carolina bay. Carolina bays are large, oval depressions in the ground, many of which are boggy and filled with water but which are named for the bay trees that typically grow around them. Lake Waccamaw has geological and hydrological characteristics that make it unique even within the odd category of Carolina bays. Because of its proximity to a large limestone deposit, the water is more neutral than its usually very acidic cousins, and so it supports a greater diversity of life. There are several aquatic creatures that live only in Lake Waccamaw, including the Waccamaw fatmucket and the silverside (a mollusk and a fish, respectively). The park draws boaters and paddlers, but the only launches are outside the grounds. Primitive campsites ($9) are available in the park.

North of Whiteville on U.S. 701 is Elizabethtown, home to **Jones Lake State Park** (4117 Hwy. 242, Elizabethtown, 910/588-4550, http://ncparks.gov, office 8am-5pm Mon.-Fri., park 8am-6pm Nov.-Feb., 8am-8pm Mar.-May and Sept.-Oct., 8am-9pm June-Aug.). You can boat on Jones Lake either in your own craft (no motors over 10 hp) or in canoes or paddleboats ($5 per hour, $3 per additional hour) rented from the park. The lake is also great for swimming ($5 over age 12, $4 ages 3-12) from late May to early September, with shallow cool water and a sandy beach. A concession stand and a bathhouse are at the beach, and camping (call for rates) is available in a wooded area with drinking water and restrooms nearby.

Singletary Lake State Park (6707 Hwy. 53 E., Kelly, 910/669-2928, http://ncparks.gov, 8am-5pm daily), north of Lake Waccamaw in Kelly, has one of the largest of the Carolina bays, the 572-acre Singletary Lake, which lies within Bladen Lakes State Forest. There is no individual camping allowed, although there are facilities for large groups, including the entrancingly named Camp Ipecac, named for the purgative herb that grows here, that date from the Civilian Conservation Corps (CCC) era. There is a nice one-mile hiking trail, the CCC-Carolina Bay Loop Trail, and a 500-foot pier extending over the bay. Some of the cypress trees in the park are believed to have been saplings when the first English colonists came to Roanoke Island.

Lumber River State Park (2819 Princess Ann Rd., Orrum, 910/628-4564, http://ncparks.gov) has 115 miles of waterways with numerous put-ins for canoes and kayaks. Referred to as both the Lumber River and Lumbee River, and farther upstream as Drowning Creek, the river traverses both the coastal plain region and the eastern edge of the Sandhills. Camping ($13) is available at unimproved walk-in and canoe-in sites and at group sites.

Yogi Bear's Jellystone Park (626 Richard Wright Rd., Tabor City, 877/668-8586, www.taborcityjellystone.com, RVs $31-67/night, tents $28-54/night, cabins $104-200/night, yurts $64-109/night) is a popular campground with RV and tent spaces, rental cabins, and yurts. The facilities are clean and well maintained, and there are tons of children's activities on-site. Some of the camping is in wooded areas, but for the most part expect direct sun.

Food

If you pass through Tabor City, have a meal at the ◖ **Todd House** (102 Live Oak St., Tabor City, 910/653-3778, www.todd-house.com, 11am-8pm Mon.-Fri., 11am-3pm Sun., under $10), which has been serving fine country cooking since 1923. The Todds are one of the oldest families in the tobacco-growing area along the state line, and the first in the restaurant business was Mary Todd, who cooked meals for visiting tobacco buyers. Through her daughter's time and subsequent owners the Todd House has continued to serve famously good barbecue, fried chicken, and other down-home specialties.

There's a take-out counter in Whiteville that chowhounds will drive an hour out of their way to reach because it's said to have the best burgers around. Next to the railroad tracks, **Ward's Grill** (706 S. Madison St., Whiteville, 910/642-2004, 7am-2pm Mon.-Thurs., 7am-1pm Wed., 7am-12pm first two Sat. of the month) has no seating, just a walk-up counter. Its burgers are famous, as are its chili dogs.

In Lumberton, try **Fuller's Old-Fashion BBQ** (3201 Roberts Ave., Lumberton, 910/738-8694, www.fullersbbq.com, 11am-9pm Mon.-Sat., 11am-4pm Sun., lunch buffet $7, dinner buffet $9.50, Sun. buffet $11.25). Fuller's has a great reputation for its barbecue, but it also makes all sorts of country specialties like chicken gizzards, chitterlings, and a 12-layer cake.

Getting There and Around

This section of southeastern North Carolina is bisected by I-95, the largest highway on the East Coast. I-95 passes near Fayetteville and Lumberton. Major east-west routes include U.S. 74, which crosses Cape Fear at Wilmington and proceeds through Lake Waccamaw and Whiteville to pass just south of Lumberton and Pembroke to Laurinburg. Highway 87 goes through Elizabethtown, where you can choose to branch off onto Highway 211 to Lumberton, or bear north on Highway 87 to Fayetteville. Highway 87 and Highway 211 are quite rural and beautiful, especially in the spring, when azaleas are in bloom and the country is greening up for summer, as well as in the fall, when cotton fields will make you do a double take, thinking you just sped past a field of snow. Take your time on these roads and be ready to pull off to take photos of farmhouses, fields, and other pastoral scenes.

FAYETTEVILLE

Fayetteville is North Carolina's sixth-largest city, and in its own quiet way has always been one of the state's most powerful engines of growth and change. In the early 1700s it became a hub for settlement by Scottish immigrants, who helped build it into a major commercial center. From the 1818 initiation of steamboat travel between Fayetteville and Wilmington along Cape Fear—initially a voyage of six days—to the building of Plank Road, which was a huge boon to intrastate commerce, Fayetteville was well connected to commercial resources in the Carolinas.

At a national level, Fayetteville serves as the location of two high-level military installations. Fort Bragg is home to the XVIII Airborne Corps, the 82nd Airborne, the Delta Force, and the John F. Kennedy Special Warfare Center and School. It's also home to many military families, and the community has a vibrant international community. Pope Air Field, home of the 440th Airlift Wing, is nearby.

Sights

The **Museum of the Cape Fear Regional Complex** (801 Arsenal Ave., 910/486-1330, http://ncmuseumofhistory.org, 10am-5pm Tues.-Sat., 1pm-5pm Sun., free) has three components, each telling different stories of Fayetteville's history. The museum has exhibits on the history and prehistory of the region, including its vital role in developing transportation in the state, as well as its military role. There is an 1897 house museum, the **Poe House,** which belonged to an Edgar Allen Poe—not the writer Edgar Allan Poe this one was a brickyard owner. The third section is the 4.5-acre **Arsenal Park,** site of a federal arms magazine built in 1836, claimed by the Confederacy in 1861, and destroyed by General Sherman in 1865.

The **Airborne and Special Operations Museum** (100 Bragg Blvd., 910/643-2766, www.asomf.org, 10am-5pm Tues.-Sat., noon-5pm Sun., noon-5pm federal holiday Mon., free, theater $4, motion simulator $5) is an impressive facility that presents the history of Special Ops paratroopers, from the first jump in 1940 to the divisions' present-day roles abroad in peacekeeping missions and war. In the museum's theater you can watch a film of what it looks like when a paratrooper makes a jump, and the 24-seat Pitch, Roll, and Yaw Vista-Dome Motion Simulator makes the experience even more exciting.

The **JFK Special Warfare Museum** (Ardennes St. and Marion St., Bldg. D-2502, Fort Bragg, 910/432-4272, www.jfkwebstore. com) tells the story of unconventional U.S. military projects, including Special Ops and Psychological Ops. The museum focuses on the

Vietnam War era but chronicles warfare from colonial times to the present. Note that ID is required to enter the base.

Looking farther back in time, the **Fayetteville Independent Light Infantry Armory and Museum** (210 Burgess St., 910/433-1612, by appointment, free) displays artifacts from the history of the Fayetteville Independent Light Infantry (FILI). FILI is still active, dedicated as North Carolina's official historic military command, which is a ceremonial duty. In its active-duty days, which began in 1793, FILI had some exciting times, particularly during the Civil War. In addition to military artifacts, the museum also exhibits a carriage in which the Marquis de Lafayette was shown around Fayetteville—the only one of the towns bearing his name that he actually visited.

The 79-acre **Cape Fear Botanical Garden** (536 N. Eastern Blvd., 910/486-0221, www. capefearbg.org, 10am-5pm Mon.-Sat., noon-5pm Sun., closed Sun. mid-Dec.-Feb., $8 adults, $2.50 ages 6-12, free under age 6, free 1st Sat. of every month and all of Apr.) is one of the loveliest horticultural sites in North Carolina. The camellia and azalea gardens are spectacular sights in the early spring, but the variety of plantings and environments represented makes the whole park a delight. Along the banks of the Paw Paw River and Cross Creek, visitors will find dozens of garden environments, including lily gardens, hosta gardens, woods, a bog, and an 1880s farmhouse garden. This is the prettiest place in Fayetteville and a fantastic spot for a picnic lunch on a long road trip down I-95.

Cross Creek Cemetery (N. Cool Spring St. and Grove St., 800/255-8217, dawn-dusk daily) is an attractive and sad spot, the resting place of many Scottish men and women who crossed the ocean to settle Cape Fear. People of other ethnicities and times are buried here, but the oldest section of the cemetery is the most poignant, where one stone after another commemorates early Scots colonists. The cemetery was founded in 1785, and the wall along the southern boundary is believed to be the oldest piece of construction still standing in Fayetteville.

Sports and Recreation

In Fayetteville you can attend a dizzying array of sporting events, from drag races to ice hockey. The **Fayetteville Fire Antz** (1900 Coliseum Dr., 910/321-0123, www. fireantzhockey.com, from $14 adults, $5 children) are an ice hockey team in the Southern Professional Hockey League, unusual for this warm climate. The **Fayetteville Swamp Dogs** (910/426-5900, www.goswampdogs.com, from $5), a baseball team in the Coastal Plains League, play home games at the J. P. Riddle Stadium (2823 Legion Rd.).

The **Rogue Rollergirls** (www.rogueroller-girls.com) is an up-and-coming all-female flat-track Roller Derby team participating in this fun fringe sport that had its heyday in the 1970s. In basketball, the **Fayetteville Crossover** (910/977-2954, http://crossover. trblproball.com) plays in the Tobacco Road Basketball League. An indoor football team, the **Cape Fear Heroes** (910/323-1100, www. capefearheroes.com, from $10), play home games at the Crown Center (1960 Coliseum Dr.).

There are two motorsports venues in Fayetteville: **Fayetteville Motor Sports Park** (4480 Doc Bennett Rd., 910/484-3677, www. fayettevillemotorsportspark.com) host drag races, and **Fayetteville Motor Speedway** (3704 Doc Bennett Rd., 910/223-7223, www. thenewfayettevillemotorspeedway.com, around $20) hosts a variety of stock car races.

GOLF

The Sandhills of North Carolina are dotted with great golf courses, and the countryside around Fayetteville is no exception: **Anderson Creek Golf Club** (125 Whispering Pines Dr., Spring Lake, 910/814-2115, www.anderson-creekgolf.com, 18 holes, par 72, greens fees from $28), **Bayonet at Puppy Creek** (349 S. Parker Church Rd., Raeford, 888/229-6638, www.bayonetgolf.com, greens fees from $30), **Cypress Lakes** (2126 Cypress Lakes Rd., Hope Mills, 910/483-0359, www.cypresslakesnc. com, greens fees from $30), and **Gates Four Golf and Country Club** (6775 Irongate Dr.,

Fayetteville, 910/425-2176, www.gatesfour. com, greens fees from $45) all offer great golf; call at least 48 hours ahead for the best chance of getting a tee time in summer, although short-notice reservations may be possible.

◖ ZIP-LINING

If you want outdoor adventure, **ZipQuest** (533 Carvers Falls Rd., 910/488-8787, www. zipquest.com, 9am-5pm Mon.-Sat., 10am-5pm Sun., $85) gives you a different sort of outdoor experience: flying through the trees on a zip line. The tour takes you over Carver's Creek and even 20-foot Carver's Falls, the only waterfall in the area. At the end of the run, you have the opportunity to get on the Swingshot, a swing that flies out over a four-story drop into the ravine below. Both the zip-line tour and Swingshot are exciting but not for the faint of heart.

INDOOR SKYDIVING

Paraclete XP SkyVenture (190 Paraclete Dr., Raeford, 888/475-9386, www.paracletexp.com, from $63) offers one of the most thrilling experiences you can have in the area: indoor skydiving. After a brief flight school, you'll step into a vertical wind tunnel with an instructor and take your first flight. If you show a little aptitude, they'll let you fly on your own (don't worry, they're never more than a couple of feet away) and even take you soaring to the top of the 51-foot tower, then rushing back down, giving you a real taste of what it's like to free fall. If you're lucky, you'll see the Golden Knights, the U.S. Army's parachute team, practicing aerial maneuvers, or maybe get to fly with world-class and even world-champion competitive skydivers, or see one of Paraclete's teams practice their wild aerial ballet.

Entertainment and Events

The **Cameo Theatre** (225 Hay St., 910/486-6633, www.cameoarthouse.com) is a cool old early-20th-century movie house, originally known as the New Dixie. Today it is "Fayetteville's alternative cinematic experience," a place for independent and art-house movies.

WILMINGTON AND CAPE FEAR

© JASON FRYE

ZipQuest's gear

Cape Fear Regional Theatre (1209 Hay St., 910/323-4233, www.cfrt.org) began in 1962 as a tiny company with a bunch of borrowed equipment. Today it is a major regional theater with a wide reputation. Putting on several major productions each season and specializing in popular musicals, it draws actors and directors from around the country but maintains its heart here in the Fayetteville arts community. The **Gilbert Theater** (116 Green St., entrance on Bow St. above Fascinate-U Museum, 910/678-7186, www.gilberttheater.com, around $10) is a small company that puts on a variety of productions throughout the year, with emphasis on classic drama and multicultural offerings.

Fayetteville's late-April **Dogwood Festival** (www.faydogwoodfestival.com) features rock, pop, and beach-music bands; a dog show; a recycled art show; a "hogs and rags spring rally;" and the selection and coronation of Miss, Teen Miss, Young Miss, and Junior Miss Dogwood Festival. In September, the **International Folk Festival** (www.theartscouncil.com) celebrates the many cultures that make up this community through food, music, art, and other cultural expressions.

Accommodations and Food

Fayetteville's lodging options are mostly chain motels, a multitude of which can be found at the Fayetteville exits along I-95. The chains have reasonable rates, but if you'd like to stay somewhere with more personality, Wilmington and Raleigh are both easily accessible. In town, **Gloria & Edgar's B&B** (3423 Dunn Rd., 910/484-6827, $80-125) is a four-bedroom bed-and-breakfast featuring private bathrooms and a spacious, sunny porch perfect for breakfast, afternoon tea, or a nightcap.

Likewise, the city's dining choices tend toward the highway chain restaurants, with some exceptions: **⟨ Hilltop House** (1240 Fort Bragg Rd., 910/484-6699, www.hilltophousenc.com, lunch 11am-2pm Tues.-Fri. and Sun., dinner 5pm-9pm Tues.-Thurs., 5pm-10pm Fri. and Sun., brunch 10:30am-2:30pm Sun., closed Sat., $20-33) serves hearty fare in an elegant setting, and was recognized in 2007 with a *Wine Spectator* magazine Award for Excellence—not surprising, given that the Hilltop House has a wine list of more than 100 bottles.

Beer lovers will prefer the **Mash House** (4150 Sycamore Dairy Rd., 910/867-9223, www.themashhouse.com, 4pm-11pm Mon.-Thurs., 4-midnight Fri., noon-midnight Sat., noon-10pm Sun., $8-16), which has a good variety of pizzas and sandwiches as well as heartier entrées and a selection of good homemade brews, or **Huske Hardware House** (405 Hay St., 910/437-9905, www.huskehardware.com, 11am-10pm Mon.-Tues., 11am-midnight Wed.-Thurs., 11am-2am Fri.-Sat., 11am-9pm Sun., entrées $10-30), a gastropub serving great food and even better beer. For a taste of Fayetteville's international cuisine, try **Sherefe** (114 Gillespie St., 910/630-3040, www.sherefe.net, 11am-9pm Mon.-Thurs., 11am-10pm Fri.-Sat., entrées $14-26), a Mediterranean restaurant. The friendly staff can point out something good, and get the Mediterranean Trio (hummus, baba ghanoush, and meze) to share.

Information and Services
Cape Fear Valley Health Services (1638 Owen Dr., 910/615-4000, www.capefearvalley.com) is a large hospital complex with full services, including acute care and a major cardiac care program.

The website of the **Fayetteville Area Convention and Visitors Bureau** (245 Person St., 800/255-8217, www.visitfayettevillenc.com, 8am-5pm Mon.-Fri.) is an excellent source of visitor information for the city. You'll find not only the basics but also detailed driving tours and extensive historical information.

Getting There and Around
Fayetteville Regional Airport (FAY, 400 Airport Rd., 910/433-1160, www.flyfay.com) has daily flights to Charlotte (US Airways), Atlanta (Delta), and Washington DC (United and US Airways). **Amtrak** (472 Hay St., 800/872-7245, www.amtrak.com, 10am-5:45pm and 10pm-5:45am daily) runs the *Silver Meteor* between New York City and Miami and the *Palmetto* between New York City and Savannah, Georgia; each train stops in Fayetteville once daily in each direction.

Fayetteville is near I-95; it is easily reached via Highway 24 from Jacksonville, Warsaw, and Clinton, and via Highway 87 from points south.

BACKGROUND

The Land

GEOGRAPHY

North Carolina's **mountains** and the **Piedmont** descend gradually until the land transforms into the **Coastal Plain.** Though I-95 is commonly regarded as the western boundary of the Coastal Plain, geologically the Sandhills section of the state is part of this region. Wedged between the Piedmont and the wetlands-rich Cape Fear Valley (the delta stretching from Fayetteville to Wilmington), the Sandhills are a zone of transition between the rich soil and rolling topography of the Piedmont and the sandy soil and dune systems of the Coastal Plain. The Sandhills are a range of sand dunes that mark where the coast was several million years ago. Since then the ocean has retreated a hundred miles or so to the coastline we know today.

The sandy soil, immense freshwater and saltwater wetlands, deep rivers, wide shallow sounds on the northern coast, and the chain of barrier islands stretching from Virginia to South Carolina make eastern North Carolina's landscape distinct. Among the wetlands are pocosins and Carolina bays, two distinct types of wetlands. Pocosins are wet, peaty expanses of moist ground that are slightly elevated in the center. Carolina bays are ovoid bodies of

Lighthouses offer a commanding view of the land and sea around them.

water on diagonal axes, and are unexplained but beautiful; they dot the landscape across the southeastern corner of the state.

The **Outer Banks** make a giant, sweeping arc from Virginia to the north out to the point at Cape Hatteras; they then turn almost due west, forming the Bogue Banks, also known as the **Crystal Coast.** Along this northerly half of the North Carolina coast, the barrier islands work with wide complexes of sounds and marshes to protect the mainland from hurricanes and smaller storms. To the south, the barrier islands are closer to the mainland, but also work with marshes, creeks, and rivers to absorb the brunt of a storm's strength. At all points along the coast, from the Outer Banks to the southern border, hurricanes can change the shape and structure of the protective islands in an instant, although the northerly barrier islands, which tend to be longer and thinner than those in the south, are often impacted more dramatically when wind and water join forces to rearrange geography.

CLIMATE

Generalizing about North Carolina's climate is difficult. It's not as hot as at the equator and not as cold as at the poles, but beyond that, each region has its own range of variables and has to be examined separately.

The mountains are much cooler than either the Piedmont or the coast, and winter lasts longer.

The central part of North Carolina, on the other hand, can be brutally hot during the summer and quite warm on spring and fall days. Cities like Fayetteville, on the edge of the coastal and Piedmont regions, can feel like the hottest places on earth in high summer; the hottest temperature recorded in the state—110°F—was at Fayetteville in 1983.

Along the coast, temperatures are more moderate than in the Piedmont. The warm Gulf Stream washes past not far off shore, influencing air temperatures in all seasons: keeping temperatures from getting too frigid in winter, bringing spring early, keeping water warm near shore and pushing storms farther inland in summer, and extending the fall season, making it a pleasant time to be here. It's windy along the coast, and these breezes help mitigate summer's heat and make the humidity more bearable.

North Carolina gets its fair share of hazardous weather to go along with beautiful summer days and crisp fall nights. Along the Outer Banks, which jut far out into the Atlantic, **hurricanes** are a particular threat. It's not just the Outer Banks that are vulnerable to these powerful storms; the coastline south of the Banks suffers plenty of hits, and even inland, hurricanes that make landfall in South Carolina can curve up through the Lowcountry and into North Carolina's Piedmont, bringing high winds and heavy rains to inland cities and dangerous floodwaters to coastal towns. Hurricane season is June to November, but toward the end of summer and the beginning of fall the risk becomes greatest. Normally there is plenty of warning before a storm hits, and by the time they hit people have had time to prepare and stock up. Wind and rain are the first effects of a hurricane, but the storm surge and high waves can cause massive damage to barrier islands, dune systems, and sensitive estuarine complexes. Flooding from inland rains as well as the coastal deluge can spell disaster. In 1999, Hurricane Floyd killed 35 people in North Carolina, caused billions of dollars of property damage, and permanently altered the landscape in places. During this storm, rivers in eastern North Carolina reached 500-year flood levels, leaving one-third of Rocky Mount under water and causing devastating damage to Tarboro, Kinston, and other towns in the region. Princeville, the oldest African American town in the United States, was nearly destroyed. Today, many towns in eastern North Carolina still carry scars to their infrastructure and economies due to Floyd.

Tornadoes, most common in the spring, can cause trouble any time of year. A rare November twister touched down in 2006, smashing the Columbus County community of Riegelwood, killing eight people and leaving a seven-mile swath of destruction. Even plain old **thunderstorms** can be dangerous, bringing lightning, flash flooding, difficult driving conditions, and even hail. **Snowstorms** are rare, and usually occur in the mountains. The Piedmont sees more snow than the Coast, which sees flurries once or twice each winter and the occasional dusting of snow. Outside the mountains, most North Carolinians are woefully inexperienced snow drivers, and the state Department of Transportation doesn't have the equipment in coastal counties to handle much more than a little snow. Along the coast, the humorous rule of thumb is that for every inch of snow that is predicted, banks, schools, and government offices shut down for a day, and for every inch of snow that actually falls, it's two days. As soon as the meteorologists mention flurries, there's a run on the most valuable snowstorm essentials: milk, bread, peanut butter, toilet paper, and magazines.

Flora

In the early 1700s, John Lawson, an English explorer who would soon be one of the first victims of the Tuscarora War, wrote of a magnificent tree house somewhere in the very young colony of North Carolina. "I have been informed of a Tulip-Tree," he wrote, "that was ten Foot Diameter; and another, wherein a lusty Man had his Bed and Household Furniture, and liv'd in it, till his Labour got him a more fashionable Mansion. He afterwards became a noted Man, in his Country, for Wealth and Conduct." Whether or not there was ever a tulip poplar large enough to serve as a furnished bachelor pad, colonial North Carolina's forests must have seemed miraculous to the first Europeans to see them.

FORESTS

Because the state is so geographically and climatically varied, there's a greater diversity in tree species than anywhere in the eastern United States. In terms of land area, more than half of the land is still forested in the Piedmont and eastern North Carolina. Coastal forests are dominated by hardwoods—**oaks** of many varieties, **gum, cypress,** and **cedar**—and the barrier islands have a few remaining patches of maritime forest where the branches of **live oak** trees intertwine to shed storm wind and their roots sink deep to keep islands stable. The best and largest remaining example of a pristine maritime forest is on Bald Head Island, where the Bald Head Island Conservancy provides education and studies the form, function, and future of barrier islands, including these important maritime forest ecosystems.

Longleaf Pine

Arguably, the most important plant in North Carolina's history is the longleaf pine, sometimes called the pitch pine. This beautiful tree is something of a rare sight today as the vast stands of longleaf pines that formerly blanketed the eastern part of the state were used extensively in the naval stores industry in the 18th and 19th centuries, providing valuable turpentine, pitch, tar, and lumber. The overharvesting of this tree has a lot to do with the disappearance of North Carolina's once-legendary pine barrens, but an unanticipated ancillary cause is the efficiency of modern firefighting. Longleaf pines depend on periodic forest fires to clear out competition from the underbrush and provide layers of nutrient-rich singed earth. In the 20th century the rule was to put out forest fires, cutting down on smoke but disturbing the natural growth cycles of these trees. In some longleaf-harboring nature preserves today, controlled burns keep the longleaf piney woods alive and healthy as crucial habitats for several endangered species, including the red cockaded woodpecker and the pine barrens tree frog.

A great place to get a feel for this ecosystem that once covered so much of the Southeast

is Weyouth Woods-Sandhills Preserve, near Southern Pines. Some of the longleaf pines here are believed to be almost 500 years old. Many of these centuries-old trees bear scars from the days of the naval stores bonanza, when turpentine makers carved deep gashes in the bark to collect the resin that bled out. The tallest and oldest longleaf pine in the state is here, and at over 130 feet tall, it's a sight.

FLOWERS

Some of North Carolina's flora puts on great annual shows, drawing flocks of admirers—the gaudy **azaleas** of springtime in Wilmington, the **wildflowers** of the first warm weather in the hills, the **rhododendrons** and **mountain laurel** of the Appalachian summer. The Ericaceae family, a race of great woody bushes with star-shaped blossoms that includes azaleas, rhododendrons, and laurel, is the headliner in North Carolina's floral fashion show. Spring comes earliest to the southeastern corner of the state, and the Wilmington area is explosively beautiful when the azaleas are in bloom. The **Azalea Festival,** held annually for more than 50 years, draws hundreds of thousands of people to the city in early to mid-April, around the time that public gardens and private yards are spangled with azaleas.

Around the end of April and into May, when spring finally arrives in the mountains but the forest floor is not yet sequestered in leafy shade, a profusion of delicate flowers emerges. **Violets** and **chickweed** emerge early on, as do the quintessentially mountainous white **trillium** blossoms and the Wake Robin, also a trillium, which looks something like a small poinsettia.

Surprisingly, one of the best places in North Carolina to view displays of wildflowers is along the major highways. For more than 20 years the state Department of Transportation has carried out a highway beautification project that involves planting large banks of wildflowers along highways and in wide medians. The displays are not landscaped but are allowed to grow up in unkempt profusion, often planted in inspired combinations of wildly

© JASON FRYE

azaleas in bloom

contrasting colors that make the flowerbeds a genuinely beautiful addition to the environment. The website of the state's **Department of Transportation** (www.ncdot.org) offers a guide to the locations and seasons of the wildflower beds.

FALL FOLIAGE

Arriving as early as mid-September at the highest elevations and gradually sliding down the mountains through late October, autumn colors bring a late-season wave of visitors to western North Carolina. Along the coast, don't expect much by way of leaf peeping, as leaves tend to go from green to brown to off the tree quite suddenly.

CARNIVOROUS PLANTS

You've probably seen **Venus flytraps** for sale in nurseries, and maybe you've even bought one and brought it home to stuff with kitchen bugs. Venus flytraps grow in the wild only in one tiny corner of the world, a narrow band of counties between Wilmington and Myrtle Beach,

South Carolina. The flytraps and their dozens of carnivorous Tar Heel kin, including Seussian sundews and pitcher plants, the abattoirs of the bug world, are fondest of living in places with nutrient-starved soil, like pine savannas and pocosins, where they have little competition for space and sunlight and can feed handsomely on meals that come right to them.

There are many species of **pitcher plants,** a familiar predator of the plant world. Shaped like tubular vases with a graceful elfin flap shading the mouth, pitcher plants attract insects with an irresistible brew. Unsuspecting bugs pile in, thinking they've found a keg party, but instead find themselves paddling in a sticky mess from which they're unable to escape, pinned down by spiny hairs that line the inside of the pitcher. Enterprising frogs and spiders that are either strong or clever enough to come and go safely from inside the pitcher will often set up shop inside a plant and help themselves to stragglers. Another local character is the **sundew,** perhaps the creepiest of the carnivorous plants. Sundews extend their paddle-shaped leaf-hands up into the air, hairy palms baited with a sticky mess that bugs can't resist. When a fly lands among the hairs, the sundew closes on it like a fist and gorges on it until it's ready for more.

There are several places where you can see wild carnivorous plants in North Carolina. Among the best are the Bluethenthal Wildflower Preserve at the University of North Carolina Wilmington, Carolina Beach State Park, and the Green Swamp Preserve and Ev-Henwood Nature Preserve in Brunswick County. There's also a good collection of them on display at Chapel Hill's North Carolina Botanical Garden.

Fauna

Among the familiar wildlife most commonly seen in the state, **white-tailed deer** are out in force in the countryside and in the woods; they populate suburban areas in large numbers as well. **Raccoons** and **opossums** prowl at night, happy to scavenge from trash cans and the forest floor. **Skunks** are common, particularly in the mountains, and are often smelled rather than seen. They leave an odor something like a cross between grape soda and Sharpie markers. There are also a fair number of **black bears,** not only in the mountains but in swamps and deep woods across the state.

In woods and yards alike, **gray squirrels** and a host of familiar **songbirds** are a daily presence. Different species of **tree frogs** produce beautiful choruses on spring and summer nights, while **fireflies** mount sparkly shows in the trees and grass in the upper Piedmont and mountains. Down along the southeast coast, **alligators** and **turtles** sun themselves on many a golf course and creek-side backyard.

The Carolina woods harbor colonies of **Southern flying squirrels.** It's very unlikely that you'll see one unless it's at a nature center or wildlife rehabilitation clinic because flying squirrels are both nocturnal and shy. They're also almost unspeakably cute. Fully extended, they're about nine inches long snout to tail, weigh about four ounces, and have super-silky fur and pink noses, and like many nocturnal animals have comically long whiskers and huge, wide-set eyes that suggest amphetamine use. When they're flying—gliding, really—they spread their limbs to extend the patagium, a membrane that stretches between their front and hind legs, and glide along like little magic carpets.

While panther sightings are more common in the mountains, big cats have been spotted in coastal areas as well. There are tales of a panther in the inland woods of Brunswick and Columbus Counties on the southeast coast.

WILD PONIES

Small herds of wild ponies have called several barrier islands in the Outer Banks home for more than 400 years. Locally known as "Banker ponies," but more properly as feral horses, they're descendants of Spanish horses, a fact established by extensive DNA testing. No one's quite sure how they arrived here, but the consensus is that they've been here since the 1500s. They may have arrived with early English colonists, who may have bought Spanish horses at a Caribbean port, or with even earlier Spanish explorers. Stories passed down here for hundreds of years say they swam ashore from long-ago shipwrecks. Today, the primary herds are on Shackleford Banks in the Cape Lookout National Seashore and in Corolla, at the extreme north end of the Outer Banks, near the Virginia border. Since they roam freely in areas open to public visitation, you may find one staring you down from behind a sand dune or a stand of scrubby cedar trees. Remember to use caution around the Banker ponies; they may resemble domestic horses, but they are wild animals. Feeding them or approaching them only ends up hurting the herd in the long run. They also pose some physical danger; all it takes for them to

A wild pony looks for food along the Outer Banks.

© BOB DECKER/123RF.COM

show you who's boss is one swift kick. You can learn more about the horses and their history at http://shacklefordhorses.org and www.corollawildhorses.com.

REINTRODUCED SPECIES

In the 1990s and early 2000s a federal program to reestablish **red wolf** colonies in the Southeast focused its efforts on parkland in North Carolina. Red wolves, thought to have existed in North Carolina in past centuries, were first reintroduced to the Great Smoky Mountains National Park. They did not thrive, and the colony was moved to the Alligator River National Wildlife Refuge on the northeast coast. The packs have fared better in this corner of the state and now roam several wilderness areas in the sound country.

BIRDS

Bird-watchers flock to North Carolina because of the great diversity of songbirds, raptors, and even hummingbirds across the state—a 2013 count put the number of species at 473—but the state is best known for waterfowl. In the sounds of eastern North Carolina, waterfowl descend en masse as they migrate. Hundreds of thousands of birds crowd the lakes, ponds, trees, marshes, and waterways as they move to and from their winter homes. Many hunters take birds during hunting season, but they're outnumbered by bird-watchers. Birders say that one of the best spots for birding in the state is around large, shallow Lake Mattamuskeet on the central coast, with 40,000 acres of water to attract incredible numbers of snow geese and tundra swans, Canada geese, and ducks. Just a few miles away, Swan Quarter National Wildlife Refuge is also a haven for ducks, wading birds, shorebirds, and their admirers.

While in eastern North Carolina, bird fanciers should visit the Sylvan Heights Waterfowl Park and Eco-Center, a remarkable park in the small town of Scotland Neck that's a conservation center and breeding facility for rare waterfowl from across the globe. Visitors can walk through the grounds, where large aviaries house bird species that, unless you're a world-traveler

© JASON FRYE

a pelican resting along the coast

REPTILES

Turtles and **snakes** are the state's most common reptiles. **Box turtles,** found everywhere, and **bog turtles,** found in the Smokies, are the only land terrapins. A great many freshwater turtles inhabit the swamps and ponds, and on a sunny day every log or branch sticking out of fresh water will become a sunbathing terrace for as many turtles as it can hold. Common water turtles include **cooters, sliders,** and **painted turtles. Snapping turtles** can be found in fresh water throughout the state, so mind your toes. They grow up to a couple of feet long and can weigh more than 50 pounds. Not only will they bite—hard!—if provoked, they will actually initiate hostilities, lunging for you if they so much as disapprove of the fashion of your shoes. Even the tiny hatchlings are vicious, so give them a wide berth. Finally, we are visited often by **sea turtles,** a gentle and painfully dwindling race of seafarers. The most frequent visitor is the **loggerhead,** a reddish-tan living coracle that can weigh up to 500 pounds and nests as far north as Ocracoke. Occasional visitors include the **leatherback,** a 1,500-pound goliath at its largest, **hawksbills, greens,** and **olive ridleys.** The Bald Head Island Conservancy on Bald Head Island has been protecting the turtles and their nests since the mid-1980s, gathering data on birth rates, nest numbers, and the mother turtles. During the nesting season, conservancy members can tag turtles along with ecologists and interns and watch them lay their eggs.

There are not many kinds of **lizards** native to North Carolina, but those that are present make up for their homogeneity with ubiquity. **Anoles,** tiny, scaly dragons that dart along almost any outdoor surface, are found in great numbers in the southeastern part of the state, up the coast, and along the South Carolina state line to west of Charlotte. They put on great shows by puffing their ruby-red dewlaps and by vacillating between drab brown and gray or lime-Slurpee green, depending on the color of the background they hide on. The ranks of lizard kind are rounded out by several varieties of **skinks** and **glass lizards,**

and a very lucky birder, you're unlikely to see elsewhere. There are more than 170 species, and you can get quite close to most of them. Bring your camera; you'll have the chance to take shots you could never get in the field.

There are many books and websites about birding in North Carolina. One of the most helpful is the North Carolina Birding Trail, both a website (www.ncbirdingtrail.org) and a series of print guidebooks. Organized by region (mountains, Piedmont, and coast), these resources list dozens of top sites for bird-watching and favorite bird-watching events throughout the state. Another good resource is the **Carolina Bird Club** (www.carolinabirdclub.org).

AMPHIBIANS

Throughout the state, **frogs** and **toads** are numerous and vociferous, especially the many species of dainty **tree frogs.** Two species, the gray tree frog and the spring peeper, are found in every part of North Carolina, and beginning in late winter they create the impression that the trees are filled with ringing cell phones.

also called glass snakes because they look like snakes, although they're not, and **fence lizards.** There are plenty of real **snakes** in North Carolina. The vast majority are shy, gentle, and totally harmless to anything larger than a rat. There are a few species of venomous snakes that are very dangerous. These include three kinds of **rattlesnake:** the huge diamondback, whose diet of rabbits testifies to its size and strength; the pigmy; and the timber or canebrake rattler. Other venomous species are the beautiful mottled **copperhead** and the **cottonmouth or water moccasin,** famous for flinging its mouth open in hostility and flashing its brilliant white palate. The **coral snake** is a fantastically beautiful and venomous species.

Most Carolina snakes are entirely benign to humans, including old familiars such as **black racers** and **king snakes** as well as **milk, corn,** and **rat snakes.** One particularly endearing character is the **hognose snake,** which can be found throughout North Carolina but is most common in the east. Colloquially known as a spreading adder, the hognose snake compensates for its total harmlessness with amazing displays of histrionics. If you startle one, it will first flatten and greatly widen its head and neck and hiss most passionately. If it sees that you're not frightened by plan A, it will panic and go straight to plan B: playing dead. The hognose snake won't simply lay inert until you go away, though; it goes to the dramatic lengths of flipping onto its back, exposing its pitiably vulnerable belly, opening its mouth, throwing its head back limply, and sticking out its tongue as if it had just been poisoned. It is such a devoted method actor that should you call its bluff and poke it back onto its belly, it will fling itself energetically back into the mortuary pose and resume being deceased.

Alligators make their reptilian kin look tiny. Tar Heel gators are most abundant in the area south of Wilmington, but they've been seen the full length of the state's coast—note how far north the Alligator River is—and as far inland as Merchants Millpond State Park near the Virginia state line. The biggest ones can reach 1,000 pounds and measure 10-15 feet long. Smaller gators are more common, and the six- and eight-foot females are small in comparison to the massive bull gators. They have approximately a mouthful of sharp teeth, and even hatchlings can pack a nasty bite. These amazing prehistoric-looking amphibious assault machines appear to spend most of their waking hours splayed out in the sun with their eyes closed, or floating motionless in the water. Don't fall for it; it's their fiendishly clever, or perhaps primitively simple, ploy to make you come closer. They can launch themselves at prey as if spring-loaded and are more than capable of catching and eating a dog, cat, or small child. It happens very rarely, but given the chance, large gators can and will eat an adult human. The best course of action, as with most wildlife, is to admire them from a distance.

History

ANCIENT CIVILIZATION

By the time the first colonists arrived and called this place Carolina, the land had already sustained some 20,000 years of human history. We know that Paleo-Indians hunted these lands during the last ice age, when there were probably more mammoths and saber-toothed tigers in North Carolina than people. Civilization came around 4000 BC, when the first inhabitants settled down to farm, make art, and trade goods. By the first century, Southern Woodland and Mississippian Indians were also living in advanced societies with complex religious systems, economic interaction among communities, advanced farming methods, and the creation of art and architecture.

When the Europeans arrived, there were more than a dozen major Native American groups within what is now North Carolina. The Cherokee people ruled the mountains while the Catawba, Pee Dees, Tutelo, and Saura, among others, were their neighbors in the Piedmont. In the east, the Cheraw, Waccamaw, and Tuscarora were some of the larger communities, while many bands occupied land along the Outer Banks and sounds.

CONQUEST

The first Europeans to land here were Spanish. We know conquistador Hernando de Soto and his troops marched around western North Carolina in 1539, but they were just passing through. In 1566, another band of Spanish explorers, led by conquistador Juan Pardo, came for a longer visit. They were making a circuitous trek in the general direction of Mexico, and along the way they established several forts in what are now the Carolinas and Tennessee. One of these forts, called San Juan, has been identified by archaeologists outside present-day Morganton in a community called Worry Crossroads. Although the troops who were garrisoned for a year and a half at Fort San Juan eventually disappeared into the woods or were killed, it's theorized that they may have had a profound impact on the course of history, possibly spreading European diseases among the Native Americans and weakening them so much that, a couple of decades later, the indigenous people would be unable to repel the invasion of English colonists.

The next episode in the European settlement of North Carolina is one of the strangest mysteries in American history, the Lost Colonists of Roanoke. After two previous failed attempts to establish an English stronghold on the island of Roanoke, fraught by poor planning and disastrous diplomacy, a third group of English colonists tried their luck. Sometime between being dropped off in the New World in 1587 and one of their leaders returning three years later to resupply them, all of the colonists—including Virginia Dare, the first English person born in the Americas—had vanished into the woods. To this day, their fate is unknown, although a host of fascinating theories are still debated and probably always will be.

The disappearance of the Roanoke colonists

did little to slow the process of the European conquest of North America. After the establishment of the Virginia colony in 1607, new English settlers began to trickle southward into Carolina, while Barbadians and Europeans from Charles Town (in present-day South Carolina) gradually began to populate the area around Wilmington. The town of Bath was established in 1706, and New Bern was settled shortly thereafter. The bloody Tuscarora War followed, and after a crushing defeat near present-day Snow Hill, in which hundreds were killed, the Tuscarora people retreated, opening the land along the Neuse River to European colonization.

COLONIALISM

The conflict between Europeans and Native Americans wasn't the only world-changing cultural encounter going on in the Southern colonies. By the middle of the 18th century, nearly 100,000 enslaved people had been brought to North Carolina from West Africa. By the end of the 18th century, many areas, especially those around Wilmington, had populations where enslaved African Americans outnumbered whites. Although North Carolina did not experience slavery on as vast a scale as South Carolina, there were a handful of plantations with more than 100 slaves, and many smaller plantations and town homes of wealthy planters, merchants, and politicians with smaller numbers of slaves. Africans and African Americans were an early and potent cultural force in the South, influencing the economy, politics, language, religion, music, architecture, and cuisine in ways still seen today.

In the 1730s the Great Wagon Road connected Pennsylvania with Georgia by cutting through the Mid-Atlantic and Southern backcountry of Virginia and North Carolina. Many travelers migrated south from Pennsylvania, among them a good number of German and Scottish-Irish settlers who found the mountains and Piedmont of North Carolina to their liking. Meanwhile, the port of Wilmington, growing into one of the most important in the state, saw a number of Gaelic-speaking Scots move through, following the river north and putting down roots around what is now Fayetteville.

The 18th century brought one conflict after another to the colony, from fights over the Vestry Act in the early 1700s, which attempted to establish the Anglican church as the one official faith of the colony, through various regional conflicts with Native Americans, and events that played out at a global level during the French and Indian War. At mid-century the population and economic importance of the Piedmont was growing exponentially, but colonial representation continued to be focused along the coast. Protesting local corruption and lack of governmental concern for the western region, a group of backcountry farmers organized themselves into an armed posse in resistance to colonial corruption. Calling themselves the Regulators, they eventually numbered more than 6,000. Mounting frustrations led to an attack by the Regulators on the Orange County courthouse in Hillsborough. Finally, a colonial militia was dispatched to

The seeds of our nation's independence were sown in North Carolina.

crush the movement, which it did at the Battle of Alamance in 1771. Six Regulators were captured and hanged at Hillsborough.

REVOLUTION AND STATEHOOD

Many believe the seeds of the American Revolution were sown, tended, and reaped in New England, but the southern colonies, particularly North Carolina, played important roles before and during the rebellion. In 1765, as the War of the Regulation was heating up, the residents of Brunswick Town, the colonial capital and the only deep-water port in the southern half of the colony, revolted in protest of the Stamp Act. They placed the royal governor under house arrest and put an end to taxation in the Cape Fear region, sending a strong message to the crown and to fellow patriots hungry to shake off the yoke of British rule. In the ensuing years, well-documented events like the Boston Tea Party, the Battles of Lexington and Concord, and the signing of the Declaration of Independence occurred, but North Carolina's role in leading the rebellion was far from over.

After the Battles of Lexington and Concord, the colonies were aflame with patriotic fervor, and Mecklenburg County (around Charlotte) passed the first colonial declaration rejecting the crown's authority. By this time, North Carolina, like the other colonies, had formed a provincial government, and it was busy in the tavern at Halifax writing the Halifax Resolves, the first official action in the colonies calling for independence from Britain. On April 12, 1776, the resolves were ratified and delegates carried them to the Second Continental Congress in Philadelphia. Other delegates were so inspired that more such resolves appeared, ultimately the Declaration of Independence was written and ratified, and the revolution was on in earnest.

Although North Carolina may have been the first to call for independence, the state was divided in its loyalties. Among the most noteworthy Loyalists was the community of Highland Scots living in and around modern-day

Fayetteville. Men from this community were marching to join General Cornwallis near Brunswick Town and Southport (then Smithville) when Patriots ambushed them at the bloody battle of Moore's Creek, killing 30 Scots and routing the Loyalist force.

North Carolinians fought all over the eastern seaboard during the Revolution, including about 1,000 who were with Washington at Valley Forge. The year 1780 brought fighting back home, particularly in the area around Charlotte, which a daunted General Cornwallis referred to as "the hornets' nest." The battle of Kings Mountain, west of Charlotte, was a pivotal moment in the war, and one that was particularly costly to the Loyalist forces. Cornwallis received another blow at the Battle of Guilford Courthouse; although technically a British victory, it weakened his forces considerably. By the time the war ended, thousands of North Carolinians were dead and the treasury was far in debt. But North Carolina was now a state with the business of statehood to attend to. The capital was moved inland to Raleigh, and 20 miles away at Chapel Hill, ground was broken for the establishment of the University of North Carolina, the first state university in the country.

THE FEDERAL ERA

The early 19th century in North Carolina was a good deal more peaceful than the previous hundred years had been. The first decade of the 1800s saw a religious awakening in which thousands of North Carolinians became devout Christians. At the same time, the introduction of the cotton gin and bright-leaf tobacco were economic boons in the state, particularly the eastern counties. Railroads and plank roads made trade immeasurably more efficient, bringing new prosperity to the Piedmont.

THE CIVIL WAR

Compared to South Carolina and a few other Southern states, North Carolina was considered politically moderate in the mid-19th century because it was less invested economically and politically in slavery. Combined with the knowledge that if secession became a reality, war would follow and North Carolina's tobacco and cotton fields would quickly become battlefields, secession was on the lips of everyone across the South. As some states voted to remove themselves from the Union, North Carolina's voters rejected a ballot measure authorizing a secession convention. As grand a gesture as that victory may have been, when fighting erupted at Fort Sumpter in Charleston Harbor, North Carolina's hand was forced and its secession was a reality. Secessionist governor John Ellis rejected Lincoln's call to federalize state militias, instead seizing control of the state and all federal military installations within its boundaries as well as the Charlotte Mint. North Carolina officially seceded on May 20, 1861, and a few weeks later Union ships began to blockade the coast. Roanoke Island in the Outer Banks fell, and a freedmen's colony (a home for enslaved people who had been freed or escaped) sprung up. New Bern, which fell in the spring of 1862, became a major focal point of Union military strategy and a thriving political base for freed and escaped African Americans. To the south, Fort Fisher, on the Cape Fear River just south of Wilmington, guarded the river's inlet and was crucial to the success of the blockade runners—smugglers whose speedy boats eluded the Union blockade. Fort Fisher kept Wilmington in Confederate hands until nearly the end of the war. When it finally did fall to Union forces in February 1865, it required what would be the largest amphibious assault in American military history until World War II. Wilmington was the last major port on the Confederacy's eastern seaboard, and its fall severed supply lines and crippled what remained of the Confederate army in the area.

The varying opinions felt by Southerners about the Civil War, in the South also called the War between the States, was particularly strong in North Carolina, where today you'll still hear whites refer to it as the War of Northern Aggression or the War of Yankee Aggression. More than 5,000 African Americans from North Carolina joined and fought in the Union Army, and there were pockets of strong Union sentiment and support among white North Carolinians, especially in the mountains. Some 10,000 North Carolinians fought for the Union. Zebulon Vance, who won the 1862 gubernatorial election and served as governor through the duration of the war, was a native of Weaverville, near Asheville, and felt acutely the state's ambivalence toward the Confederacy. Much to the consternation of Richmond (the Confederate capital), Governor Vance was adamant in his refusal to put the interests of the Confederacy over those of his own state. Mountain communities suffered tremendously during the war from acts of terrorism by deserters and rogues from both armies.

The latter years of the Civil War were particularly difficult for North Carolina and the rest of the South. Approximately 4,000 North Carolina men died at the Battle of Gettysburg alone. After laying waste to Georgia and South Carolina, General William T. Sherman's army entered North Carolina in the spring of 1865, destroying homes and farms. His march of fire and pillage spared Wilmington, which is one reason the town contains such an incredible collection of Federal architecture. The last major battle of the war was fought in North Carolina, when General Sherman and Confederate General Joseph Johnston engaged at Bentonville. Johnston surrendered to Sherman in Durham in April 1865.

By the end of the war more than 40,000 North Carolina soldiers were dead—a number equivalent to the entire present-day population of the city of Hickory, Apex, or Kannapolis.

RECONSTRUCTION AND THE NEW SOUTH

The years immediately after the war were painful as well, as a vast population of newly free African Americans tried to make new lives for themselves economically and politically in the face of tremendous opposition and violence from whites. The Ku Klux Klan was set up during this time, inaugurating an era of horror for African Americans throughout the country. Federal occupation and domination of the Southern states' political and legal systems also exacerbated resentment toward the North. The state's ratification of the 14th Amendment on July 4, 1868, brought North Carolina back into the Union.

The late 1800s saw large-scale investment in North Carolina's railroad system, launching the industrial boom of the New South. Agriculture changed in this era as the rise of tenancy created a new form of enslavement for many farmers—black, white, and Native American. R. J. Reynolds, Washington Duke, and other entrepreneurs built a massively lucrative empire of tobacco production from field to factory. Textile and furniture mills sprouted throughout the Piedmont, creating a new cultural landscape as rural Southerners migrated to mill towns.

THE 20TH CENTURY AND TODAY

The early decades of the 1900s brought an expanded global perspective to North Carolina, not only through the expanded economy and the coming of radio, but as natives of the state scattered across the globe. About 80,000 North Carolinians served in World War I, many of them young men who had never before left the state or perhaps even their home counties. Hundreds of thousands of African Americans migrated north during what became known as the Great Migration. The communities created by black North Carolinians in the Mid-Atlantic and the Northeast are still closely connected by culture and kinship to their cousins whose ancestors remained in the South. The invasion of the boll weevil, an insect that devastated the cotton industry, hastened the departure of Southerners of all races who had farmed cotton. The Great Depression hit hard across all economic sectors of the state in the 1930s, but New Deal employment programs were a boon to North Carolina's infrastructure, with the construction of hydroelectric dams, the Blue Ridge Parkway, and other public works.

North Carolina's modern-day military importance largely dates to the World War II era.

Installations at Fort Bragg, Camp Lejeune, and other still-vital bases were constructed or expanded. About 350,000 North Carolinians fought in World War II, and 7,000 of them died.

A few old-timers remember World War II quite vividly because they witnessed it firsthand: German U-Boats prowled the waters off the coast, torpedoing ships and sinking them with frightening regularity. These German submarines were often visible from the beach, but more often the evidence of their mission of terror and supply-chain disruption—corpses, wounded sailors, and the flotsam of exploded ships—washed up on the shore. More than 10,000 German prisoners were interned in prisoner-of-war camps, in some parts of the state becoming forced farm laborers. In Wilmington, just a few blocks from downtown, is an apartment complex that was part of a large prisoner-of-war compound for U-boat officers.

In the 1950s and 1960s, African Americans in North Carolina and throughout the United States struggled against the monolithic system of segregation and racism enshrined in the nation's Jim Crow laws. The Ku Klux Klan stepped up its pro-segregation efforts with political and physical violence against Native Americans as well as African Americans; in the famous 1958 Battle of Maxton, 500 armed Lumbee people foiled a Klan rally and sent the Knights running for their lives. Change arrived slowly. The University of North Carolina accepted its first African American graduate student in 1951 and the first black undergraduates four years later. Sit-ins in 1960 at the Woolworth's lunch counter in Greensboro began with four African American men, students at North Carolina A&T. On the second day of their protest they were joined by 23 other demonstrators; on the third day there were 300, and by day four about 1,000. This was a pivotal moment in the national civil rights movement, sparking sit-ins across the country in which an estimated 50,000 people participated. You can see the counter today at the International Civil Rights Center and Museum in Greensboro. Even as victories were won at the level of Congress and in the federal courts, as in *Brown v. the Board of Education* and the 1964 Civil Rights Act, actual change on the ground was inexorably slow and hard-won. North Carolina's contribution to the civil rights movement continues to be invaluable for the whole nation.

Government and Economy

POLITICAL LIFE
Liberal Enclaves
Although historically a red state, North Carolina's large population of college students, professors, and artists has created several boisterous enclaves of progressive politics. The outspoken archconservative U.S. Senator Jesse Helms supposedly questioned the need to spend public money on a state zoo in North Carolina "when we can just put up a fence around Chapel Hill." The Chapel Hill area is indeed the epicenter of North Carolina's liberalism, with its smaller neighboring town of Carrboro at its heart. Would-be Democratic presidential candidates and politicians on the campaign trail regularly stop here to bolster support in the state.

Although you'll find a mixture of political views statewide, the Triangle is not the only famously liberal community. In Asheville, lefty politics are part of the community's devotion to all things organic and DIY. Significant pockets of liberalism also exist in Boone, the cities of the Triad, and Wilmington.

Famous Figures
Several major players in modern American politics are from North Carolina. The best-known politician in recent years is former U.S. Senator John Edwards, who made two runs for the

White House, the first leading to a vice presidential spot on the Democratic ticket. Edwards was born in South Carolina but grew up here in the Sandhills. At the other end of the political spectrum, Monroe native Jesse Helms spent 30 years in the U.S. Senate, becoming one of the most prominent and outspoken conservative Republicans of our times. Upon his retirement, Helms was succeeded in the Senate by Salisbury-born Duke University graduate Elizabeth Dole, who had previously served in Ronald Reagan's cabinet and George H. W. Bush's cabinet. She was also president of the American Red Cross and had a close brush with the White House when her husband, Kansas Senator Bob Dole, ran for president in 1996.

MAJOR INDUSTRIES

Over the last 20 years, North Carolina has experienced tremendous shifts in its economy as the industries that once dominated the landscape and brought wealth and development declined. The **tobacco** industry ruled the state's economy for generations, employing innumerable North Carolinians from field to factory and funding a colossal portion of the state's physical and cultural infrastructure. The slow decline of the tobacco industry worldwide from the 1980s changed the state dramatically, especially the rural east, where tobacco fields once went from green to gold every fall. Other agricultural industries, especially **livestock**— chickens and hogs—are still important in the east. The **textile** industry, a giant for most of the 20th century, suffered the same decline as manufacturers sought cheaper labor overseas. Likewise, the **furniture** industry slipped into obscurity. Today, the once-thriving **fishing** industry is in steep decline, largely due to globalization and overfishing.

While these staple industries have fallen off, new industries and fields have sprouted across the state. **Pharmaceutical** and **biotech** companies have set up in the Research Triangle, formed by Raleigh, Durham, and Chapel Hill. The **film industry** has made Wilmington a hub of feature film production, Charlotte is a major production center for television programming and commercials, and Raleigh is home to a number of visual-effects studios that contribute to films and TV. **High-tech** leaders like Apple have set up in North Carolina, and other tech giants have followed, locating database and network centers here. Charlotte is second only to New York City among the country's largest **banking** centers. **Tourism** continues to grow and contribute in a major way to the state's economy. **Agriculture** continues to remain relevant, though it is increasingly becoming more specialized, especially as the demand for organic products and locally and regionally sourced products continues to be a trend.

Tourism

North Carolina has always drawn visitors to its mountains, waters, beaches, and cities. As the economy evolves, the tourism sector has become even more important. Beach landscapes sell themselves, but competition is strong to be the town visitors think of first. **Heritage tourism** is also enormously important, with a number of guidebooks and driving trails established or under development to promote history, traditional music, folk arts, and literary achievements. The state's Department of Commerce estimates that nearly 46 million people visit North Carolina every year, bringing in more than $19 billion, and that close to 200,000 state residents work in industries directly related to and dependent on tourism.

DISTRIBUTION OF WEALTH

For the most part, North Carolina is basically working-class. Pockets of significant wealth exist in urban areas, and as more and more retirees relocate to North Carolina, there are moneyed people in the mountains and coastal counties. Extensive white-collar job availability makes the Triangle a comparatively prosperous region, with average household incomes in 2010 exceeding $60,000, much higher than the state's average of just over $40,000.

The state also experiences significant **poverty.** The proportion of people living in poverty has been rising since 2000, partly due to the ongoing worldwide economic slowdown

© JASON FRYE

A number of modern day blacksmiths carry on this centuries-old tradition.

but also due to the derailment of many of North Carolina's backbone industries. As recently as 15 years ago, a high school graduate in small-town North Carolina could count on making a living wage in a mill or factory; nowadays those opportunities have dried up, and the poverty rate in 2011 was just over 16 percent. Even more distressing, the number of children living in poverty is just over 24 percent, and for children under age 6 climbing to 28 percent.

The northeastern quadrant of North Carolina is the most critically impoverished, which points to **financial inequality** correlating to race, as the region has a significant African American population. Broken down by ethnicity, the data reveal that 10 percent of urban and rural whites live in poverty, while 20-30 percent of rural and urban Latinos, African Americans, and Native Americans live in poverty.

Several hardworking organizations and activists are trying to alleviate the economic hardship found in North Carolina. National organizations like **Habitat for Humanity** (www.habitat.org) and regional groups like the **Southern Coalition for Social Justice** (http://southerncoalition.org) and the **Institute for Southern Studies** (www.southernstudies.org) bring community activism and research to the state. There are also excellent North Carolina-based advocates in groups such as the **North Carolina Rural Economic Development Center** (www.ncruralcenter.org), the **North Carolina Justice Center** (www.ncjustice.org), the **Black Family Land Trust** (www.bflt.org), and **Student Action with Farmworkers** (http://saf-unite.org).

People and Culture

DEMOGRAPHICS

The 10th most populous state in the union, North Carolina's population of 9.75 million residents is slightly larger than New Jersey and slightly smaller than Georgia. More than two-thirds of North Carolinians are white, primarily of German and Scottish-Irish descent, and not quite one-quarter are African American. The state's population is about 8.6 percent Latino, and has the seventh-largest Native American population of any state after California, Arizona, Oklahoma, New Mexico, Washington, and Alaska.

More than 40 percent of North Carolinians are between the ages of 25 and 59, but the older population is steadily rising, due in large part to the state's popularity with retirees. The majority—about 70 percent—of North Carolinians live in family groups, with married couples constituting about half of those, and married couples with children (not mutually exclusive data sets) making up almost one-quarter of households. Of the remaining one-third of the state's population who live in "nonfamily households"—that is, not with blood relatives or a legally recognized spouse—the vast majority are individuals living on their own. Unmarried couples, both straight and gay, have a much lower rate of cohabitation here than in more urban parts of the United States, but such households are common and accepted in the Triangle, Asheville, Charlotte, and other urban areas.

Native Americans

Many Americans have never heard of the **Lumbee people** despite the fact that they claim to be the largest Native American nation east of the Mississippi. This is in part due to the federal government's refusal to grant them official recognition, although the state of North Carolina does recognize them. The Lumbee are primarily based in and around Robeson County in the swampy southeastern corner of the state, their traditional home. In the Great Smoky Mountains, the town of Cherokee on the Qualla Boundary, which is Cherokee-administered land, is the governmental seat of the **Eastern Band of the Cherokee.** The Eastern Band are largely descended from those Cherokee people who escaped arrest during the deportation of the Southeast's Native Americans on the Trail of Tears in the 19th century, or who made the forced march to Oklahoma but survived and walked home to the mountains again. The Lumbee people and Cherokee people are both important cultural groups in North Carolina. Several other Native American communities are indigenous to the state as well; those recognized by the state are the **Waccamaw-Siouan, Occaneechi Band of the Saponi Nation, Haliwa-Saponi, Coharie, Sappony,** and **Meherrin.**

© JASON FRYE

Small-town life still thrives in North Carolina.

Latinos

North Carolina has one of the fastest-growing Latino populations in the United States, a community whose ranks have swelled since the 1990s, in particular as hundreds of thousands of **Mexican and Central American laborers** came to work in the agricultural, industrial, and formerly booming construction trades. Their presence in such large numbers makes for some unexpectedly quirky cultural juxtapositions, as in small rural towns that are now majority Latino, or in Charlotte, where the Latino population has made Roman Catholicism the most common religion.

Other Immigrants

Significant numbers of non-Latino immigrants also live in North Carolina. Charlotte is a dizzying hodgepodge of ethnicities, where native Southerners live and work alongside **Asians, Africans,** and **Middle Easterners,** where mosques and synagogues and *wats* welcome worshipers just down the street from Baptist churches and Houses of Prayer. Many **Hmong** and other **Southeast Asian** immigrants have settled in the northern foothills and the Piedmont Triad, and the dense thicket of universities in the Triangle attracts academics from around the world.

RELIGION

As early as the 17th century, North Carolina's religious landscape foreshadowed the diversity we enjoy today. The first Christians in North Carolina were Quakers, soon followed by Anglicans, Presbyterians, Baptists, Moravians, Methodists, and Roman Catholics. Native American and African religions, present in the early colonial days, were never totally quashed by European influence, and Barbadian Sephardic Jews were here early on as well. All of these religions remain today, with enrichment by the presence of Muslims, Buddhists, and an amazing mosaic of other Christian groups.

North Carolina claims as its own one of the world's most influential modern religious figures, Billy Graham, who was raised on a dairy farm outside Charlotte and experienced his Christian religious awakening in 1934. After preaching in person to more people around the world than anyone in human history, and being involved with every U.S. president since Harry Truman, Billy Graham is now home in his native state, where he divides his time between Charlotte and Montreat, outside Asheville.

LANGUAGE

Few states can boast the linguistic diversity of North Carolina. North Carolina speech varies widely by region and even from county to county. These variations have to do with the historical patterns of settlement in a given area—whether Scots-Irish or German ancestry is common, how long Native American languages survived after the arrival of the Europeans, the presence or lack of African influence—as well as other historical patterns of trade and communication.

Of our distinct regional accents, the **Outer Banks brogue** is probably the best known. Much like the residents of the Chesapeake islands in Maryland and Virginia, "Hoi Toiders," as Outer Bankers are jokingly called, because of how they pronounce the phrase "high tide," have a striking dialect that resembles certain dialects in the north of England. "I" is rounded into "oi," the *r* sound is often hard, and many distinctive words survive from long-ago English, Scottish, and Irish dialects. Not dissimilar is the Appalachian dialect heard through much of the mountains. The effect is more subtle than in the Outer Banks, but "oi" replaces "I" in Appalachian English too, and *r*'s are emphasized. A telltale sign of upcountry origins is the pronunciation of the vowel in words like bear and hair, which in the mountains is flattened almost inside-out so that the words are pronounced something like "barr" and "harr." This is similar to mountain accents in Tennessee, West Virginia, Virginia, and Kentucky.

There are a great many smaller linguistic zones peppered throughout the state. Folks from up around the **Virginia border** in eastern North Carolina may have a distinctively Virginian accent. Listen for the classic telltale word *house*. Southside Virginians and their neighbors south of the state line will pronounce it "hease," with a flat vowel. **Cherokee English,** heard in the Smokies, combines the Appalachian sound with a distinctively Cherokee rhythm, while **Lumbee English,** spoken in and around Robeson County in the southeast, combines sounds somewhat like those of the Outer Banks or deep mountains with a wealth of unusual grammatical structures and vocabulary of unknown origin. Oft-cited examples are the Lumbee construction "be's," a present-tense form of "to be," and words like *ellick* for coffee and *juvember* for slingshot: "Get me some more ellick, please, if you be's going to the market." Residents of the **Sandhills** area, bounded by the Uwharries to the west, Sanford to the north, and Southern Pines to the southeast, have a highly unusual rhythm to their speech—a rapid, soft, almost filigreed way of talking, delivered in bursts between halting pauses. Down around Wilmington and south to the South Carolina state line, African American English, and to a lesser extent white English, have some of the inflections of the **Gullah language** of the Lowcountry. These are only a few of the state's dialects, and even these have subvariations. Old-timers can pinpoint geographical differences within these categories—whether a

Lumbee speaker is from Prospect or Drowning Creek, for example, or whether a Banker is from Ocracoke or Hatteras.

Of course, English is hardly the only language spoken here. If you visit Cherokee, you'll see that many street and commercial signs bear pretty, twisty symbols in a script that looks like a cross between Khmer or Sanskrit and Cyrillic; **written Cherokee** uses the script famously devised by **Sequoyah** in the early 19th century. Cherokee also survives as a spoken language, mostly among the elders in traditional communities such as Snowbird, near Robbinsville, and many younger Cherokee people are determined to learn and pass on their ancestral tongue, but the small pool of speakers points to the slow death of the language. **Spanish** is widely spoken throughout the state as the Latino population continues to grow rapidly, and within Latino communities here are many national and regional dialects of Spanish. Some Central American immigrants who speak indigenous languages arrive unable to understand English or Spanish. Anyone who doubts that newcomers to this country are dedicated to the task of integrating into American society need only consider the incredibly difficult task faced by such immigrants, who must first learn Spanish before they can enroll in ESL programs to learn English.

The Arts

As much as North Carolinians like to brag about the beaches and mountains and college sports teams, it's the artists across the state who help North Carolina distinguish itself. There is an incredibly rich and complex cultural heritage here that has strong support from the North Carolina Arts Council and a vast network of local and regional arts organizations. These groups have supplied inspiration, financial and emotional support, and sustenance for generations of remarkable musicians, writers, actors, and other artists.

LITERATURE

Storytelling seems to come naturally to Southerners. From the master storytellers of Jack Tales in the Blue Ridge to the distinguished journalists we see every night on television, North Carolinians have a singular gift for communication. Thomas Wolfe was an Asheville native, and O. Henry, whose real name was William Sidney Porter, was born and raised in Greensboro. Tom Robbins (*Even Cowgirls Get the Blues*) was born in Blowing Rock. Charles Frazier (*Cold Mountain*) is from Asheville. Sarah Dessen (*Just Listen*) is from Chapel Hill. Kaye Gibbons, Lee Smith, Fred Chappell, Randal Kenan, and Clyde Edgerton, leading lights in Southern fiction, are all natives or residents of North Carolina. Also closely associated with the state are Carl Sandburg, David Sedaris, Armistead Maupin, and Betsy Byars, who have all lived here at some point in their lives. Arts programs focused on creative writing have sprung up across the state, imbuing the literary scenes in towns like Wilmington, Greensboro, Asheville, and Chapel Hill with talented undergraduate and graduate students and their professors. Notable writers teaching creative writing programs include poet A. Van Jordan, essayist David Gessner, and novelist and short story writer Jill McCorkle.

North Carolina has also given the world some of the giants of 20th-century journalism. Edward R. Murrow, Charles Kuralt, David Brinkley, and Howard Cosell were all sons of Carolina, and Charlie Rose carries their torch today.

MUSIC

It's hard to know where to begin in describing the importance of music to North Carolinians. With fiddlers conventions, renowned symphony orchestras, busy indie-rock scenes, and a thriving gospel-music industry, there is no escaping good music here. Since the earliest days of recorded country music, North Carolinians have shared their songs with the world. Charlie Poole and Wade Mainer were among the first to record, and became influential artists in the 1930s. By 1945 a banjo player named Earl Scruggs was helping create what would become the quintessential sound of **bluegrass** music, particularly his three-fingered picking style. Bluegrass greats like Del McCoury helped further define the sound. Today, bluegrass is alive and well in North Carolina; Steve Martin's collaboration with the Steep Canyon Rangers sells out concerts around the world and garners awards at every turn, and the late Doc Watson's annual **MerleFest** is still going strong. **Country** musicians like Ronnie Milsap, Donna Fargo, Charlie Daniels, and Randy Travis made

big names for themselves from the 1970s to the 1990s; more recently, Kellie Pickler and Scottie McCreery (of *American Idol* fame) and Eric Church have made waves on the country charts.

The growth of **jazz** and **funk** would be unimaginably different if not for a number of notable innovators that make North Carolina nearly as important as New Orleans to the development of these genres. John Coltrane was raised in High Point, Thelonious Monk was a native of Rocky Mount, Nina Simone hails from Tryon, and Dizzy Gillespie grew up just over the South Carolina state line but contributed greatly when he studied music in Laurinburg. On the funk side of the coin, what would the genre be without George Clinton, founder of Parliament and Parliament-Funkadelic? Saxophonist Maceo Parker and his brother, drummer Melvin Parker, played with Clinton and with South Carolina's favorite son and the Godfather of Soul, James Brown, to help develop the classic funk sound and influence the groove-driven side of **soul** music.

In North Carolina, you're never far from some good **gospel** music. On the coast, African American choirs blend spirituality and faith with showmanship and serious talent to perform beautiful inspired sets. In the mountains, you're more likely to find gospel quartets and old-time gospel music, which is more inspired by bluegrass and traditional music, at camp meetings and gospel sings on weekend nights. The state's Native American communities also have thriving gospel traditions of their own.

Artists that include James Taylor, Tori Amos, Clay Aiken, the Squirrel Nut Zippers, the Avett Brothers, Fred Durst (from Limp Bizkit), rapper and producer Jermaine Dupri, Corrosion of Conformity, Ben Folds Five, Daughtry, Southern Culture on the Skids, and Megafaun have all had a hand in shaping the state's musical legacy.

THEATER

Regional theater companies such as the venerable Flat Rock Playhouse near Hendersonville make great theater accessible in small towns

Antiquing and antique restoration are big across the state.

and rural areas. Wilmington is home to Thalian Hall and the Thalian Association, a group founded in 1788 that was named the Official Community Theatre of North Carolina thanks to their long-running commitment to the arts in Wilmington. The North Carolina School for the Arts in Winston-Salem mints great actors and filmmakers, among other artists. The film and television industries have long recognized North Carolina as a hotbed of talent as well as a place with amazing locations to film at.

For some reason, **outdoor historical dramas** have long flourished in North Carolina. The most famous is North Carolina playwright Paul Green's *Lost Colony,* which has been performed every summer since 1937 on Roanoke Island, except during World War II when German U-boats lurked nearby. The Cherokee people depict emblematic episodes in their history in the outdoor drama *Unto These Hills,* in production since 1950. The community of Boone has presented *Horn in the West* since 1952, and it is joined by Valdese and several other communities in North Carolina in turning to performance tableaux to commemorate their heritage. It's especially important to note that among the characteristics of outdoor drama in North Carolina is the fact that the cast, crew, and often the producers and playwrights are members of the communities whose stories the plays tell.

ARTS AND CRAFTS

Folk art and studio craft show vitality in North Carolina. Several communities are known worldwide for their local traditions, and countless individual artists, studios, and galleries can be found across the state.

As people become more accustomed to a world where almost every object we see and use was mass-produced far away, we develop an ever deeper appreciation for the depth of skill and aesthetic complexity that went into the production of everyday objects in past generations. North Carolinians have always been great crafters of utilitarian and occupational necessities. As you travel through the state, keep an eye out for objects that you might not immediately recognize as art—barns, fishing nets, woven chair bottoms—but that were made with the skill and artistry of generations-old traditions. In North Carolina, art is everywhere.

Food

You'll probably have heard of North Carolina's most famous specialties—**barbecue, Brunswick stew,** and **hush puppies**—but are you brave enough to venture deeper into the hinterlands of Carolina cooking? Few snacks are more viscerally craved by locals, and more revolting to non-Southerners, than **boiled peanuts.** The recipe is simple: Green peanuts are boiled in their shells in bulk in water as salty as the chef deems necessary. Once they're soft and slimy, the peanuts are dumped into a strainer and are ready to eat. All you need to make them is a big kettle and a fire, so boiled peanuts are often made and sold in small bags at roadside stands, primarily in the Lowcountry and coastal plain, but increasingly in the mountains as well. Often these roadside stands are themselves folk art, with handmade signs reading "Bolit P-Nuts Here," with a collection of carvings or sculptures for sale in the bed of a truck nearby. To eat a boiled peanut, pick it up by the ends with your thumb and forefinger and place it lengthwise between your front teeth. Gently crack open the shell—don't bite through it—and detach the halves. Pry off half of the shell, and nip or slurp the peanuts out as if you're eating an oyster (boiled peanuts often show up at Lowcountry oyster roasts). Toss the shell out the window—chances are you're driving as you eat—and have another. Be sure you have a lot of something to drink close at hand, because you'll soon get thirsty.

Many cultures have a recipe that makes thrifty use of the leftover meat scraps that are too small or too few or too disgusting to be served alone. For upper Piedmont Carolinians, particularly those of German ancestry raised in the wavy ribbon of towns between Charlotte and Winston-Salem, that delicacy is **livermush.** Some folks say that if you're from the Mid-Atlantic and are familiar with scrapple, you'll have a pretty good idea of what livermush is like; that's not true—livermush is much worse and tastes like some bitter combination of burning hair and pepper. Under North Carolina law (really), livermush must contain at least 30 percent hog liver, which is supplemented with sundry scraps from hog heads, sometimes some skin, and cornmeal. At the factory, it's mashed up and cooked in loaves. In the kitchen, it's sliced and fried. You can eat it at breakfast like sausage, in a sandwich, or even on a stick if you go to the annual livermush festivals in Drexel and Shelby. Should you try it? Yes, at least a bite; plenty of people like it.

In the eastern part of the state, a similar aesthetic underlies the creation of **hog hash,** best made directly after an old-time hog killing, when the animal's organs are pulled steaming hot out of the carcass in the frosty fall morning. The liver, lungs, and a variety of other organs and appendages are dumped in a kettle with potatoes, a liquid base (broth, milk, or just water), and some vegetables and seasonings. Unlike livermush, hog hash is served in bowls or tubs as a dark, musky stew; it's not common.

Another food that you have to look pretty hard for is **dandoodle,** also called **tom thumbs,** seen in far northeastern North Carolina and the bordering Virginia counties. At hog-killing time, the animal's stomach is removed and stuffed with sausage and flavorings. It's then tied shut and hung in the smokehouse for seasoning with hickory smoke. Like livermush, dandoodle comes out in a sort of loaf shape, held together by the stomach membrane. Some people toss their tom thumbs in a pot to boil, either alone or with greens, while others slice them and lay them out with sliced boiled eggs.

You can read all about these and other acquired tastes at **NCFOOD** (www.ncfolk.org) or **Our State Eats** by *Our State* magazine (www.ourstate.com), two food blogs devoted to Carolina cooking, or on the **Southern Foodways Alliance** (www.southernfoodways.com) and **Dixie Dining** (www.dixiedining.com) websites.

Vegetarians and devotees of organic food, fear not; North Carolina is an unusually progressive state when it comes to healthy and homegrown grub. Nevertheless, if you want to avoid meat, you have to be cautious when ordering at a restaurant: Make sure the beans are made with vegetable oil rather than lard, ask if the salad dressing contains anchovies, beware of hidden fish and oyster sauce. Traditional Southern cooking makes liberal use of fatback (cured pork fat) and other animal products; greens are often boiled with a strip of fatback or a hambone, as are most soups and stews. Even pie crusts are still made with lard in many old-time kitchens.

In the major cities, you'll find organic grocery stores. Earth Fare and Whole Foods are the most common chains, but there are also plenty of small independent markets. Farmers markets and roadside stands are so plentiful that they almost have to fight for space. Visit the state Department of Agriculture's **North Carolina Farm Fresh** (www.ncfarmfresh.com) for directories of farmers markets and pick-your-own farms and orchards.

ESSENTIALS

Getting There

BY AIR

The state where air travel began has over 70 public airports, almost 300 privately owned airfields, and about 20 "fly-in" communities where residents share an airstrip and have their own hangar space. Nine airports have regularly scheduled passenger service, and two of them host international flights. The state's Department of Transportation estimates that more than 35 million people fly in and out of North Carolina every year. The main hubs are North Carolina's international airports in Charlotte, Greensboro, and Raleigh-Durham; Wilmington has more limited service.

To reach the coast by air, your nearest airports are in Wilmington and Raleigh, depending on your end destination. From either airport, you'll need a rental car or a friend. The **Wilmington International Airport** (ILM, 1740 Airport Blvd., Wilmington, 910/341-4125, www.flyilm.com) is only 15 minutes from Wrightsville Beach. **Raleigh-Durham International Airport** (RDU, 2400 W. Terminal Blvd., Morrisville, 919/840-2123, www.rdu.com) is farther from the coast. Located in Wake County about midway between Raleigh and Durham, it has flights to most domestic hubs as well as London,

© IOFOTO/123RF.COM

Toronto, and Cancún, Mexico. Hourly and daily parking is available for reasonable rates within walking distance of the terminals and in satellite lots linked by shuttle buses. The nearest beach to Raleigh is Wrightsville Beach, two hours south; drive for another 15-20 minutes to reach Carolina Beach and Kure Beach. Topsail Island (north of Wilmington and Wrightsville Beach) is two and a half hours away. To reach the central beaches of the Crystal Coast and the southern beaches of Brunswick County, you'll need almost three hours of windshield time from Raleigh. It will take you between three and four hours to reach the Outer Banks, depending on which beach town you're visiting. Ocracoke is a whopping five hours from Raleigh, thanks in large part to a long ferry ride to this one-time pirate haven.

The eighth busiest airport in the country, **Charlotte Douglas International Airport** (CLT, 5501 Josh Birmingham Pkwy., Charlotte, 800/359-2342, http://charmeck. org) has more than 730 daily departures and is served by dozens of airlines. There are nonstop flights to 140 U.S. cities as well as international flights to Latin America and the Caribbean, London, Frankfurt, Munich, and Toronto. Parking is abundant and inexpensive, with parking shuttle buses operating from 5am. Arriving in Charlotte isn't necessarily ideal for a visit to the beach. By car from Charlotte, it's four hours to Wrightsville Beach, four and a half hours to Topsail Island, and five hours to the beaches of Brunswick County. The drive is long and isolated, with few spots to stop for gas or food. If you're flying into Charlotte, look into a commuter flight into the Wilmington Airport. It will be worth the money.

In addition to the Wilmington airport, several smaller airports offer regularly scheduled domestic passenger service. **Fayetteville Regional Airport** (FAY, 400 Airport Rd., Fayetteville, 910/433-1160, www.flyfay.com), **Pitt-Greenville Airport** (PGV, 400 Airport Rd., Greenville, 252/902-2025), **Coastal Carolina Regional Airport** (EWN, 200 Terminal Dr., New Bern, 252/638-8591), and the **Albert J. Ellis Airport** (OAJ, 264 Albert

An airplane waits on the runway at Charlotte Douglas International Airport.

Ellis Airport Rd., Richlands, 910/324-1100) near Jacksonville and Richlands are all on or within a couple hours drive of the coast. You can fly Delta or US Airways into any of them, and United offers service into Pitt-Greenville Airport. Pitt-Greenville Airport has flights to Charlotte, and New Bern's Coastal Carolina Regional Airport has flights to Atlanta and Charlotte. Albert J. Ellis Airport has flights to Atlanta, Charlotte, and Washington DC.

Private aircraft can fly into any of over 75 regional, county, and municipal air strips statewide; **NC Airports Association** (www.ncairports.org) has a full list with phone numbers, website links, navigational information, airstrip specifications, and aerial photos. For historical reasons there are more municipal airports in the central and western parts of the state. When the state government started handing out grants for small public airstrips in the 1950s, there were already many surplus military airfields in the eastern part of the state, a legacy of World War II.

BY CAR

Several major interstate highways run through North Carolina, so if you're driving and would prefer that your trip be efficient rather than scenic, you've got several choices. From anywhere along the eastern seaboard, I-95 slices through the eastern third of the state, providing easy access to the beaches, which are mostly one or two hours east of I-95, and to the Triangle area, under an hour west of I-95 via U.S. 64, U.S. 70, or I-40. From the north, you might choose to veer southwest at Richmond, Virginia, on I-85; this is an efficient route to Durham and Chapel Hill as well as to the Triad and Charlotte regions.

I-40 starts in California and runs east to Wilmington. It's a fast road all the way through North Carolina, although weather—ice in the fall, winter, and spring, and fog any time of year—might slow you down considerably

between Knoxville, Tennessee, and Asheville. U.S. 64 and I-77 connect North Carolina to the Midwest. I-77 cuts through the toe of Virginia, in the mountains, straight to Charlotte, while U.S. 64 meanders east through the Triangle all the way to Roanoke Island and the Outer Banks. From the Deep South or Texas, the best bet is probably I-20 to Atlanta, and from there I-85 to Charlotte, or U.S. 19 or U.S. 23 if you're going to the mountains.

There are no checkpoints at the state line to inspect vehicles for produce or animals, but sobriety checkpoints are established and staffed throughout the year.

BY BUS

Travel around North Carolina can be accomplished easily and cheaply by bus. **Greyhound** (800/231-2222, www.greyhound.com) offers daily service to many towns and cities on or near the coast, although there is currently no Greyhound service to the Outer Banks. Before you reserve bus tickets, be sure to check out special discounts on the Greyhound website. There are often regional promotions as well as special "Go Anywhere" fares as low as $29 each way with 14-day advance booking, for example, as well as regular discounts for students and seniors.

These days, the large buses used by Greyhound and its local subsidiaries are clean and comfortable, and if you make a reservation ahead of time, you can choose your seat. One word of caution is that some bus stations are located in seedy parts of town, so make sure taxi service is available at your destination station after dark.

BY TRAIN

Train service is not currently available along the coast, but **Amtrak** (800/872-7245, www.amtrak.com) does have service in Raleigh and Charlotte, making those cities starting points for coastal exploration.

Getting Around

BY CAR

North Carolina's highway system, with the largest network of state-maintained roads in the country and a good interstate grid, provides access to the whole state. I-95 crosses north-south, demarcating the eastern third of the state, and I-85 runs northeast-southwest from north of the Triangle area through Charlotte. I-40 is the primary east-west route, from Wilmington through the Smoky Mountains to Knoxville, Tennessee. The highest speed limit, which applies to some rural interstates and four-lane roads, is 70 mph. Highways in developed areas have much lower speed limits, and in residential areas it's a good idea to keep it under 25 mph.

You can take your pick of car-rental agencies at the major airports at Charlotte, Winston-Salem, and Raleigh-Durham; there are fewer choices at smaller regional airports. There are also car-rental pickup and drop-off offices in many towns. Rental car companies in North Carolina include Alamo (800/462-5266, www.alamo.com), Avis (877/222-9075, www.avis.com), Budget (800/218-7992, www.budget.com), Dollar (800/800-4000, www.dollar.com), Enterprise (800/261-7331, www.enterprise.com), Hertz (800/654-3131, www.hertz.com), National (877/222-9058, www.nationalcar.com), Thrifty (800/847-4389, www.thrifty.com), and Triangle Rent-A-Car (800/643-7368, www. trianglerentacar.com). To rent a car you must be at least 25 years old, and have both a valid driver's license and a credit card, although some companies will accept a cash security deposit in lieu of credit.

Driving to and through the Outer Banks can be a bit complicated, depending on your destination, because there are not many bridges. The northern banks are linked to the mainland by bridges between Point Harbor and Kitty Hawk, and from Manns Harbor over Roanoke Island to just south of Nags Head. There are no bridges to Hatteras, and none until you get all the way to the southern end of the banks, where bridges link Morehead City and Cedar Point to the towns along Bogue Banks. The state's excellent ferry system connects the Outer Banks to the mainland; it's a fun way to travel. Detailed information is available from the state Department of Transportation (www.ncdot.gov/ferry). Several ferries link mainland points across sounds and rivers, while ferries from Currituck to Knotts Island, and from both Swan Quarter and Cedar Island to Ocracoke, will carry you to the Outer Banks.

Highway Safety

Write "*HP" (*47) on a sticky note and affix it to your dashboard. That's the direct free hotline to the North Carolina Highway Patrol, which will send help if you're trouble. North Carolinians don't hesitate to report aggressive, reckless, or drunk motorists to the highway patrol, and you might be reported by another

DRIVING TRAILS

The state of North Carolina and a variety of regional organizations have created a wonderful network of "trails"–thematic itineraries showcasing North Carolina's treasures. Check out the destinations on this sampling of trails.

- **Civil War Traveler:** www.civilwartraveler.com/east/nc/index.html
- **Core Sound Itinerary:** www.ncfolk.org
- **Discover Craft North Carolina:** www.discovercraftnc.org
- **Historic Albemarle Tour (Northeast coast):** www.historicalbemarletour.org
- **North Carolina Scenic Byways:** www.ncdot.gov/travel/scenic

driver if you're tailgating, speeding, weaving, or driving aggressively. What passes for normal driving in the Northeast, Florida, and many other parts of the United States is regarded as aggressive driving in the South. It's not that people are being unfriendly by turning others in; they just don't want to be endangered by someone else's impatience.

Pull well off the road and turn on your hazard lights if you have an accident. If you can't safely pull your vehicle out of traffic, at least get away from the roadway. A distressing number of motorists with disabled vehicles as well as pedestrians are struck and killed by cars every year.

Some rules to remember while driving in North Carolina: Wearing your seat belt is required by law; child safety seats are mandatory for anyone under age 8 or weighing less than 80 pounds; and if it's raining hard enough to need windshield wipers, you must also turn your headlights on.

Weather Considerations

If you're driving in the mountains in the morning or at night, you may run into heavy fog. Because the clouds perch on and around mountaintops, you may find yourself in clear weather one moment and only seconds later in a fog with little visibility. It can be dangerous and frightening, but if this happens, slow down, keep an eye on the lines on the road, watch for other cars, and put on your low beams. As in any kind of bad weather, it's always best to find a safe place to pull off the road and wait for the weather to improve. Fog can dissipate as quickly as it appears.

In the winter you might encounter icy roads in any part of the state, but you're most likely to find that weather in the mountains. Many Southerners on the coast and in the Piedmont tend to panic when snow is forecast. In anticipation of a half-inch dusting of snow, schools and businesses may close, fleets of sand and salt trucks hit the highway, and residents mob the grocery stores. This overreaction to snow makes the roads a little safer because many folks are more likely to stay home, but those who do drive in winter weather are less likely to know how to drive on ice than the average Yankee or Midwesterner. That can make the roads hazardous, so even if you are an experienced snow driver, stay alert.

Wildlife on the Road

A final note about highway travel: Be conscious of wildlife. Deer, rabbits, turtles, foxes, coyotes, raccoons, and opossums litter the highways. Head-on collisions with deer can be fatal to both species, and smaller animals die because drivers are going too fast to avoid them. If you see an injured animal and are able to help it without putting yourself in danger, you'll find a phalanx of wildlife rehabilitators throughout the state to give it the care it needs.

The large number of deer in urban and rural areas makes them frequent victims of highway accidents. In clear weather when there's not much oncoming traffic, use your high beams so that you'll see them from farther away. If you see a deer cross the road in front of you, remember that they usually travel in small herds, and there may be several more waiting to jump out.

Road Etiquette

Certain informal rules of road etiquette apply in North Carolina, and they help make driving less stressful. North Carolina drivers willingly let others vehicles get in front of them, whether merging onto the highway or exiting a parking lot. Wave to say thanks when someone lets you in; positive reinforcement helps keep these habits alive. Folks will often wave at drivers in oncoming traffic on two-lane country roads, and there is an expectation of a quick wave from drivers and pedestrians as well. It's not a big production; simply lift two or three fingers off the steering wheel. A general rule of thumb is that if you're able to discern the facial features of someone outside your car, waving to that person is appropriate.

Drivers are legally obligated to pull over to let emergency vehicles pass. There's also an old tradition of pulling over to allow funeral processions to pass. Very few drivers are willing to merge into or cross a train of cars headed for a funeral, but in rural areas you will still see drivers pulling all the way off the road and waiting for a procession to pass before resuming driving. It's meant as a gesture of respect to the deceased and the mourners.

In all of these situations, safety should be the top priority. You don't need to wave or make eye contact with someone you feel is threatening, and don't pull off the road if there's no safe place to do so. But if you show courtesy to other drivers when you're able, you'll find that traffic karma will work its way back around to you when it's needed.

BY BUS

Municipal bus services operate in larger towns and some of the more popular tourist areas. **Hatteras Tours** (www.hattarastours.com, 252/986-2995) offers narrated tours of the islands of the Outer Banks, with a focus on the region's colorful history. There are ghost tours, Christian tours, farm tours, home and garden tours, Civil War history tours, ecology tours, and many other specialized tours, as well as tours of historic sites within many cities and towns; see www.visitnc.com to search for bus tours by town, region, or keyword. The state **Department of Transportation** (www.ncdot.gov/nctransit) maintains an index of information on the state's 99 public transportation systems, including those that serve rural counties.

BY BICYCLE

Before the Wright brothers made history as the first aviators, they were bicycle men. While the mountains offer the challenge of elevation, the relatively flat terrain along the coast offers challenges of its own. There are hundreds of organized bicycling events every year, many of them in support of charities, and they welcome participants from all over. The most popular bike events are held spring to fall, including a six-day Ocracoke Vacation Tour from New Bern to the tip of the Outer Banks. Other public cycling events include January's New Year's Day Breakfast Ride in Jacksonville and March's Rumba on the Lumber 5K Run and Bike Ride in Lumberton. June has bicycling events as part

You can use many modes of transportation to travel around North Carolina.

of the North Carolina Blueberry Festival in Burgaw. In late September is the state-spanning Annual Mountains to the Coast Ride that even goes to the islands of the Outer Banks by ferry; approximately 1,000 cyclists take part. For a full roster of events, see the official **Calendar of Bicycling Events** (www.ncdot.gov/bikeped/bicycle/events).

Baggage cars on **Amtrak**'s *Piedmont* trains are equipped with bicycle racks; call 800/872-7245 to reserve bike space on a train. You can also take your bicycle on any of the seven **North Carolina Ferries** (800/293-3779, www.ncdot.gov/ferry).

BY TRAIN

North Carolina has good rail connections among the major cities in the central part of the state, but lacks service to the coast.

BY FERRY

For hundreds of years, ferries were a crucial link between points on North Carolina's coast, and they still provide an essential service today. The **North Carolina Department of Transportation's Ferry Division** (877/293-3779, www.ncdot.gov/ferry) operates seven primary ferry routes along the coast. All ferries have restrooms, and some can accommodate cars and allow pets. Commercial ferries also operate throughout the coastal region.

Conduct and Customs

GREETINGS

Common courtesy, such as saying "please" and "thank you," being deferential to the elderly, and demonstrating concern for others, is hardly proprietary to the South. No matter where you're from, chances are your parents raised you to "act like folks," as people say here. The difference is that in North Carolina and elsewhere in the South, manners are somewhat more ritualized.

If you're unfamiliar with Southern ways, the thing you may find strangest is the friendliness of strangers. When passing a stranger on the sidewalk or in a corridor, riding together in an elevator, or even washing hands in the restroom, eye contact and a quick greeting are usually in order. Most common greetings are "Hey," "How you doing," and "How you," spoken as a statement rather than a question. The reply is usually equally casual: "Doing good, how about you," pronounced with just four syllables, "Doin' good, 'bout you," again spoken as a statement rather than a question. Often that's the end of the conversation, although passengers on elevators sometimes wish each other a good day when one gets out. In these encounters, eye contact needn't be lingering, there's no expectation of false pleasantries, and there is certainly no obligation to engage someone who makes you uncomfortable.

It's standard courtesy in a retail or similarly casual transaction to inquire as to the well-being of the person serving you. It takes little time, especially when delivered in the spoken shorthand most Southerners use. For instance, a cashier at McDonalds in another part of the country might greet you with "What would you like?" or simply wait for your order and not speak until asking for your money. The transaction here would more likely start with the "How you," "Doin' good, 'bout you," exchange. With that two- or three-second dialogue, a bit of human warmth and mutual respect is shared.

It's expected that people hold doors open for each other and thank each other for doing so. In addressing someone elderly that you don't know well, the standard courtesy is to use a title, Mr. or Ms. with the last name, or in friendlier situations, Mr. or Ms. the first name. The South was way ahead of the curve in adopting the "Ms." designation; Southerners have always pronounced both "Mrs." and "Miss" as "miz." North Carolinians will likely address you as ma'am or sir regardless of your age; it doesn't mean they think you're old.

TIPPING

Besides restaurant servers, tip motel and hotel housekeeping staff, bartenders, cab drivers, bellhops, redcaps, valet parking staff, and other service workers. Standard tipping rates are 20 percent for meals, 15 percent for a taxi ride, and $1 per piece of luggage for a redcap or porter, although tipping extra for good service is always gracious and appropriate.

Tips for Travelers

GAY AND LESBIAN TRAVELERS

North Carolina offers no legal protection against discrimination based on sexual orientation or gender identity. The effects of the landmark 2013 Supreme Court decision on the Defense of Marriage Act have yet to play out. The state's sodomy law, which applied to straights and gays alike, was struck down in 2003, but there hasn't been much progress since. Hate-crimes statutes do not address violence targeting victims because of their sexual orientation or gender identity. Despite all this, don't close the book on North Carolina. While the laws may be retrogressive, the people are not; much of North Carolina is gay-friendly.

Despite being a red state, North Carolina has a strong purple streak. Metropolitan areas have active and open queer communities with numerous organizations and social groups, publications, human rights advocacy services, and community centers. Like anywhere in the United States, smaller and more rural communities are less likely to be gay-friendly, although there are exceptions and pleasant surprises. As a general rule, a same-sex couple will attract little attention holding hands in North Carolina, but they may not be received warmly at the Big Al's Shuckin' Shack in Bay Creek Waters (not a real place, but you get the idea).

Gay, lesbian, bisexual, and transgendered travelers planning to visit North Carolina can learn a great deal about community resources and activities at **QNotes** (www.q-notes.com), **North Carolina Pride** (www.ncpride.org), and **NC Gay Travel** (http://ncgaytravel.com).

VACATION RENTALS

In addition to hotels and bed and breakfasts in eastern North Carolina, vacation homes are available from a number of rental companies:

THE OUTER BANKS
- **Beach Realty** (800/635-1559, www.beachrealtync.com)
- **Resort Realty Vacations** (800/458-3830, www.resortrealty.com)
- **Sun Realty** (888/853-7770, www.sunrealtync.com)
- **Twiddy** (866/457-1190, www.twiddy.com)

THE CRYSTAL COAST
- **Bluewater Real Estate and Vacation Rentals** (866/231-5892, www.bluewaternc.com)
- **Crystal Coast Escapes** (252/6456-2900, www.crystalcoastescapes.com)

- **Rent A Beach** (www.rentabeach.com)
- **Spectrum Properties** (800/334-6390, www.spectrumproperties.com)

WILMINGTON AND THE BRUNSWICK BEACHES
- **Bald Head Island Limited** (800/432-7368, www.baldheadisland.com)
- **Brunswickland Realty** (800/842-6949, www.brunswicklandrealty.com)
- **Bryant Real Estate** (800/322-3764, www.bryantre.com)
- **Holliday Vacations** (888/256-2911, www.hollidayvacations.com)
- **Seashore Realty** (910/328-3400, www.seashorerealtync.com)
- **Tiffany's Rentals** (910/457-0544, www.tiffanysrentals.com)

SENIOR TRAVELERS

North Carolina has attracted a tremendous number of retirees in recent years, especially in the mountains and coast. It's also an increasingly popular destination for older travelers. For those who want to visit the state through organized programs, **Elderhostel** (www.road-scholar.org) is a great choice. Tours and classes are available throughout the state; the offerings in the mountains are particularly rich, with a great variety of courses and hands-on workshops about Appalachian culture and crafts. The North Carolina chapter of the **AARP** (866/389-5650, www.aarp.org/nc) is a good resource for senior issues and information. **VisitNC** (800/847-4862, www.visitnc.com) can also answer questions about activities and accessibility.

WOMEN TRAVELERS

Women from other parts of the country might find male strangers' friendliness a little disconcerting, but keep in mind that while some of them may be flirting with you, it's just as likely that they are simply being courteous. When a Southern man holds a door open for you, offers to help you carry something, or even calls you "honey," "darlin'," or "dear heart," it usually implies no ulterior motives and isn't intended to be condescending; he's probably just showing that he was raised up right. Again, manners should never preclude safety, so if some sketchy character is coming on to you in a way that gives you the creeps, trust your instincts.

TRAVELERS WITH DISABILITIES

Access North Carolina (800/689-9090, TDD 919/733-5924, www.ncdhhs.gov) is an excellent up-to-date guide on the accessibility of hundreds of cultural, recreational, historical, environmental, and commercial sites of interest and a goldmine for travel planning. Download a copy or phone to ask for the current edition, published by the state Department of Health and Human Services. The guide is set up by region and county, and sites and venues are described and rated in terms of accessibility.

Health and Safety

CRIME

As nice a place as North Carolina is, it's not immune to crime. Common sense about safety applies, particularly for women. Lock your doors immediately when you get into the car, park in well-lit areas as close as possible to your destination, and don't hesitate to ask a security guard or other trustworthy type to see you to your car. Don't carry too much cash on you. Pepper spray might save your life if you're attacked, whether by a person or by a bear.

Note that 911 emergency phone service is available everywhere in the state, but cell phone signals are not dependable everywhere. The deep mountains and more remote parts of western North Carolina and isolated stretches of the coast are more likely to have cell-phone dead zones.

SPECIAL WEATHER CONCERNS
Hurricanes

Hurricanes are a perennial danger, but luckily there tends to be plenty of warning when one is approaching. Evacuation orders should always be heeded, even if they are voluntary. It's also a good idea to leave sooner rather than later to avoid being trapped in traffic when the storm hits. The state **Department of Crime Control and Public Safety** (www.nccrimecontrol.org) posts a map online every year showing evacuation routes. You'll also see evacuation routes marked along the highways.

Tornadoes

Tornadoes can happen in any season and have killed people here in recent years. Pay close

Many beaches have lifeguards, but a number do not.

attention to tornado watches and warnings, and don't take chances: Find a safe place to shelter until the danger is over.

Rip Currents

More than 100 people die every year on U.S. beaches because of rip currents. Also called riptides, these dangerous currents can occur on any beach and can be very difficult to identify by sight. In rip current conditions, channels of water flow swiftly out toward deep water, and even if you are standing in relatively shallow water, you can suddenly be swept under and out into deep water. Rip current safety tips are available on the National Oceanic and Atmospheric Administration's National Weather Service website (www.ripcurrents. noaa.gov). Among their advice: "Don't fight the current. Swim out of the current, and then to shore. If you can't escape, float or tread water. If you need help, call or wave for assistance." Heed riptide warnings, and try to swim within sight of a lifeguard. Even good swimmers can drown in a rip current, so if you have any

doubts about your swimming abilities or water conditions, play it safe and stay close to shore.

ANIMAL THREATS

There are a handful of dangerous creatures across the state, ranging in size from microscopic to monstrous, that can pose risks to health and safety. Be on the lookout for mean bugs: **Ticks** can carry Lyme disease and Rocky Mountain spotted fever, both serious and lingering conditions. Most likely to climb on you if you are walking through brush or bushes but liable to be lurking about anywhere, ticks come in many sizes and shapes, from barely visible pinpoint-size to that thing that looks like a grape hanging off your dog's neck. Wear insect repellent if you're going to be tramping around outside, and check your body and your travel companions thoroughly—your clothing as well as your skin—for stowaways. They'll attach themselves to any soft surface on your body, but they particularly like people's heads, often latching on to the scalp an inch or so behind the ears. If you find a tick on you or a human or canine companion, don't remove it roughly, no matter how freaked out you are. Yanking can leave the tick's head buried in your skin, increasing the risk of infection. Grasp the tick in a pinching motion, and pull slowly but firmly. You may have to hang on for several moments, but eventually it will decide to let go. Dab the bite with antiseptic, and over the next several weeks be alert for a bull's-eye-shaped irritation around the bite and for flu-like symptoms such as fever, achiness, malaise, and fatigue. If you have any of these signs, visit your doctor for a blood test.

Mosquitoes can carry West Nile virus, La Crosse encephalitis, and eastern equine encephalitis. Wear insect repellent and clothing that covers your arms and legs to avoid bites. Although not disease vectors, **fire ants** are among the state's most feared insects. It's easy to stumble onto one of their nests, and before you realize what you've stepped in, they can be swarming up your legs and biting you. Certainly this is a painful and frightening experience, but it's also potentially dangerous if you're allergic to bees. There have been documented cases in recent years of adult humans being swarmed and killed by fire ants. Watch where you step, and keep an eye out for areas of disturbed ground and turned-up soil. Sometimes their nests look like conventional anthills, sometimes like messy piles of dirt, and other times just soft spots on the ground.

Another reason to mind where you tread: snakes. The vast majority of snakes in North Carolina are harmless and shy, but we do have a few pit vipers. **Copperheads** are quite common in every part of the state and in wooded or semiwooded terrain—even in backyards, where they can lurk in bushes and leaf piles, under porches and in storage sheds, and even in the walls of a house. They have a gorgeous pattern of light and dark brown splotches, which makes them incredibly difficult to spot against the ground in fall. Copperheads are usually less than three feet long. Their bite is poisonous but usually not fatal.

Found in the eastern half of the state and up into the Sandhills, **cottonmouths**—also called water moccasins—are very dangerous. They range in color from reddish brown to black, can grow up to 5.5 feet long, and are easily mistaken for harmless water snakes (and vice versa). They sometimes venture into the woods and fields, but cottonmouths are most commonly seen on or near water. Be especially careful walking along creek beds or in riverside brush. When threatened, they display the inside of their mouths, a startling and beautiful cottony white. Their bite is potentially lethal.

Coral snakes are endangered in North Carolina, but if you're going to be in the woods in the southeastern quarter of the state, keep an eye out. These jewel-toned snakes are generally small and slim, rarely more than a couple of feet long. Like the harmless scarlet king snake and scarlet snake, coral snakes have alternating bands of red, yellow, and black. The way to tell coral snakes from their harmless kin is to note the order of colors. On coral snakes, the yellow bands separate the black and the red, whereas on their imitators, red and black touch. An adage advises, "Red and black, friend of Jack; red and yellow, kill a fellow." Coral snakes can also be identified by their sinister black snouts, making them look like cartoon burglars, whereas scarlet snakes and scarlet king snakes have red clown noses. That's a lot to remember in that instant of panic when you notice a coil of red and yellow and black stripes at your feet looking up at you testily. Rather than stopping to figure out if the snake is friend or foe, it's better just to step away fast. Coral snakes' venom works on its prey's respiratory system, and it can kill humans. They're cousins of cobras and are some of the most beautiful snakes in these parts, but locals fear them more intensely than the huge, lumpy-headed, tusky-fanged vipers that appear more threatening.

There are also three poisonous native rattlesnakes: The **eastern diamondback rattlesnake** is the largest of rattlesnakes and can grow to nearly six feet long and as fat around as an adult human's arm. They are extremely dangerous—powerful enough to catch and eat rabbits, and willing, if provoked, to kill a person. Eastern diamondbacks are rare but can be found in the southeastern sandy swamp counties. Also large are **canebrake rattlers,** more formally known as timber rattlers. They are found throughout the state, including the mountains. Their bite can be fatal to humans. To make them even scarier, they too can grow to nearly six feet in length, and in cold weather they like to congregate in large numbers to hibernate. **Pygmy rattlesnakes** are found along the state's coastline, up into the Sandhills, and around Crowder's Mountain. Generally up to about a 1.5 feet long, pygmies are also venomous.

Alligators are incredible creatures, scaly submarines that can exceed 15 feet snout to tail (females generally mature at around 10 feet) and can weigh 1,000 pounds, with a steel-trap maw of 75-80 fangs. They are found through much of eastern North Carolina, as far north as Merchants Millpond State Park near the Virginia border, but they are most common from Wilmington south. You don't have to trek into the depths of a swamp to see gators; they like to sun themselves on golf courses, next to roadside drainage ditches, even in yards that

Gators look docile, but they're dangerous. Admire from a distance.

© JASON FRYE

adjoin fresh water. Their behavior is deceptive, because they seem to spend 90 percent of their time in a motionless stupor; but they can awaken and whirl around to grab you before you have time to back away. They also spend much of their time submerged, sometimes entirely underwater, and more often drifting just below the surface with only their nostrils and brow ridges visible. Be aware of floating logs as they may have teeth attached. Alligators will gladly eat dogs that venture too close, so it goes without saying that small children should never be allowed to wander alone near potential alligator habitats. An adult alligator can kill an adult human, and even the cute little ones will be only too happy to help themselves to your foot, so don't tempt fate for the sake of a photo or a closer look. If you're determined to get a close-up picture, visit one of the state's aquariums.

Bear attacks are rare and usually defensive, but considering that the creatures can weigh up to 800 pounds, caution would seem to be indicated. They are present in the woods in various parts of the state, especially up in the mountains and in the deep swamps and pocosins along the coast. They're quite shy and apt to gallop into the brush if they see a human coming. They will investigate potential meals, though, so securing your food when camping is crucial. If your car is nearby, lock the food in it; otherwise, hoist it into a tree with a rope, too high to reach from the ground and out of reach from the tree trunk. The National Park Service recommends the following course of action if a bear approaches you. First, try backing away slowly. If the bear follows, stand your ground. If it continues to menace you, try to scare it: Make yourself look bigger and more threatening by standing on a rock or next to your companions. Try waving sticks and throwing rocks. In the extremely unlikely event that you actually find yourself in hand-to-hand combat with a bear, remember the Park Service's advice to "fight back aggressively with any available object." Your chances of seeing a bear in North Carolina, much less being threatened by one, are pretty slim.

DISEASES AND NATURAL THREATS

Among the invisible villains here is **giardia,** a single-celled protozoan parasite that can be contracted by drinking untreated water. Hikers and campers should avoid drinking from streams unless they first boil the water vigorously for at least one minute. Filtering water with a filter of 0.1 to 1 micron absolute pore size or chemically treating it with iodine or chlorine is less reliable than thorough boiling.

There's a fairly high incidence of **rabies** in North Carolina's raccoons, bats, foxes, ground-hogs, and skunks. If you're bringing a pet into the state, be sure that its vaccinations, including rabies, are up-to-date. If you plan to go hiking with your dog, it may even be wise to bring a copy of its rabies vaccination certificate in case you have to prove its immunity. If you are bitten by a wild animal, seek medical help immediately, even if you're out in the woods. Rabies is deadly to humans and it's extremely important to start treatment immediately.

HEALTH PRECAUTIONS
Emergencies

As elsewhere the United States, calling 911 in North Carolina will summon medical help, police, or fire fighters. On the highway, blue road signs marked with an "H" point the way to hospitals, but if you're experiencing a potentially critical emergency, it's best to call 911 and let the ambulance come to you. There are plenty of rural places in the state where cell-phone coverage is spotty to nonexistent, so if you have a medical condition from which an emergency could arise, keep this in mind.

Summer Weather

Heat, humidity, and air pollution often combine in the summer to create dangerous conditions for children, the elderly, and people with severe heart and lung conditions. Even if you're young and healthy, don't take chances in the heat. Carry drinking water with you, avoid exertion and being outside in the hottest part of the day, and stay in the shade. Even young healthy people can die from the heat. Remember that even if it doesn't feel very warm outside, children and pets are in grave danger when left in cars. Temperatures can rise to fatal levels very quickly inside closed vehicles, even when it's not terribly hot outside.

Information and Services

MONEY

For international travelers, currency-exchange services can be found in the big cities at some major banks and at currency-exchange businesses. Numerous money-transfer services, from old familiars like Western Union to a multitude of overseas companies, are easily accessible. The easiest place to wire or receive money is at a grocery store—most have Western Union or a proprietary wiring service—or at a bank. Banking hours vary by location and chain, but most are closed on Sunday and federal holidays. ATMs are located at most bank branches as well as in many grocery stores and convenience stores.

COMMUNICATIONS AND MEDIA
Newspapers and Radio

North Carolina has several major news-papers, the largest of which is the Pulitzer Prize-winning **Charlotte Observer** (www.charlotteobserver.com). In addition to the print edition, the *Observer* has extensive online-only content for travelers. The Raleigh **News & Observer** (www.newsobserver.com) serves the Triangle area and much of central Carolina. Other prominent newspapers include the Wilmington **Star-News** (www.starnewsonline.com). Among the many local and regional radio stations is a number of NPR affiliates.

There are few parts of the state where you won't be able to tune in to a clear NPR signal.

Magazines

Our State magazine (www.ourstate.com) is a widely distributed monthly that tells the stories of the people, places, and history across North Carolina. As a travel resource, it will give you a feel for the people you're likely to encounter, but it will give you an even better idea of places to eat and towns you may not have thought to visit. Their website has an extensive collection of archived stories arranged by topic. In most larger cities in North Carolina it isn't hard to find magazines covering the local arts scene or guiding area parents to the best the town has to offer for kids. Look at news racks outside grocery stores and on street corners to pick up free publications like *Salt, Wilma!* and *Encore* in Wilmington and *North Brunswick Magazine* in and around Brunswick County.

Internet Access

Internet access is widespread. Coffee shops are always a good place to find Wi-Fi, usually free but sometimes for a fee. A few small towns have free municipal wireless access. Most chain motels and major hotels offer free wireless access, and smaller hotels and bed-and-breakfasts often do too. This is true for some remote areas as well The deep mountains are the most difficult place to get a reliable Internet connection, but you'll probably be able to get online at your place of lodging or the coffee shop in town.

Cell Phones

Cell phone coverage is not consistent across North Carolina. You'll get a signal in all of the cities and most areas in between, but service can be spotty in the eastern and western parts of the state. On the coast and in rural eastern North Carolina, there are plenty of areas where you could drive 20 miles before finding any reception. Spotty cell-phone coverage is a safety issue; if you're treed by a bear or run out of gas on a backwoods track, 911 may be unreachable.

MAPS AND VISITOR INFORMATION

Among the best sources for travel information in North Carolina is the state's tourism website, **VisitNC** (www.visitnc.com). They maintain an up-to-date list of festivals and events, tours and trails, and almost anything else you might want to know. Also excellent is the magazine *Our State* (www.ourstate.com), available at grocery stores, drugstores, and bookshops. Their website monitors upcoming events as well.

North Carolina Welcome Centers, located at several major highway entry points to the state, are sources for more free brochures and maps than one person could carry. They are located at the Virginia state line on I-77 near Mount Airy, on I-85 in Warren County, and on I-95 in Northampton County; at the Tennessee state line on I-26 in Madison County and on I-40 in Haywood County; and along the South Carolina state line on I-26 in Polk County, I-85 in Cleveland County, I-77 just outside Charlotte, and I-95 in Robeson County.

For basic planning, the maps on the VisitNC website will give you a good sense of the layout of the state and its major destinations. Many areas are experiencing rapid growth, particularly around Charlotte and the Triangle, so if your map is even a little out of date, you may not know about the newest bypass. For features like mountains, rivers, back roads, and small towns that don't change, atlas-style books of state maps are useful. My own favorite is DeLorme's *North Carolina Atlas & Gazetteer;* I live here and find it indispensable.

RESOURCES

Suggested Reading

TRAVEL

Daniels, Diane. *Farm Fresh North Carolina.* Chapel Hill: UNC Press, 2011. This guidebook will help you find the perfect place to pick apples, cut Christmas trees, visit a pumpkin patch, pick a bushel of blueberries, and shop at every farmers market across the state. You'll find recipes from chefs and farmers as well.

Duncan, Barbara, and Brett Riggs. *Cherokee Heritage Trails.* Chapel Hill: UNC Press, 2003; online companion at www.cherokeeheritage.org. A fascinating guide to both the historic and present-day home of the Eastern Band of the Cherokee in North Carolina, Tennessee, and Georgia, from ancient mounds and petroglyphs to modern-day arts co-ops and sporting events.

Eubanks, Georgann. *Literary Trails of the North Carolina Mountains: A Guidebook.* Chapel Hill: UNC Press, 2007. This book and its companion books *Literary Trails of the North Carolina Piedmont: A Guidebook,* 2010, and *Literary Trails of Eastern North Carolina: A Guidebook,* 2013, introduce fans of Southern literature to the places that produced and inspired various scribes. Also included are the best bookstores and book events across the state.

North Carolina Atlas and Gazetteer. Yarmouth, ME: DeLorme, 2012. Since I was in Boy Scouts, I have always been partial to DeLorme's state atlases. This series represents in great detail the topography and other natural features of an area, giving far more useful and comprehensive information than the standard highway map.

Our State. www.ourstate.com. For a lively and informative look at North Carolina destinations and the cultural quirks and treasures you may find in your travels, *Our State* magazine is one of the best resources around. The magazine is easy to find, sold at most bookstores and even on grocery store and drugstore magazine racks. It covers arts, nature, folklore, history, scenery, sports, and lots of food, all from a traveler's perspective.

HISTORY AND CULTURE

Cecelski, David. *The Waterman's Song: Slavery and Freedom in Maritime North Carolina.* Chapel Hill: UNC Press, 2001. A marvelous treatment of the African American heritage of resistance in eastern North Carolina, and how the region's rivers and sounds were passages to freedom for many enslaved people.

Powell, William S. *North Carolina: A History.* Chapel Hill: UNC Press, 1988. A readable, concise account of our fascinating and varied past.

Powell, William S., and Jay Mazzocchi, editors. *Encyclopedia of North Carolina.* Chapel Hill: UNC Press, 2006. A fantastic compendium of all sorts of North Carolina history, letters, and politics. If you can lift this mammoth book, you'll learn about everything from Carolina basketball to presidential elections to ghosts.

Setzer, Lynn. *Tar Heel History on Foot: Great Walks through 400 Years of North Carolina's Fascinating Past.* Chapel Hill: UNC Press, 2013. This book sends you on a series of short walks in all parts of the state—coastal and mountain, city and country, historic sites and state parks—to discover the history of the state. The walks are arranged by theme

and location, making it simple to find one near you.

Wright, David, and David Zoby. *Fire on the Beach: Recovering the Lost Story of Richard Etheridge and the Pea Island Lifesavers.* New York: Oxford University Press, 2002. The riveting tale of the first African American captain of a U.S. Life Saving Station and his all-African American crew. Spanning the time from just before the Civil War to the turn of the 20th century, it's a fascinating look at life for enslaved people and former slaves on the Outer Banks.

Internet Resources

NEWSPAPERS
North Carolina newspapers have unusually rich online content, and are great resources for travel planning.

Fayetteville Observer
http://fayobserver.com
News and culture from Fayetteville and the surrounding towns.

StarNews
www.starnewsonline.com
Daily news coverage of Wilmington and neighboring towns.

Outer Banks Sentinel
www.womacknewspapers.com/obsentinel
News and events pertinent to Outer Banks towns.

ARTS AND CULTURE
North Carolina's arts and history have an ever-growing online dimension, telling the story of the state in ways that paper and ink simply can't.

North Carolina Folklife Institute
www.ncfolk.org
The website will fill you in on the many organizations across the state that promote traditional music, crafts, and folkways. You'll also find a calendar of folk life-related events in North Carolina, and travel itineraries for weekends exploring Core Sound, and Cherokee heritage in the state.

NCFOOD
www.ncfolk.org/category/food
This wonderful food blog, maintained by the Folklife Institute, features articles about the culinary back roads of the state.

North Carolina Arts Council
www.ncarts.org
The Arts Council provides information about performing arts, literature, cultural trails, galleries, and fun happenings.

North Carolina ECHO
www.ncecho.org
ECHO stands for "Exploring Cultural Heritage Online," and this great site has links to hundreds of online exhibits and brick-and-mortar museums.

Our State
www.ourstate.com
The online companion to this print publication provides expanded coverage of the history, people, food, and arts across North Carolina. An extensive archive of stories lets you look back several years for the best the state has to offer.

OUTDOORS
Great online resources exist for planning outdoor adventures in North Carolina, where rich arts and blockbuster sports are matched by natural resources.

North Carolina Sierra Club
http://nc2.sierraclub.org
Find information about upcoming hikes and excursions as well as an overview of the state's natural areas and environmental issues.

North Carolina Birding Trail
www.ncbirdingtrail.org
Covering bird-watching across the state, this site contains information about dozens of pristine locations and active flyways along the coast, in the Piedmont, and in the mountains.

Carolina Canoe Club
www.carolinacanoeclub.com
A clearinghouse of statewide canoeing resources.

Carolina Kayak Club
www.carolinakayakclub.org
A repository for flat-water kayaking information, resources, trails, and activities across the state.

CanoeNC
www.canoenc.org
A nice starting point for planning a flat-water paddling trip in eastern North Carolina.

North Carolina Sportsman
www.northcarolinasportsman.com
Covering hunting and fishing news, destinations, and seasonal trends across the state.

North Carolina Outdoors
www.northcarolinaoutdoors.com
This privately operated site is full of excellent information and cross-referenced sources for state and national parklands and wilderness throughout the state.

Friends of the Mountains to Sea Trail
www.ncmst.org
Find details, hike-planning tools, and resources for a day or longer on the 1,000-mile-long Mountains to Sea Trail that crosses North Carolina.

NC Hikes
www.nchikes.com
All things hiking-related, including trails in every corner of the state, books, and trip recommendations.

Index

List of Maps

Acknowledgments

Without the following people helping, pushing, prodding, editing, traveling, and working with me, this book would not have been possible.

To Lauren, the best cheerleader, travel companion, research assistant, and wife I could ask for. You make every day fun, even the rainy ones when you have a long drive ahead.

To Billy and Tammy for taking me to North Carolina for the first time.

To Bob and K.D. for teaching me to see and appreciate this state from a new perspective.

To Aaron, Melody, Connie, Mitzi, and all the other folks who helped me put trips together and introduced me to the people and places in your corner of North Carolina.

To the North Carolina Division of Tourism for the introductions, tips, and contacts.

To my editors at Avalon Travel, without your help, this book wouldn't be nearly as good.

To you, North Carolina, for being awesome, beautiful, and fun.

And finally, to the travelers, adventure seekers, foodies, and explorers who will pick up this book and discover new favorite places.

www.moon.com

DESTINATIONS | ACTIVITIES | BLOGS | MAPS | BOOKS

MOON.COM is ready to help plan your next trip! Filled with fresh trip ideas and strategies, author interviews, informative travel blogs, a detailed map library, and descriptions of all the Moon guidebooks, Moon.com is all you need to get out and explore the world—or even places in your own backyard. While at Moon.com, sign up for our monthly e-newsletter for updates on new releases, travel tips, and expert advice from our on-the-go Moon authors. As always, when you travel with Moon, expect an experience that is uncommon and truly unique.

f 🐦 KEEP UP WITH MOON ON FACEBOOK AND TWITTER
JOIN THE MOON PHOTO GROUP ON FLICKR

MAP SYMBOLS

Expressway		Highlight		Airfield		Golf Course
Primary Road	○	City/Town	✈	Airport	ⓟ	Parking Area
Secondary Road	◉	State Capital	▲	Mountain		Archaeological Site
Unpaved Road	◉	National Capital	✚	Unique Natural Feature		Church
Trail	★	Point of Interest				Gas Station
Ferry	•	Accommodation		Waterfall		Glacier
Railroad	▼	Restaurant/Bar	▲	Park		Mangrove
Pedestrian Walkway	■	Other Location		Trailhead		Reef
Stairs	ʌ	Campground		Skiing Area		Swamp

CONVERSION TABLES

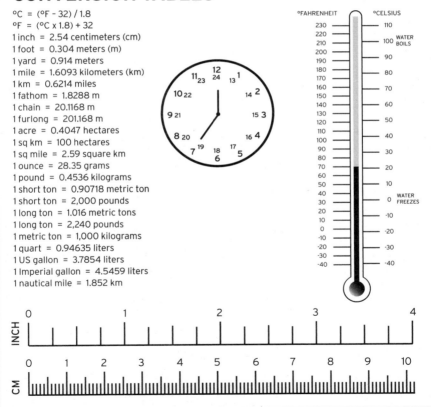

°C = (°F - 32) / 1.8
°F = (°C x 1.8) + 32
1 inch = 2.54 centimeters (cm)
1 foot = 0.304 meters (m)
1 yard = 0.914 meters
1 mile = 1.6093 kilometers (km)
1 km = 0.6214 miles
1 fathom = 1.8288 m
1 chain = 20.1168 m
1 furlong = 201.168 m
1 acre = 0.4047 hectares
1 sq km = 100 hectares
1 sq mile = 2.59 square km
1 ounce = 28.35 grams
1 pound = 0.4536 kilograms
1 short ton = 0.90718 metric ton
1 short ton = 2,000 pounds
1 long ton = 1.016 metric tons
1 long ton = 2,240 pounds
1 metric ton = 1,000 kilograms
1 quart = 0.94635 liters
1 US gallon = 3.7854 liters
1 Imperial gallon = 4.5459 liters
1 nautical mile = 1.852 km

MOON NORTH CAROLINA COAST
Avalon Travel
a member of the Perseus Books Group
1700 Fourth Street
Berkeley, CA 94710, USA
www.moon.com

Editors: Elizabeth Hansen, Nikki Ioakimedes
Series Manager: Kathryn Ettinger
Copy Editor: Christopher Church
Graphics Coordinator: Elizabeth Jang
Production Coordinator: Elizabeth Jang
Cover design: Faceout Studios, Charles Brock
Moon logo: Tim McGrath
Map Editor: Kat Bennett
Cartographer: Stephanie Poulain
Indexer: Greg Jewett

ISBN-13: 978-1-61238-512-9
ISSN: 2333-049X

Printing History
1st Edition — June 2014
5 4 3 2 1

Text © 2014 by Jason Frye and Avalon Travel.
Maps © 2014 by Avalon Travel.
All rights reserved.

Some photos and illustrations are used by permission and are the property of the original copyright owners.

Front cover photo: sunset at the Whalehead Club in Corolla © Alice Mullen Drake/www.alicedrake.com

Title page photo: Jennette's Pier © Jason Frye

Interior color photos: p. 4 sunrise over the marsh near Southport © Jason Frye; p. 5 (top) closeup of the lens of the Currituck Beach Lighthouse © Kenneth Keifer/123rf.com, (bottom left) oyster shells on Bald Head Island © iofoto/123rf.com, (bottom right) sailing the waters off Southport © Jason Frye; p. 6 (top left) azaleas in full bloom in Wilmington, (top right) Old Baldy, (bottom) Virginia Dare statue in the Elizabethan Gardens, all © Jason Frye; p. 7 (top) pelican, (bottom left) path to the beach on Oak Island, (bottom right) turtle, all © Jason Frye; p. 8 sunset over the docks © Jason Frye; p. 9 (top) marsh boat house on Bald Head Island © Jason Frye, (bottom left) the Old Burying Ground in Beaufort © Kenneth Keifer/123rf.com, (bottom right) the spiral staircase of Cape Hatteras Lighthouse © Jason Frye; p. 12 − 16 all © Jason Frye; p. 17 © Kenneth Keifer/123rf.com; p. 18 Bob Decker/123rf.com; p. 20 © Jason Frye

Back cover photo: the Cape Hatteras Lighthouse © Kenneth Keifer/123rf.com

Printed in Canada by Friesens

KEEPING CURRENT

If you have a favorite gem you'd like to see included in the next edition, or see anything that needs updating, clarification, or correction, please drop us a line. Send your comments via email to feedback@moon.com, or use the address above.